# Narrative Mediation

## A New Approach to Conflict Resolution

John Winslade

Gerald Monk

Jossey-Bass Publishers • San Francisco

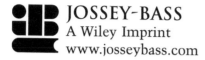

## JOSSEY-BASS
### A Wiley Imprint
### www.josseybass.com

www.josseybass.com

Jossey-Bass books and products are available through most bookstores. To contact Jossey-Bass directly, call (888) 378-2537, fax to (800) 605-2665, or visit our website at www.josseybass.com.

Substantial discounts on bulk quantities of Jossey-Bass books are available to corporations, professional associations, and other organizations. For details and discount information, contact the special sales department at Jossey-Bass.

We at Jossey-Bass strive to use the most environmentally sensitive paper stocks available to us. Our publications are printed on acid-free recycled stock whenever possible, and our paper always meets or exceeds minimum GPO and EPA requirements.

**Library of Congress Cataloging-in-Publication Data**

Winslade, John, 1953-
   Narrative mediation: a new approach to conflict resolution / John Winslade, Gerald Monk.—1st ed.
      p. cm.
   Includes bibliographical references and index.
   ISBN 0-7879-4192-1 (alk. paper)
   1. Conflict management. 2. Mediation. 3. Storytelling. 4. Discourse analysis, Narrative.
I. Monk, Gerald. II. Title.
HM1126.M66   2000
   303.6'9—dc21                                                              99-048273
FIRST EDITION

*HB Printing*   10  9  8  7  6  5  4

# Contents

*To*
*Maida and Norman Winslade*
*Geoff and Joan Monk*

# Preface

Many books and articles on mediation and conflict resolution are published each year. A quick scan of the amazon.com list of books with mediation and conflict resolution in the title shows fifty-nine new publications in the last two years. That represents a small sample of the mass of material published in the mediation field on a regular basis. There is enormous interest in finding peaceful means to settle human conflict.

This interest is not coincidental. The stakes for our survival on the planet are growing. Despite the end of the nuclear-arms-driven cold war, the continuing threat of a localized war involving nuclear weapons by accident or design continues to grow. Since the end of the Second World War, the so-called war to end all wars, there have been 150 major wars (conflicts resulting in more than one thousand deaths per year). The death toll since that time is more than 23,142,000.[1]

Ninety percent of all casualties resulting from wars and civil conflicts are civilian. Forty million people are uprooted at present due to war or civil conflict. More than forty major conflicts are occurring in more than thirty countries as this book goes to press.[2]

On the domestic scene, the statistics are equally disturbing. A minimum of 16 percent of American couples experienced an assault during the year in which they were asked about it, and about 40 percent of these assaults involved severely violent acts, such as kicking, biting, punching, choking, and attacks with weapons.[3]

During the 1990s, domestic violence has been identified as one of the major causes of emergency room visits by women. It is estimated that 20 to 30 percent of women who are seen by emergency room physicians exhibit at least one or more symptoms of physical abuse.[4] FBI data indicate that more than half of the 5,328 women murdered in 1990 were killed by someone they knew, half or more of them by a husband or boyfriend.[5]

We do not need further evidence to know that as a species we continue to demonstrate a capability to commit acts of human violation of the most grievous kind.

Because of the prevalence of violence and conflict throughout the ages, many people, including academic researchers, claim that human beings are inherently aggressive, that it is our nature to be so. A widely accepted argument is that because human beings have been violent throughout history, there is every reason to think that we are naturally inclined to continue to be violent.

You will quickly discover when reading this book that we do not support the notion that conflict is caused by an inherently aggressive human nature. Neither do we support the idea that conflict is a necessary product of needs and interests thwarted by the acts of another person—a popular concept in mediation theory. In our defense we cite evidence of communities living side by side in peaceful coexistence even when external duress has threatened them and their quality of life.

For these reasons we think it is important to keep working on ideas for bringing about a more peaceful and just world. This book by no means offers answers to all of the problems of conflict in the world. It is, however, an attempt to introduce some new ideas into the field. Goodness knows we need as many ideas as possible.

## Theories of Mediation

Mediation theory and practice are built on the views that people hold about the way the world works. Some mainstream mediation theories are predicated on the idea that human beings are motivated primarily to fulfill their own personal interests. Taking this assumption as a given, interest-based theories of mediation work toward assisting disputing parties to find an underlying shared interest that was not identified earlier in the dispute so they can become motivated to address the presenting conflict. In this way they will not experience the deprivation of having to give up something in order to get something—a compromising approach to solving disputes. We would characterize most of the approaches to mediation that exist in the literature as variants on this interest-based or problem-solving approach.

Narrative mediation is different from problem-solving approaches in its character and in its basic assumptions. It does not subscribe to the assumption that what people want (which gets them into conflict) stems from the expression of their inner needs or interests. Rather, it starts from the idea that people construct conflict from narrative descriptions of events.

We argue for an approach to mediation that changes the way individuals see themselves in a particular conflict so as to open up new possibilities for resolution. The narrative approach is less grueling than problem-solving mediation, especially with long-standing conflicts. It concentrates on developing a relationship that is incompatible with conflict and that is built on stories of understanding, respect, and collaboration. Parties are invited to reflect on the effects that these stories have had on them before they are asked to address the matters that cause separation. In this way, people move more quickly toward resolution.

At the risk of oversimplifying the mediation process, we compare narrative mediation with other approaches to mediation as an "outside-in" phenomenon rather than as an "inside-out" phenomenon. For example, the outside-in perspective looks at conflict as produced in the sociocultural milieu, where meanings are contested within the social fabric of community, while the inside–out perspective looks at conflict as created within the so-called natural desires, interests, and needs emanating from the individual. This approach is built on the assumption that the individual is unitary and context-independent.

A narrative approach to mediation helps mediators and their clients make sense of the complex social contexts that shape conflicts. The mediation context is riddled with strong cultural narratives that form around ethnicity, gender, class, education, and financial wealth, for example. Mediators have often failed to grapple with these complex cultural stories. This has led to strong criticisms of mediation practice by indigenous peoples and some feminist groups. We think that narrative mediation offers mediators some potent linguistic tools for changing their practice in ways that address some of these criticisms.

# Origins and Audience of the Book

This book arose from a number of sources. The success of our first book—*Narrative Therapy in Practice: The Archaeology of Hope*[6]— encouraged us to build on the work that John Winslade and Alison Cotter presented in their chapter on narrative mediation. We received many requests to develop the mediation ideas presented in that book. Considerable interest was generated by an article we authored that was published in *Negotiation Journal* in 1998.[7] We were greatly heartened by the editor's decision to rush our article into print, and by a reviewer's comment that our approach was fresh and exciting and approximated what he or she had been searching for over a twenty-year period.

This book speaks to a variety of professionals who have an interest in dispute resolution. We have in mind an audience of marriage and family counselors, professional mediators, and lawyers working in the field of family conciliation and in the wider dispute resolution field. There is a lot in here for mediators who have been working with mainstream mediation theory and practice and are ready for something quite new. We offer practitioners a range of useable ideas that can transform how they engage disputing parties in mediation.

Narrative approaches to dealing with problems are currently riding a wave of popularity in North America and elsewhere. Narrative therapy in particular has a strong following among many social workers, counselors, psychotherapists, and psychologists. Many of these practitioners also do mediation work, often family and community mediation. We offer narrative practitioners an exciting array of new ideas, techniques, and strategies to use in their mediation work, where they can push the limits of the narrative metaphor still further.

Narrative mediation is embedded within a social constructionist framework. Many social science researchers are writing about and reflecting on the practical applications of social constructionist theory and the postmodern movement, of which social constructionism is a growing part. We have made efforts to link the mediation practices described in this book to the traditions arising from postmodern theory.

Central to the link with postmodernism is the role that language plays in constructing who we are and how we engage or behave with others. We provide numerous practical illustrations of the theory-practice relationship, emphasizing the constitutive function of language in a social constructionist epistemology. This book offers postmodern enthusiasts a body of practical material through which to consider the implications of the postmodern movement for applied helping professions. We hope this material triggers a variety of new thoughts and opinions that will serve to advance your own theoretical and practical work. For others it may act as a springboard for further discussion that might critique and possibly expand the ideas we present here.

Some readers will find some of our language and terminology distinctively different from that featured in many other mediation texts. We do not want to burden you with jargon. Because narrative mediation theory and practice are so decisively different from many other mediation models, we have had to use a number of very precise but perhaps unfamiliar concepts to accurately depict the workings of this orientation. We do not apologize for this. Any new conceptual process requires a unique set of linguistic descriptions to explain the nature of the activity.

## Contents of the Book

The first chapter provides an overview of the narrative approach to mediation by taking you through an actual mediation scenario. The example provides you with an opportunity to see a mediator at work using the narrative metaphor. The chapter links you to the other chapters in the book, where narrative concepts are fleshed out in considerable detail.

Chapter Two reviews some of the mainstream assumptions about mediation theory and practice. We deconstruct the epistemologies underpinning the problem-solving interest-based models. By way of contrast, we present the theoretical premises of the narrative approach and demonstrate the intimate relationship between our theoretical posture and its application in the mediation room. We explore the significance of the postmodern turn in the helping professions and its expression in social constructionism.

In Chapter Three we walk you through the major features of the narrative mediation process. We explain our view of how conflict relates to the ways in which discourses position people in relation to one another. We show how conflict-saturated stories narrow people's focus in relationships onto particular problem issues, and how they obscure nonproblematic resources that might be drawn on in the resolution of disputes. We describe the kind of deconstructive listening that provides parties to mediation with an entry point for reviewing their circumstances. In this way they can be invited to change their original stance.

Chapter Four highlights the liberal discourse of ownership out of which people construct their understandings of what they believe they are entitled to. We think that this discourse is central to how conflict develops. It is rooted in individualism and is dominant in our legal systems. However, despite the liberal rhetoric, the entitlements that become legitimate in our social worlds are not equal. Discourses of gender, race, class, disability, and education (and others) position people in disputes in ways that grant them differing entitlements. Out of these entitlements people then construct their feelings, thoughts, and stories. Disputes arise when people perceive that others are encroaching on their entitlements, and they resort to anger, blame, rigidity, abuse, and violence to protect those entitlements. Mediation can deconstruct entitlements and help people access alternative knowledges from which relations can be built that feature more equitable entitlements. Numerous examples of this idea from mediation contexts are given to illustrate the argument.

The stance of the mediator toward the parties and toward the problem is presented in Chapter Five. This is a stance of collaborative respect in which the parties are regarded as the experts in the resolution of the dispute, already in possession of much information about how the conflict can be resolved. The mediator's task is to work alongside the parties and to appreciate the neglected knowledge the parties have about how to author a new relationship. We argue for the advantages of caucusing in mediation and against the idea that the mediation proper begins only when both parties are together. This chapter describes ethical principles that are implicit in narrative mediation, and the practices that flow from them.

Disarming the conflict is the focus of Chapter Six. In this chapter we demonstrate with examples and stories the kind of deconstructive listening that narrative mediation features. There are sections on curiosity, externalizing conversations, and mapping the influence of conflicts on each person and on the relationship, including the identification of relational trends.

Chapter Seven explores the kinds of questions that generate new positions in conflict situations by inviting parties to explore their commitments to alternative relational patterns. These questions break down the polarizing tendency of disputes and encourage the appreciation of multiplicity and complexity. Examples show how ways forward in conflict situations can be constructed out of the resources that then become available.

Chapter Eight shows how narrative mediation builds momentum and motivation to create a more productive relationship between the parties. The process of elaborating on the emerging new story is demonstrated in response to the questioning described in the previous chapter. Events or moments of relationship that contrast with the conflict story, once found, can be developed into the authoring of a new version of what was in dispute, one that is more inclusive of both parties' experience. A new description of the relationship based on this new story can then be sought and the description can be enlivened by coming to understand its history and its possible future.

Getting unstuck is the theme of Chapter Nine. We explore some of the more difficult aspects of mediation and discuss a narrative approach to a number of specific issues that can arise, such as how to deal with relationships in which there is violence or harassment that seems to be an obstacle to the emergence of a new story. The chapter also covers how to support solution-bound narratives that survive the honeymoon period.

The last chapter focuses on the process of creating and making use of forms of documentation of the new story. These include written agreements, letters from the mediators to the parties, and conversations that review the progress of the new story.

*November 1999*                                    JOHN WINSLADE
                                                   *Hamilton, New Zealand*
                                                   GERALD MONK
                                                   *San Diego, California*

## Notes

1. Project Ploughshares, *Armed Conflicts Report* (Waterloo Institute of Peace and Conflict Studies, 1997).
2. American Refugee Committee, unpublished paper (Minneapolis, Minn.: International Headquarters, American Refugee Committee, 1999).
3. Straus, M. A., and Smith, C., "Family Patterns and Primary Prevention of Family Violence," *Trends in Health Care, Law and Ethics,* 1993, *8*(2), 17–25.
4. Henry, S. L., Roth, M., and Gleis, L. H., "Domestic Violence: The Medical Community's Legal Duty," *Journal of the Kentucky Medical Association,* 1992, *90*(4), 162–169.
5. Kellerman, A. L., and Mercy, J. A., "Men, Women and Murder: Gender-Specific Differences in Rates of Fatal Violence and Victimization," *Journal of Trauma,* 1992, *33,* 1–5.
6. Monk, G., and Winslade, J. (eds.), *Narrative Therapy in Practice: The Archaeology of Hope* (San Francisco: Jossey-Bass, 1996).
7. Winslade, J., Monk, G., and Cotter, A., "A Narrative Approach to the Practice of Mediation," *Negotiation Journal,* 1998, *14*(1), 21–42.

# Acknowledgments

This project would not have germinated and grown into this book if it had not been for the wonderful professional and personal nurturance and encouragement we received from an awesome group of friends and colleagues who offered us their time, support, and expertise.

We want to salute the efforts of Alison Cotter and Tim Clarke; their wonderful support, professional input, and expertise have helped us present some of the narrative ideas we have developed together over the last few years. Our heartfelt appreciation goes to Alison for her painstaking reviews of our draft chapters and for her thoughtful advice and guidance. A special thank you goes to Wally McKenzie for sharing his creativity and genius with us in complex and challenging mediations. Chapter Nine is based on many of Wally's ideas, developed over years of professional practice.

We would like to thank the large group of mediators at Waikato Mediation Services, who provided us with the professional stimulation that inspired us to document and celebrate the achievements and successes we experienced in those heady days when the agency was established. Specifically, we would like to thank David Swain, Richard Te Ao, Chris Jacques, Stephen Hooper, Yvonne Smolenski, Richard Cohen, Rae Brooker, Saskia Schuitemaker, Eileen Suttor, and Bill Anderson. We also want to thank Waikato Mediation Society for continuing to act as a catalyst for the further evolution of our mediation practices. Our appreciation goes to David Lang, Marg Robbie, Margaret Craig, and Marijke Boers.

The school community conferencing project funded by the Ministry of Education in New Zealand provided another forum in which to explore and reflect on narrative approaches and their compatibility with other mediation models emerging from Restorative Justice and Maori concepts of mediation. We want to thank Angus MacFarlane, Timoti Harris, and Jan Robertson.

Thanks to Linda Fletcher for her clear feedback on style and organization in some of the chapters. Thanks also to Sue Turner-Jones for her willingness to help us on short notice with the graphics that illustrate some of the theoretical concepts in the book.

Finally, we want to thank our dear friends and colleagues in the counselor education program, Wendy Drewery and Kathie Crocket, for their ongoing support in helping us explore the narrative metaphor in new fields of inquiry. The University of Waikato and the Department of Education Studies provided us with opportunities to travel to conferences and to offer professional forums to apply these ideas in the community, and time to synthesize our ideas and put them together in some accessible fashion.

# Narrative Mediation

# Chapter One

# Narrative Mediation: What Is It?

*The universe is transformation: our life is what our thoughts make it.*
(MARCUS AURELIUS ANTONINUS, "MEDITATIONS")

*Healing is a matter of time, but it is sometimes also a matter of opportunity.*
(HIPPOCRATES, "PRECEPTS")

Greg wanted the custody of the children to be decided in the family court. "I'm sick of the bloody arguments," he said. "She keeps changing her bloody mind. One day she's all understanding and wanting me to be involved and the next day she's trying to keep me from having a say. I've had enough! I can't see how this mediation is going to make any difference. I don't want to have to rework this issue for one more day. She's made up her mind. It's like talking to a frigging brick wall. How are you going to make any difference? This mess has been going on for months!"

For those who have been involved in divorce mediation, such a scenario will not be unfamiliar. It presents many challenges for a mediator to start to work with. In this book we introduce you to how we would approach the process of mediation in such a situation. We think that the model we are proposing is significantly different from other approaches to mediation, particularly the commonly espoused problem-solving model of mediation.[1] We call our approach *narrative* to signify some of the ways in which we conceptualize mediation

1

and also to link it to the work of other people who use this metaphor to describe their work.

To start, we tell you a story. It is the story of a mediation between Greg and Fiona. We usher you through this story to illustrate the approach we flesh out in the following chapters. This first chapter is like a snapshot; the more detailed moving picture comes later.

The story shows narrative mediation in action. This method has both a theoretical robustness and some creative ideas for practice to recommend it. The story provides an overview of some of the narrative moves used in mediating a conflict between Greg and Fiona. The challenges thrown up by this conflict are rich opportunities for demonstrating a range of mediation moves to help create preferred outcomes.

### A Mediation Story

Greg was not enamored with the idea of mediation. (The comment at the beginning of this chapter is from his first meeting with the mediator.) He wanted a family court judge to put a stop to Fiona's "controlling and manipulative behavior." The judge would surely make a "sensible" decision and give Greg custody of the children. Greg was sure that the judge would understand his story.

Fiona had initiated the mediation. She had outlined to the mediator in a telephone conversation that she had interim custody of the three children and was highly motivated to avoid the agony of an expensive and lengthy court hearing. She did not think this ugly dispute was going to be solved by a judge.

Fiona was also sick of Greg's threats. She knew he would tell the mediator that she deserved to lose all the children, that she was to blame for the breakup of their marriage of fourteen years. Fiona was most upset about how Greg would run her down in front of her friends in their small rural community. He would tell her friends that she had no morals and that she had deceived him when she had an affair with Greg's friend three years previously.

Fiona and Greg had a well-developed problem-saturated narrative about the conflict.[2] Each described the other in unidimensional, fixed, and unyielding terms. Elements of this problem narrative had such a tangible and reified quality that both Fiona and Greg experienced their own storied account as the only true description of the events of the conflict.

# The Storying Process

The narrative perception is that people tend to organize their experiences in story form. The narrative metaphor draws attention to the ways in which we use stories to make sense of our lives and relationships.[3] People grow up amid a multitude of competing narratives that help shape how they see themselves and others. They tell stories about themselves and about others. They act both out of and into these stories, shaping the direction of the ongoing plot as they do so. Descriptions of problems are typically told in narrative terms. Such problem narratives have often been rehearsed and elaborated over and over again by participants in a conflict.

Mediators who use a narrative orientation are interested in the constitutive properties of conflict stories. In other words, whether a story is factual or not matters little to the potential impact it has in someone's life. Our emphasis is on how the story operates to create reality rather than on whether it reports accurately on that reality. Stories therefore are not viewed as either true or false accounts of an objective "out there" reality. Such a view is not possible, because events cannot be known independently of the dominant narratives held by the knower. It is therefore more useful to concentrate on viewing stories as constructing the world rather than viewing the world as independently known and then described through stories.

Practitioners who use this approach are only too aware of the difficulties that arise when mediators seek an objective account of "what really happened" in order then to coach the parties into a more balanced way of looking at the problem. We would even expect such efforts to meet with resistance. From within a dispute it makes perfect sense for conflicted parties to "story" the conflict in their own terms. It is therefore more helpful for a mediator to validate explicitly the stories through which people experience the conflict and then to seek out the points where the story might incorporate some different perspectives.

### Beginning the Mediation

Greg was mandated to attend at least one mediation session before the matter could be taken further in the family court. Although he was reluctant to attend, he still had a lot to say about his present circumstances and about his desire for custody of the children.

Greg had established his own courier company over recent years and described not having the time he would have liked to spend with his children and, now, his ex-wife, Fiona. He reflected back on these times with some regrets. Yet there was a great deal he was proud of. He was now a self-made man. He enjoyed a very good income and employed a growing fleet of drivers and a competent administrative staff to cater to the demands of his burgeoning business.

At first Greg was clear that his full commitment to his career and the establishment of a strong financial foundation were the best contributions he could have made to his family's development. He recollected clearly the financial struggles his parents had experienced in his early youth and the shame his father had suffered in barely managing to look after the basic needs of the family. Greg did not want to put his family through the money worries of his childhood. Indeed, Fiona had enjoyed a financially comfortable life with Greg in recent years and, while married, had needed to work only part-time, so she was able to follow interests outside of the family.

Greg and Fiona's children—Frank (fifteen), Jessie (eleven), and Thomas (six)—were receiving a high-quality education at a private school and had had some wonderful vacations with their mother in the last few years. Greg had missed most of these vacations because of the demands made on his time by work pressures. Clearly he regretted missing out on so much of the children's childhood. Earlier in the marriage he had wished that he was more nurturing toward Fiona, but now he was bitter about how she was behaving toward him. Greg was against the separation that Fiona had instigated some seven months before. Although he was still angry at her betrayal and the agitation she had caused him, he still loved her, he said.

Greg explained that it had taken time to build up his business. But now that it was virtually running itself, he imagined he could devote more time to the children, even if he couldn't be with Fiona. In fact, he saw that it was now his right to help shape the children's moral development.

Following his separation from Fiona, Greg had become reinvolved in a Christian fellowship from which he had been disengaged since his teens. He was keen to imbue a strong Christian presence into the children's lives. Greg explained that Fiona was now spending significant amounts of time socializing with friends and, in his view, was not providing the quality of care he thought the children deserved.

Greg was also agitated about the implications for his business of a matrimonial settlement that was still to be finalized through Greg's and Fiona's lawyers. Greg did not think Fiona was entitled to half of their assets. He felt it had been due to his own efforts that the business had gone so well. He recognized that legally he would very likely have to pay out a significant share to Fiona, but he wanted to minimize the size of this payout in order to maintain business solvency.

Greg was certainly unwilling to give up the family home. Fiona had moved into a two-bedroom apartment with Frank, Jessie, and Thomas. Greg, however, wanted the children to live with him in the family home. For her part, Fiona was convinced that the children were better off with her.

## Opening Up Space in a Tightly Woven Story

Judgment and accusation are typically woven so tightly around the participants in a conflict that there does not seem to be any space for other descriptions of what has taken place or what could take place. We refer to these descriptions as *totalizing descriptions;* that is, they sum up a complex situation in one description that purports to give a total picture of the situation or of a person in it.[4] Totalizing descriptions of the conflict and of the conflict's protagonists tend to become highly evolved before the mediator has an opportunity to be part of the conversation.

One of the major tasks of a mediator is to destabilize the totalizing descriptions of conflict so as to undermine the rigid and negative motivations that the conflicted parties ascribe to each other. A variety of strategies can be employed by a mediator to loosen these negative attributions. These strategies help to create a context from which a preferred story line can be developed. They may include the following:

- Building trust in the mediator and in the mediation process
- Developing externalizing conversations
- Mapping the effects of the problem on the person
- Deconstructing the dominant story lines
- Developing shared meanings about the conflict and its solutions

These strategies are elaborated in considerable detail in the following chapters. However, here we briefly introduce them in relation to the scenario presented earlier, to give you the flavor of the narrative mediation process.

## Building the Relationship in Mediation

Building trust with each of the disputing parties is crucial to the successful outcome of any mediation. When people feel hurt by the actions of another, they tend to rework aspects of the conflict story to reinforce their own sense of injustice, betrayal, victimization, or mistreatment. The mediator can use the narrative metaphor to convey to each of the parties that the mediator has grasped the depth of their distress, without appearing to collude with each party's problem-saturated descriptions of the other.

Mediators are interested in employing strategies that will take some of the intensity out of the conflict and destabilize it to the point where alternative stories can be considered. Careful, respectful listening is a key part of this process. Respect is demonstrated through taking seriously someone's story and avoiding making assumptions about underlying deficit in the person. The starting assumption of the narrative approach is that it is likely that everyone is doing their best to deal with the conflict with the resources they have at hand.

## Externalizing Conversations

Externalizing conversations, discussed in more detail in Chapter Six, are one of the most powerful methods that narrative practitioners can use to help disputing parties disidentify with the problem story and begin to develop shared meanings, understandings, and solutions.[5] Externalizing conversations reverse the common logic in both popular and academic psychology that increasingly focuses explanations for events inside the person. Externalizing conversations focus attention on the relational domain. As mediators externalize a problem, they speak about it as if it were an external object or person exerting an influence on the parties but they do not identify it closely with one party or the other.

In the first meeting with Greg, it was helpful for the mediator to prepare for an externalizing conversation with Greg by identifying some of the dominant themes in Greg's account of the problem. Certainly distrust, betrayal, and neglect featured prominently in Greg's descriptions of what was happening to him in his relationship with Fiona. The mediator could then speak of these themes as if they are the problem, rather than identifying Greg or Fiona as the problem.

The mediator asked Greg to identify what he thought were some of the central difficulties that had led to the current conflict over the custody of the children. After pondering the mediator's request briefly, Greg said, "Fiona has caused me a great deal of grief."

As is typical of parties caught in a prolonged conflict, Greg stayed with an internalizing, blaming description of Fiona. The grief he was experiencing was storied as originating from within Fiona, either as a deliberate desire to hurt him or as a result of her character. Externalizing conversations help separate the problem from the person and open space for a perspective in which blame and shame become less significant. Mediators who explore the use of externalizing conversations need not be disheartened by the blaming responses of the parties to one another despite the efforts of the mediator to externalize the problem. Careful listening by the mediator along with curiosity and enthusiastic persistence are useful in reconstructing problem narratives in less blaming terms.

The mediator next asked Greg, "If we could name this account of the difficulties you have experienced with Fiona 'a great deal of grief caused by distrust, betrayal, agitation, and neglect,' would that come close?" Greg wasn't exactly sure but he thought this description was close enough for now.

In interactions with Greg, the mediator often referred to the dispute over custody of the children as "this conflict" or "this betrayal," "this distrust" or "this neglect," or "this grief." The externalizing descriptions used depended on the direction of the conversation. Staying with the externalization of relational themes that underpinned Greg's blame of Fiona created an atmosphere in which Greg could focus on the effects of the conflict on his life and on the children. This helped him to avoid focusing on the character flaws and inadequacies he might have otherwise emphasized about Fiona.

## Mapping the Effects of the Conflict History on Disputing Parties

Fuller descriptions of what is going on give the mediator much more information about how individuals construct problem issues. In the case of Greg and Fiona, the mediator explored the effects of the problem-saturated story in order to gain a richer description of the parties' different understandings of the conflict.[6] The mediator paid particular attention to fleshing out the history of this account of the problem. The ebb and flow of the conflict could then be storied from its origins in an externalized fashion to help the parties understand the impact that the evolution of the conflict had had on them.

A historical account allows for a time orientation to emerge. This time orientation offers an enriched perspective. The rhythms and patterns of the conflict are more clearly perceived by each of the parties as they gain clarity about how the conflict is changing and possibly escalating. Naming when the conflict began and tracing how it developed provide openings for the mediator to inquire about experiences that stand outside the conflict. The skills required to historicize the effects of the problem are discussed in Chapter Six.

The mediator asked Greg, "When did you first became aware of the problems around custody of the children?" Greg stated that the problems started when he objected to Fiona's "declining ability to care for the children." One of the children had mentioned that their mother had gone out one night with a girlfriend and left Frank, the oldest child, in charge. She hadn't come home until midnight. Greg reported being furious on hearing about what he described as a "serious lapse" in her parenting. He now doubted her ability to provide consistent quality care for the children. Greg also reported that he worried about the children not getting an appropriate spiritual education. He added that he would be taking the children to church and Sunday school if the children were in his care.

The inclusion of *relative influence questions* or *mapping-the-effects questions* often builds momentum and volition within the parties.

These questions map the effects of the conflict on each person associated with it. They assist the parties to come to grips with how much the conflict has cost them in both personal and material terms.

The mediator asked Greg how the conflict had been affecting his well-being. Greg reported that he was living with additional stress in his life. He was worried about the legal costs of gaining custody of the children and how he would fare in the pending court hearing. He said that his sleep patterns were disrupted and he had not been eating regular meals. He expressed concern about the toll it was all taking on his physical and emotional well-being. He was feeling desperately lonely and was painfully aware that he was not in a psychological space to develop a relationship with anybody else. The matrimonial property issues were weighing heavily on him.

But the effects of the conflict were not just on Greg and Fiona. The mediator wanted Greg to include in his story of the problem an account of the impact of the conflict on the children. There is value in helping disputing parties see how a conflict spills over into other domains in their own and other people's lives.

The mediator asked Greg, "What effect is the growing lack of trust with Fiona having on the children?"

"I haven't got the faintest idea," Greg said slowly but thoughtfully. "I am seeing so little of the children right now that I don't really know what shape they are in."

Greg was initially reluctant to consider seriously how the conflict had been touching the children's lives. After further discussion, it became clear to him that the children had been suffering as a result of the escalating dispute between him and Fiona. He was concerned about this. The lack of trust between Greg and Fiona was troubling the children, although at this point Greg was holding Fiona completely responsible for the conflict.

Jessie, the middle child, seemed to be suffering the most. Her teacher had reported that Jessie's grades had been deteriorating and she appeared to be mildly depressed. It seemed that the negative effects of the conflict were growing. The mediator asked Greg if he thought the lack of trust and grief were going to do further damage to himself and the children given the direction in which the conflict was moving. Greg stated that he thought the damage could get worse but it could be averted if the family court judge were to rule in Greg's favor soon. Even as he said this, Greg recognized that a ruling on custody was many months away.

In the course of such an inquiry into the effects of a problem on the people involved, a story develops about the functions of the conflict in everyone's lives. After sufficiently mapping these effects, the mediator asked Greg whether he would like to do something to change the direction of the conflict. These same lines of inquiry were followed with Fiona as well.

The mediator asked Greg, "Are you willing to continue adjusting to the growing deterioration of trust while waiting for a judge to take action, or are you interested in doing some damage control by building some trust in the meantime?" Greg was not sure what he could do, because it depended to a large extent on what Fiona did. He stated, however, that he would certainly be willing to do the best he could on his side to halt any further erosion of trust.

The significance of inviting the parties to make a judgment about the effects of the problem is elucidated in Chapter Seven.

## Constructing Solution-Bound Narratives

It is significant for a mediator when one of the parties clearly states that he or she does not want to participate in escalating the conflict. This decision can open the door to a very different conversation. The mediator was now able to ask Greg if there had been any brief periods when there were interactions with Fiona in which he thought trust was building rather than diminishing. This move in narrative mediation is based on the notion that people in dispute are likely to have had experiences that were not completely dominated by the history of the conflict.[7]

In this initial session it was possible to begin to *coauthor* with Greg an alternative, non-problem-bound narrative that could serve as the rudimentary stage of a resolution to the problem. Greg could recall a few instances when his interactions with Fiona were not filled with angst. Although initially it was a struggle for him to remember, he recalled how Fiona and he had calmly discussed plans for Jessie's birthday. Greg described how a month earlier he had managed to spend a cordial and at times friendly evening with Fiona at Jessie's party.

Narrative mediators put effort into tracking non-problem-bound interactions. Through a series of questions about these interactions, the mediator and Greg were beginning to assemble some alternative descriptions of Greg's relationship with Fiona that were not completely dominated by lack of trust and bad feeling. Greg was beginning to open the door to building trust in his parenting relationship with Fiona. He did not need to put everything on hold while he waited for a decision from a family court judge. He was able to recall a number of other examples of collaborative and cooperative interchanges within recent months.

In their conversations thus far, Greg and the mediator had made the following progress:

- Greg was gaining a fuller appreciation of the toll the conflict was having on him and his family.
- He and the mediator were coauthoring an alternative account of Greg and Fiona working together.
- Greg was much more engaged in the mediation process and was beginning to recognize that establishing a cooperative parenting relationship with Fiona was necessary.

*Fiona's Account*

A separate meeting was arranged with Fiona. The mediator asked her to express her views on the present difficulties and to provide a brief overview of the history of the conflict with Greg.

Fiona was adamant that her marriage was over. She described many years of feeling empty and alone in the marriage. She felt that Greg had been consistently emotionally unavailable for long periods. Even a short while after marrying, Fiona had noticed a change in Greg. She remembered that he had been very attentive, available, and loving when they had lived together. All that had seemed to change after they got married. Fiona described Greg as losing himself in his work. He would be gone early in the morning and would often return late in the evening. He would be exhausted and spend little time with the children, even though he cared about them. All of this discussion supported a view of the negative effects on Fiona of Greg's single-minded focus on being a successful material provider.

Fiona indicated that she was completely responsible for attending to the children's psychological and emotional needs. She would attend to their distress, deal with their disappointments and conflicts, and delight in their successes. She granted that Greg did his best to play with the children and attend school functions, but he was usually unavailable. Fiona claimed that Greg would often lose his patience with the children and become short-tempered and somewhat aggressive with them.

It is useful for the mediator to store away such commentary because it provides a rich background picture in which some of the dominant cultural patterns that have influenced the direction and shape of the conflict can later be identified.

An assumption of narrative mediation is that conflict is produced within competing cultural norms. The mediator was therefore interested in eliciting from Fiona some of the dominant cultural norms that had had an impact on her. The mediator asked Fiona to discuss some of her ideas about marriage and what she had hoped for in her relationship and in the family she and Greg had developed.

Fiona believed that in the early part of her marriage both she and Greg had expected that Fiona would be the homemaker and take charge of the domestic duties. She said they had never really negotiated this but had found themselves caught up in patterns that had been modeled by their parents. By adopting a curious and naive posture, the mediator helped Fiona to name how in both her and Greg's family of origin the women were primarily responsible for the psychological support of their husbands and children. Featured were traditional gendered patterns for the division of labor in which the male was responsible for the primary income and the female was responsible for the care of the home and the raising of the children.

The mediator asked Fiona what her attitude was toward these cultural imperatives. She felt resentful about her predicament and wished that she had been more assertive with Greg about what she wanted. She had dedicated herself to being a good mother and homemaker. She had done her best to be responsive and caring toward Greg, but she felt she had gotten little in return other than temporary financial security. Now that too was gone. She did not have a career and she wished that she had insisted on support from Greg to commence some studies. She felt betrayed by Greg's "neglect of the family's psychological needs." Fiona was now immediately faced with minimal income. She would get a meager financial benefit from the state and she could supplement this income with her part-time work.

Fiona felt entitled to at least half of the business assets because of the sacrifices she had made in raising the children and taking care of Greg's needs in the home. Yet she also felt guilty about the extra pressures this would put on Greg to find some way of keeping his business while dividing his assets in half to pay Fiona her share of the matrimonial property. This was an issue she would have to face.

Fiona was clear that Greg was in no position to have custody of the children. Currently he had the children in his care every second weekend and set aside one afternoon per week to spend time with them after school. In Fiona's view, the children did not want to live with their father, though she recognized that Jessie had a stronger psychological tie with Greg. Fiona thought that Jessie felt responsible for providing some care and company for her father. Jessie had said to Fiona that she was worried about her Dad living all alone and that he needed somebody to look after him. Fiona was strongly against splitting up the custodial care of the children.

As Fiona told her story she began to get a clearer understanding of some of the dominant cultural messages that had affected her while she was married to Greg. It was important for her to identify these messages because it subsequently assisted her to be less dogged by guilt and self-blame for ending the marriage. By linking the gendered themes of servitude and submission implicit in Fiona's problem-saturated narrative, the mediator helped her to recognize that she was much more vulnerable to verbal attacks from Greg because of her dominant feelings of guilt and self-doubt.

During this meeting, the mediator asked Fiona what guilt and self-blame had done to her when the marriage had begun to unravel. Fiona responded that guilt and self-blame had been extremely costly for her. However, she had also spent long periods wondering whether she should try to repair the damage done to her relationship with Greg. This had left her feeling confused and had led her to give inconsistent messages to him about where their relationship stood. Sometimes, in an effort to alleviate the guilt, she had conveyed to Greg that there was still some hope for their relationship. At other times she was very clear that she could not return to the habitual pattern of relating that had characterized so much of their relationship. It had been too costly for her.

This interview with Fiona achieved a number of narrative mediation purposes:

- The effects of the problem narrative on her life were storied.
- Descriptions of a preferred future parenting relationship with Greg were explored.
- Preconceived notions about marriage and relationship that had been problematic for Fiona were identified.
- The features of the cultural context that had caught her in a particular pattern of relating to Greg were also identified. She could see how this pattern undermined her own sense of confidence and well-being. She could also see how this pattern created confusion and disruption for Greg.

## Disassembling Cultural Prescriptions

Fiona had been positioned (not so much by Greg as by conventional cultural discourse) as the domestic server and social-emotional caregiver of the family. Throughout her marriage she had felt obliged to take complete care of the children's psychological well-being and had assumed that this was her primary role in life. She now realized that over the years this role had taken its toll. The moral weight of it was particularly burdensome, because there was no sign that Greg would be relieving her of this responsibility.

Cultural norms invoke particular patterns or styles of relating that are enacted in repetitive ways. The mediator, using a narrative orientation, focuses on those cultural constraints that limit the possibilities available to individuals to address their concerns. Engaging carefully in a conversation about preferred experiences that lie outside the domain of the problem opens up new discursive or cultural possibilities.[8] These openings can lead to a resolution of the conflict. The significance of the sociocultural context for the mediator in addressing conflict is expanded and developed in Chapter Two.

Narrative mediation is not merely a set of techniques that can be clipped onto existing mediation models. This approach invites mediators to think very carefully about how their own constructions of the mediation process can significantly influence the outcome. The mediator in this conflict needed to be aware of his own gendered constructions about marriage and relationship, and he needed to consider how his own beliefs might contribute to shaping the conversation. Dominant cultural story lines are likely to influence the kinds of questions the mediator asks and how he hears and understands the parties' concerns. For example, if the mediator has fixed ideas about the kinds of roles men and women should play in a marriage, at some subtle level these views will have an impact on the mediation. We argue that neutrality and impartiality are severely constrained by the cultural location of the mediator.

Many mediation researchers suggest that the mediator should attend to the psychological relationships and to procedural or process matters and be less involved in the substantive or content aspects of any dispute.[9] For example, in the preceding scenario, many mediators would stress the importance of building a strong relational connection with the parties in early mediation interchanges and establishing appropriate procedural guidelines.

Yet there is also significant variation in how mediators respond to relational, process, and substantive issues because of the influence of their theoretical persuasions. For example, some mediators working with family conflict perform as advocates for children. They become keenly involved in substantive issues, particularly when children's needs have been neglected.[10] From this perspective, mediators are directly involved in the content discussions of the mediation. Other mediation researchers suggest that it is not appropriate for mediators to influence the parties directly in shaping content matters.[11]

We do not believe that the separation of process and content issues is as simple as it can be made to sound. Process issues shape the content that can arise, and any process will privilege some content issues over others. In practice, we argue, relationship, process, and content issues are all interwoven in the very fabric of mediation.

## Naming Dominant Discourses

Because narrative mediators are interested in tracking the background narratives and identifying the themes that underpin the conflict, it is useful to record the dominant themes. Such recordings will of course be affected by the discursive themes that have an impact on the mediator. In the first session with Fiona, for example, the mediator noted the following background discursive themes that appeared to be a feature of her relationship with Greg:

- A wife should be submissive to the needs of her husband.
- A wife should gain her sense of pleasure and satisfaction through the achievements of her husband.
- A woman is responsible for the social and emotional needs of her husband and children.
- A woman should put aside her own career aspirations.

It seemed that Fiona was still heavily influenced by these discursive influences. However, mapping their effects on her sharpened her sense of the cost that these cultural prescriptions were exacting from her sense of well-being. She was clear too that she did not have to keep subjecting herself to these cultural norms or continue to seek fulfillment through being a dutiful wife and partner. This knowledge had assisted her decision to create a life independent of Greg. The clarity she was gaining from the early mediation session was enabling her to be more consistent with Greg about her intentions.

## A Deconstructive Conversation with Greg

The mediator met individually with both Greg and Fiona one more time before a joint session was held. Greg was not keen to meet with Fiona until he felt better prepared. From the mediator's perspective, there was potential value in strengthening Greg's degree of engagement in the mediation. The mediator also wanted an opportunity to understand further Greg's perspectives on the problem.

Before this second session with Greg, the mediator wrote down some of the discursive themes from the first session. The mediator saw Greg as being strongly positioned by a "head of the household discourse" that invited Greg into the position of making executive decisions—in this case, about what was required to resolve the conflict. In addition, in his understanding of Christianity, Greg saw himself as the appropriate moral educator for the children.

Greg felt entitled to be the custodial caregiver for the children. (We discuss how such entitlements are built from a discursive perspective in Chapter Four.) His sense of entitlement was founded on what he identified as Fiona's betrayal of her marriage vows and the damage he perceived the divorce would do to the children. In passing he did suggest that he would accept joint custody if it was not possible to have sole custody. He believed, however, that Fiona's unwillingness to try to rebuild their relationship was evidence of her lack of moral fiber. From the mediator's perspective, Greg was strongly positioned by a fundamentalist patriarchal stance.

This discursive imperative often invokes a rigid position in a custodial conflict. In the second session with Greg, the mediator explored with him other possible discursive imperatives that were influencing his view of what he was entitled to. They identified the following background discourses:

- Men contribute to the family by being primary income earners.
- The man is the head of the household and should take charge when the family is threatened.
- A good male provider is a good income earner.
- A woman who leaves her husband has betrayed the family. She loses her right to have any say over the welfare of the children. She has breached her contract.
- A Christian life is superior to an agnostic life. A practicing Christian is a better parent than a nonbeliever.

The mediator then went on to explore with Greg the effects of the statement, "A good male provider is a good income earner." The mediator developed an externalizing conversation in order to name the effects of this particular discourse on Greg, Fiona, and the children.

The mediator asked Greg whether he felt burdened by "being a good provider," and to what extent he had felt morally obliged to make so many work sacrifices. Greg described feeling the full weight of this responsibility and how it persuaded him into a quest to provide for Fiona and the children in a manner that he might have only dreamed about as a child.

The mediator then asked a relative influence question: "Greg, what have been the effects on you of feeling the full moral weight of responsibility for being a generous and successful provider?"

Greg responded, "I think I have done a great job in providing security for the family. I also feel genuinely proud of what I have accomplished in my work life, but I do have regrets. You know, I have sacrificed a lot, but I now wonder whether it was all worth it."

The mediator asked Greg to elaborate (a simple use of *narrative curiosity*).[12] Greg responded, "Well, I missed out on some of the most special times in the children's growing up, including vacation time. Their childhoods are almost half over and I'm only now beginning to realize the painful consequences of being so preoccupied with work commitments."

The mediator asked Greg about other costs of the "man is the provider" discourse. Greg had been suffering from high blood pressure and regular migraine headaches. He thought that these physical ailments were effects of the physical demands he had placed on himself. The stress of fighting for the custody of the children was currently exacerbating some of these physical symptoms.

Such questions helped "unpack," or *deconstruct,* some of the discursive content in Greg's story of Fiona's "betrayal." He had done his best to meet the demands of the dominant discourse. Fiona's initiative to separate from him and her rejection of the authority of this discourse appeared to discount this effort. The mediator's questions helped crystallize for Greg the role that being a good provider had played in this sense of betrayal, as well as its effects on his health.

Greg stated a wish to be freed from the discursive dictate to work slavishly at being a successful provider. He was already moderating his work to give him more quality time with the children and for his church activities. We would describe this wish as an expression of a desire to reposition himself within the provider discourse. However, the patriarchal discourse still had a very strong influence over him. The mediator did not want to be too directive in exploring the discursive underpinnings of Greg's identity as a father, for fear of coming across as intrusive or judgmental. Therefore, the mediator sought to acknowledge Greg's commitment to being a better parent. However, Greg's certainty about his custodial rights still provided little opportunity for creating leverage in the mediation. For significant movement to take place in the custodial dispute, Greg would also need to loosen his certainties about his role as the executive decision maker.

## A Deconstructive Conversation with Fiona

When the mediator met with Fiona again, they continued to develop the deconstructive conversation they had begun in their first meeting. Here two parts of that conversation are highlighted.

The mediator asked Fiona what she needed in preparation for the joint session with Greg. She said she wanted to shore up her ability to manage guilt and to limit the effects of self-blame. The mediator asked Fiona a relative influence question about her growing ability to resist guilt and self-blame. She responded that increasingly she wanted to reposition herself as a woman making her way in the world independently of her husband. While Greg had continued to subscribe to traditional discursive prescriptions in the marriage, Fiona had over time clearly revised her own understanding of what it meant to be in partnership. Her current view was very different from what it had been when she began the relationship.

The mediator then asked Fiona what had influenced her to change her thinking. Fiona identified some alternative discourses that were emerging influences in her identity. At the end of the second session, she was clearly more comfortable with the following discursive themes:

- Addressing the other person's emotional and psychological needs should be reciprocal in a partnership.
- A woman has a right to develop her own career aspirations within a marriage.
- A male partner should take on a more equitable role in taking care of the psychological needs of the children.
- A female partner should have an equal role in the making of decisions in the home.

This kind of discursive analysis maps out the territory from which ways out of the conflict can be found. As we live, we "perform meaning" around such statements. We also offer one another positions from which to relate. The statements that embody dominant or alternative discourses are not compulsory requirements for living, however. As we weave stories around them, they come to express the realities of the relations between us.

In this case, there were some clear discrepancies between the discursive themes from which Greg and Fiona were operating. No amount of negotiation on substantive issues, or even negotiation on the basis of underlying interests, was going to shift that discrepancy. What was needed was a set of discursive statements in which both parties could feel included. Then some compelling stories would need to be woven around those themes before a way forward could be found in the conflict.

## Introducing the Children's Voices

One of the options in a situation like this, where two competing stories were casting the two protagonists, Greg and Fiona, into conflict with each other, was to widen the conversation and include other voices. Other voices would alter the dynamics; they would call forth new responses so that Greg and Fiona would not simply respond to each other's voices (and each other's discursive positions).

In this case, further perspectives could be introduced by involving Greg and Fiona's children in the decision-making process. Frank, Jessie, and Thomas were all old enough to have their own perspectives on the kind of caregiving plan their parents could devise. Although Greg initially placed little weight on the children's views, he was willing to consent to the children being interviewed to determine their interest in where they might receive custodial care. The mediator's hunch was that introducing the children into the conversation could make it possible for Greg to review his claims to executive authority.

The mediator interviewed the children both separately and together. He paid particular attention to the use of *relative influence questions* to explore the children's reactions to the idea of living with either their father or mother or both at different times. In response to the mediator's careful questions, the children disclosed their preference for living with their mother, despite having to live in more cramped conditions, although Jessie acknowledged that she wanted also to live with her father, primarily because she felt responsible for monitoring his well-being. She was the only female child and seemed influenced by the story that girls and women are responsible for looking after brothers, fathers, and children. But if she were to consider her own preference, she wanted the status quo.

This is an instance in which the mediator's own values are present in the conversational moves. The mediator did not support the position taken by Greg that he should have an executive role in deciding where the children would live. The mediator saw the children as having a legitimate say in decisions about their future. He wanted them to have an opportunity to tell their father and mother, in an unthreatening context, their views about their care. He contracted with the children that they did not have to answer any questions they did not want to answer.

This stance is not a neutral one. It contradicts the dominant legal discourse that still sees children as chattel of their parents who are not expected to have a voice of their own.

## The Family Meeting

Greg, Fiona, and the children all attended the next session. The mediator invited the children to speak about their own views on their caregiving arrangements. It was clearly difficult for Jessie to talk. She did not want her father to think she was abandoning him. The mediator supported Jessie's desire not to say anything while Frank and Thomas made their views clear to their father. They spoke frankly about their wish to keep the caregiving arrangements the same.

One of the tasks of mediation is to create contexts in which the participants in a conflict have opportunities to reflect on and examine their positions. This needs to be done in a fashion that does not create defensiveness and guardedness in the participants. Providing a context within the mediation where the children could speak about their desires and wishes was one such context. It enabled the parents to examine their views and reposition themselves in relation to the children's views as well as in relation to each other.

The mediator asked Greg to make meaning out of what the children had said. What had he heard them say and what did it mean to him? It became obvious to Greg, perhaps for the first time, that his children had clear ideas about what they wanted that were in contrast to his own. Again, the mediator inquired about the significance of this information. Greg recognized that to insist on his plans and make the children do something to which they were vigorously opposed would begin to alienate them from him. He began to rethink his role in the family.

This was a *unique outcome* in the conflict story.[13] It was the beginning of Greg's repositioning himself in relation to the custody dispute. Inviting the children into the mediation process proved to be significant. They stepped out of the position of being objects of their parents' discourse. As the parents made room in the conversation for the children's voices, their own positions were altered, both in relation to the children and in relation to each other. As Greg in particular revised his position about what he wanted for the children, it became possible to start to build a caregiving consensus between him and Fiona.

## Moving Toward Consensus

In two subsequent sessions, Fiona became more flexible in her dealings with Greg as he softened his formerly authoritative stance. The mediator exercised his curiosity about the details of their ideas about caregiving arrangements. This led them to develop greater fluidity in these arrangements, particularly in relation to holiday plans for the children.

Greg was now willing to entertain some challenges to his patriarchal ideas about parental and marital roles. This was evident in his revisions of his relationship with the children. He was now less insistent and less sure that having the children live with him was the right option. Frank's and Thomas's comments had hit Greg hard. The boys had spoken eloquently about their wishes, and Frank had also explained that Jessie felt torn about wanting to live with Greg because of her feelings of responsibility for him. Greg was ready to hear these comments and clearly was revising what he thought should happen.

In addition, he was now less focused on blaming Fiona for the pain she had caused him and was more concerned about bringing this stressful conflict to a close. He agreed with the mediator's comment that Greg seemed less in need of controlling the caregiving arrangements, and he added that a lot of the tension and struggle he had been feeling for months was beginning to subside.

In the last session with Greg and Fiona, the mediator noticed a lightness in their voices as they talked about planning a surprise birthday party for Frank. Trust was building in their parenting relationship. Negotiating the caregiving arrangements for the children now seemed much more straightforward. Greg accepted that Fiona would continue as the primary caregiver but he would become more involved in the children's day-to-day lives. It was arranged that on the weekend the children were with Fiona, Greg would pick up Thomas and Jessie and take them to church. Frank and Jessie often wanted time with their friends on the weekends. Sometimes this meant they would not be with Fiona or Greg on one of the weekend nights. Greg was now much more accommodating of these requests.

## Holding to the Preferred Story

Fiona and Greg were now beginning to disengage from their totalizing descriptions of the other as hurtful and destructive. They were developing more understanding of what it meant to move from a couple relationship to a parenting one. In other words, they were developing a different story about their relationship. It was the mediator's concern to keep asking questions to help them elaborate this story.

In response to these questions, Greg was certainly able to distance himself more from his earlier struggles to control the outcome of the battle for custody of the children. He had been able to hear, perhaps for the first time, the wishes of his children, which were separate from what he desired for them. He was also beginning to realize that part of his fight for the custody of the children was his attempt to punish Fiona.

Fiona, for her part, was willing to be much more empathetic toward Greg as she saw him beginning to shift away from the authoritative, controlling stance he had demonstrated earlier. Although some mediators might conclude that the work was now done, a further session would prove to be an important investment in settling the somewhat fragile negotiations.

Many mediators prize the sweet taste of success when helping parties resolve a long-standing acrimonious conflict. It is therefore disheartening for a mediator to find his or her hard work unraveling when the conflicting parties return to the earlier interactional pattern that had escalated the original conflict. The narrative perspective makes sense of this backsliding by seeing it as a possible outcome of the competition between stories. The story of conflict has sufficient pull to upset the fledgling new story until the new story is knitted fully into the fabric of the participants' lives. For this reason, it is preferable in a mediation to spend time finding ways to strengthen the solution-bound narratives that emerge when greater understanding is achieved. It can take only one or two negative encounters to reactivate problem-saturated narratives.

A follow-up session with Greg and Fiona took place three weeks after the meeting with the children. Both appeared comfortable and reasonably relaxed. Although they reported that there had been no major disagreements about the caregiving arrangements over the last three weeks, they were both on tenterhooks about the matrimonial property settlement meeting that was scheduled for the following week. They were to meet together with their respective lawyers.

The mediator asked Greg and Fiona to reflect on the last six weeks and identify what they were particularly pleased about in their dealings with each other. Both commented that they appeared to be showing much more respect toward each other when they needed to discuss matters related to the children. They both continued to worry about Jessie because her school work was still deteriorating. What was different now was that they could support each other rather than blame each other for Jessie's difficulties. They both visited Jessie's teacher to discuss their concerns. They also reported that Frank's surprise birthday party had been a great success. Although Fiona had virtually organized it on her own, Greg had paid for the catering. They felt that they had both contributed but in different ways, and no bitter interactions followed.

The following interactional sequence took place.

*Mediator:*  I have to say that I am quite surprised by the way you are being with one another given how six weeks ago you had trouble discussing things without getting into a major disagreement. Can you see how I could be surprised?

*Fiona:*  I think I am the one who is most surprised about how well we are getting along. However, I am really worried about how we are going to get on dealing with the matrimonial property issues. We might find that everything is going to come crashing down around our ears. Still, Greg, I feel your whole attitude has changed.

*Greg:* Yeah, I am worried about the money issues that are inevitably going to be tough issues to work through.

## Thickening the Plot

It was quite understandable for Greg and Fiona to turn to the difficulties they were about to face in the next week. A degree of trust had developed in the mediation sessions that provided safety for them to talk about these difficult issues that would otherwise be too upsetting to discuss on their own. Although they were ready to focus on the matrimonial property issues, the mediator wanted to stay with reflecting on the changes Greg and Fiona were making in their relationship. He felt that this discussion would give more fullness to the positive parenting narrative they were establishing for themselves and their children. "Thickening the plot" of the preferred narratives of a parenting partnership, would, the mediator believed, serve them both well in managing the difficult matrimonial property issues.[14]

*Mediator:* I can appreciate that you want to discuss the implications for your parenting relationship given the financial issues you want to address. However, my hunch is that if you can get clearer about your abilities to work through problems together, this may better prepare you to negotiate your way through some of the specific financial issues that are coming up next week. Are you interested in taking a few minutes to reflect on what you have been able to achieve to date, and on some of the reasons for this, before discussing the matrimonial property issues?

The mediator wanted to stay with a curious and inquiring stance about Greg and Fiona's desired relational abilities. He believed that this approach would give further substance and strength to their cooperative parenting narrative. He needed to be respectfully persistent with this aim, but only with their consent. He did not want to take over as a knowing expert the delineation of what they were permitted to talk about, and thereby diminish their knowledge. He wanted, however, to state his preference for the kind of conversation that he believed would most support the growth of the alternative story. So he stated his interest and asked their permission to follow it. This approach is in line with the narrative stance called *coauthoring*.[15] Greg and Fiona agreed to follow the mediator's line of inquiry.

Next, the mediator focused on a narrative cluster of questions called *unique account questions*.[16] These questions are designed to help people identify how they were able to achieve their successes. This line of questioning added more richness and depth to the co-parenting narratives.

*Mediator:*   How do you make sense of the fact that you are both able to work so well together? You made a success of Frank's birthday, you are working together to address Jessie's schooling difficulties and depression, and you have been following a caregiving plan for the children that you developed yourselves.

*Greg:*   Well, I think I let go of trying to make things go in a direction that I wanted but that didn't seem to fit for the kids. I think I just listened to what the kids had to say and what they wanted.

*Fiona:*   I think we are starting to find a way of liking one another as parents even though there are still some big wounds there.

These interactions helped to name some of the relational strengths that were emerging. Specifically, Greg's response provided an opportunity for him to acknowledge his ability to listen to others' points of view even when they were not what he wanted to hear. Fiona's response demonstrated a willingness to let go of her susceptibility to the story that she had betrayed Greg, and to let go of her resentment over the years that he was unavailable to help with the parenting of the children. She was now able to concentrate on what was happening in the present parenting relationship. Further interactions followed that storied Greg's ability to listen and be attentive, and fleshed out in more detail Fiona's ability to be more trusting of Greg's motives.

The mediator asked Fiona and Greg what it said about them that they were developing a parenting partnership with attentive listening, growing trust, and diminishing bad feelings. This question was seeking a description of personal and relational qualities. It asked them to explore their experience and bring forth aspects of their character that previously had been unstoried. In response to such questions, favored events can be gathered together and storied into a robust account of cooperation. These questions are often difficult to answer but they are worth pursuing because of the potential for relational identity reconstruction they offer. Greg and Fiona were shifting from being an angry, feuding couple with few resources for solving their parenting issues, to being parents living separately who could make wise choices about what their children required. After some thought, Fiona was able to make the following statement:

> I think I am a quite trusting and forgiving person deep down and I am also beginning to appreciate that Greg sincerely believed that the way he was being a father of the children in our marriage was motivated by his best intentions. It has helped me see another side of him that I couldn't see before. However, too much has happened to want to try again. I guess that is just the way it is.

Greg followed shortly with his own summary of how he saw himself:

> Well, all I can say is that it has been a painful experience that I never want to repeat. I've learned a lot going through this and I can't say I am fully there yet. I have been really knocked around by this whole issue. However, I think I am a better man for it. I would like to think that I have the ability to put my family first, and under the circumstances I think I have taken a pretty unselfish view of things. I know that the financial settlement issues will hit me hard, but they have to be faced, and I now say the sooner the better so I can pick up my life again and go on.

## Storying the Future

These statements were enormously important because they were to help Greg and Fiona construct a positive foundation from which to tackle some of the more difficult issues they were about to face. I asked them whether they had learned some strategies that would help them deal with the challenging matrimonial property issues. Greg thought they had moved their relationship into a parenting and business partnership and, because they had built a greater degree of trust, he was not anticipating major problems with the property settlement. Already he was preparing to work with Fiona so that she would receive a just share of their assets. Greg wanted Fiona to be fairly resourced so that she could purchase her own home, one that would be much more appropriate for the children. Fiona, for her part, was going into the deliberations with the confidence that she was seeking a just share of their joint assets, and she was going to take considerable care in the way this would be handled.

The mediator then inquired further about how the changes they were now making were going to be kept intact. He was interested in what rescue plans they had devised, or planned to devise, to help them hold onto the progress they had made, in the event of any difficulties arising in the asset negotiation.

This question invited Greg and Fiona to reflect on future possibilities and to plan how to handle future difficult issues, at least in principle. *Unique possibility questions* prepare the way for the parties who were formally in conflict to reflect on the strategies, techniques, and problem-solving abilities they are putting in place.[17] Fiona and Greg were thoroughly involved in this process. A new chapter in their coparenting relationship was about to unfold.

This is also the end of the first chapter. No doubt this chapter has raised many questions about the narrative approach to mediation. We have made many allusions without providing full explanations. Our purpose has been to whet your appetite. The story we have told serves an introductory purpose for this book. We want it to convey a flavor rather than amount to complete coverage. In the next chapter we explain how a narrative approach is built on assumptions different from those that underlie the problem-solving approach. We then turn to a theoretical review of narrative mediation that underpins all of the important moves and strategies taken up in the mediation process. Later we speak more about the practice aspects of crafting a narrative conversation.

**Notes**

1. Moore, C., *The Mediation Process: Practical Strategies for Resolving Conflict* (San Francisco: Jossey-Bass, 1996); Fisher, R., and Ury, W., *Getting to Yes: Negotiating Agreement Without Giving In* (Boston: Houghton Mifflin, 1981).
2. White, M., and Epston, D., *Narrative Means to Therapeutic Ends* (New York: Norton, 1991); Monk, G., Winslade, J., Crocket, K., and Epston, D., *Narrative Therapy in Practice: The Archaeology of Hope* (San Francisco: Jossey-Bass, 1997); Freedman, J., and Combs, G., *Narrative Therapy: The Social Construction of Preferred Realities* (New York: Norton, 1996).
3. Bruner, E., "Ethnography as Narrative," in V. Turner and E. Bruner (eds.), *The Anthropology of Experience* (Chicago: University of Illinois Press, 1986).
4. Winslade, J., and Monk, G., *Narrative Counseling in Schools* (Thousand Oaks, Calif.: Corwin Press, 1999).
5. White, M., "The Externalizing of the Problem," *Dulwich Centre Newsletter,* 1989, special edition, pp. 3–21.
6. White, M., "The Process of Questioning: A Therapy of Literary Merit?" in M. White, *Selected Papers* (Adelaide, Australia: Dulwich Centre Publications, 1989).
7. White and Epston, *Narrative Means to Therapeutic Ends;* Monk, Winslade, Crocket, and Epston, *Narrative Therapy in Practice;* Freedman and Combs, *Narrative Therapy;* Dickerson, V., and Zimmerman, J., *If Problems Talked: Narrative Therapy in Action* (New York: Guilford Press, 1996).
8. White, M., "Deconstruction and Therapy," in D. Epston and M. White (eds.), *Experience, Contradiction, Narrative and Imagination* (Adelaide, Australia: Dulwich Centre Publications 1992); Fairclough, N., *Discourse and Social Change* (Cambridge, England: Polity Press, 1992); Weedon, C., *Feminist Practice and Poststructuralist Theory* (Oxford, England: Blackwell, 1987).
9. Moore, *The Mediation Process.*
10. Coogler, O. J., *Structured Mediation in Divorce Settlement* (San Francisco: New Lexington Press, 1978); Saposnek, D. T., *Mediating Child Custody Disputes: A Systematic Guide for Family Therapists, Court Counselors, Attorneys, and Judges* (San Francisco: Jossey-Bass, 1983).

11. Stulberg, J., *Citizen Dispute Settlement: A Mediator's Manual* (Tallahassee: Supreme Court of Florida, 1981).

12. Amunsden, J., Stewart, K., and Valentine, L., "Temptations of Power and Certainty," *Journal of Marital and Family Therapy*, 1993, *19*(2), 111–123; Hoffman, L., "A Reflexive Stance for Family Therapy," in S. McNamee and K. Gergen (eds.), *Therapy as Social Construction* (Thousand Oaks, Calif.: Sage, 1992); Anderson, H., and Goolishian, H., "The Client Is the Expert: A Not-Knowing Approach to Therapy," in S. McNamee and K. Gergen (eds.), *Therapy as Social Construction* (Thousand Oaks, Calif.: Sage, 1992).

13. White and Epston, *Narrative Means to Therapeutic Ends;* Monk, Winslade, Crocket, and Epston, *Narrative Therapy in Practice;* Freedman and Combs, *Narrative Therapy;* Dickerson and Zimmerman, *If Problems Talked.*

14. White, M., *Narratives of Therapists Lives* (Adelaide, Australia: Dulwich Centre Publications, 1997).

15. Epston, D., and White, M., "Consulting Your Consultants," in D. Epston and M. White (eds.), *Experience, Contradiction, Narrative and Imagination* (Adelaide, Australia: Dulwich Centre Publications, 1992).

16. White, "The Process of Questioning."

17. White, "The Process of Questioning."

# Chapter Two

# Theoretical and Philosophical Issues in Narrative Mediation

*When, with a failing heart and throbbing brow*
*I must review my captured truth, sum up*
*Its value; trace what ends to what begins,*
*Its present power with its eventual bearings,*
*Latent affinities, the views it opens*
*And its full length in perfecting my scheme*
*I view it sternly circumscribed, cast down*
*From the high place my fond hopes yielded it . . .*
(ROBERT BROWNING, "PARACELSUS")

The mediation literature is currently dominated by a problem-solving or interest-based approach to resolving disputes. This model has been so pervasive in the philosophy and practice of mediation in the West that scant attention has been given to conceptualizing the mediation process in alternative ways. Problem-solving approaches to mediation are predicated on a handful of assumptions about conflict and about human intentions and relations.[1] These assumptions are open to challenge if we look at them squarely. Indeed, in recent years they have been subjected to a series of challenges. This chapter outlines some of these assumptions and the challenges that have been raised to them. It then lays out the theoretical assumptions behind the narrative perspective on mediation and makes explicit the assumptions on which we have built our work in this area.

Some readers may find a description of the theoretical landscape inessential and want to skip over this chapter. We urge you not to do so, because narrative practices in mediation are built more on entering into a philosophical position than on learning some techniques. Those who grasp the philosophical position will relatively easily and quickly master the practices. They are also likely to generate new developments in the field. Those who undertake narrative mediation through a simplistic practical orientation often flounder after a short time and fail to embody the spirit of the approach. It is our experience that these ideas are powerful and that they can transform practice in subtle ways, many of which have yet to be described. Therefore, we urge you to persevere in reading the challenging ideas presented in this chapter.

## Assumptions Built into the Problem-Solving Approach

At the heart of the problem-solving approach is the idea that when human need or interest is frustrated, some form of conflict results. According to this view, conflict occurs when the attainment of the interests or the satisfaction of the needs of one party is found or perceived to be incompatible with the attainment of interests or satisfaction of needs of another party. This position has been expressed clearly in statements like the following: "Problem-solving is an orientation to negotiation which focuses on finding solutions to the parties' sets of underlying needs and objectives."[2] The theory is that the opposition created by competing interests hardens into positions around which polarization occurs. The parties then concentrate on defending these positions while seeking to attack or undermine the position of the other party.

Some underlying premises come with these ideas. One is the assumption that conflict is based on a psychology that focuses primarily on the individual (rather than a psychology that begins with a social view of human being). The primacy of the individual in this model of mediation is such that even when a conflict involves groups, the model directs us to make sense of it in terms drawn from individual psychology. Individuals are seen as prime movers in their own worlds, and communities are portrayed as made up of distinct human beings who act independently and are accountable for their choices. The identification of an individual's needs and the accommodation of her or his interests are viewed as the object of a community and as the essential ingredient of a successful mediation.

The second major assumption built into the problem-solving model is that individuals are driven primarily by internally generated needs, which are expressed in mediation as their interests. Such needs are posited to have their origin in human nature rather than in, say, cultural patterns of thinking. Implicit in this theory is that each party in the conflict is pursuing a path of self-interest and that both parties must meet their respective needs in order to succeed in any negotiation. The needs of the individual in this framework rely on a set of psychological assumptions that have been accepted in many psychological theories. For example, both Sigmund Freud's account of the individual's psychodynamic struggles and Abraham Maslow's hierarchy of needs assume an inherent self-interested pleasure-seeking principle at a basic level of individual human motivation.[3] Individual needs-based assumptions direct our focus away from cultural, collective, or relational aspects of personhood. As a result, we are more likely to view people's claims of entitlement in mediation as biologically essential (inalienable rights?), once we have sorted out what those basic interests are and distinguished them from polarized posturing.

It is not only mediators who account for human behavior with these assumptions in mind. Needs-based assumptions are part of common discourse in the modern world. These widely held, taken-for-granted assumptions provide a lens through which people construct their needs and desires. These assumptions influence people's expectations and behavior, affect the way they respond to other people, and inform what they find acceptable about their social arrangements. Expectations, in turn, construct people's understandings of what moves or responses are possible, what outcomes are desirable, and what role a mediator should play in the process. In other words, these expectations become the dominant norms to which people subscribe and around which they perform meaning in their day-to-day dealings in a variety of contexts.

The third major assumption is about conflict itself. It follows from the assumption about the drive to fulfill individual needs. Conflict is assumed to happen because individual needs are not being met. Disputes transpire when individuals, in the attempt to fulfill their needs, encounter others who believe that their own need-fulfillment goals are threatened. The frustration of needs not being fulfilled leads to a deficit condition, which fuels the motivation for need satisfaction. Thus, a personal deficit (an unmet need) is considered to be the underlying motivational drive for conflict. This deficit can be removed and the need satisfied when a solution is found to the conflict.

A biological metaphor of homeostasis lies behind this idea. Unmet need equals disequilibrium. The biological organism is driven to return to a steady state (homeostasis). A solution is found. Homeostasis, or equilibrium, is restored. What, then, is the task of mediation from this perspective? It is to find solutions that will meet the needs of each of the parties (individuals) and restore homeostasis.[4]

Roger Fisher and William Ury illustrate interest-based mediation by telling their now-famous story of two individuals who are disputing over the temperature of a room.[5] One person is too hot and wants to open a window so as to have air circulating in the room. The other person is concerned that if the window is opened the draft will be unpleasant and possibly chill them. Fisher and Ury suggest an alternative to the traditional problem-solving method, in which the individuals compromise and give up part of what they would like (perhaps leaving the window partially open). In the alternative, the emphasis is on identifying the underlying shared need for a more favorable temperature in the room. The problem gets resolved by both people recognizing that opening a window in an adjacent room will allow cooler air to circulate without creating a draft. Thus the needs for fresh air and even temperature are met.

The fourth assumption built into the problem-solving model is that the mediator is an objective, neutral third party. If the parties to a dispute have needs, the mediator is neutral in regard to those needs. If the parties have interests, the mediator is disinterested. If the parties want to address substantive goals, the mediator cares only about the process and about creating the opportunity for both parties to reach their goals in a win-win resolution. The ultimate model for the mediator is that of the scientist-practitioner, the detached neutral observer applying the knowledge generated within modernist scientific traditions, in which the concept of problem-solving is well entrenched. The emphasis in this tradition is on the generation and application of universal cultural truths. Issues of culture and gender contribute to the kind of bias and distortion that good models of practice seek to eliminate.

## Critiques of the Problem-Solving Assumptions

First, we do not want to argue that these assumptions are necessarily wrong. Rather, the narrative perspective leads us to consider these implicit assumptions about how conflict is to be understood and resolved as only one conceptualization of negotiation or mediation practice. They constitute a plausible story of how conflict occurs and how it can be resolved. We presume that this story arises out of a context in which it makes sense, that it expresses a cultural slant and represents a particular historical set of circumstances. Even when such stories are served up in the guise of science, we expect them to be contextually located. Conversely, we assume that other contexts, cultural and historical, would lead to different formulations and different emphases. In the language of social constructionism, ideas are constructed out of the available discourse that circulates in the communities in which we live, as are our thoughts, feelings, and experiences. Therefore, ideas formed out of an individualistic, needs-based discourse constitute only one way of viewing, judging, and making sense of the world.

Disquiet about the problem-solving method and the assumptions built into it has been expressed from a variety of quarters in recent years. The existence of these critiques seems, to us, to indicate that other plausible perspectives on conflict resolution are possible. We review some of these critiques before advancing the social constructionist perspective more explicitly.

The assumption of a neutral, disinterested stance in relation to the needs that disputing parties present to a mediator has been strongly questioned in the mediation literature. In the process, the way in which cultural values are often implicit within such needs has been highlighted. Janet Rifkin, Jonathan Millen, and Sara Cobb have commented that there has been less "theorizing" about the neutrality of the mediator than development of a "folklore of neutrality."[6] The idea of the mediator as neutral facilitator of the process, who "makes no assessments, judgments, or value interventions" but is "wholly supportive of all actors, and adopts a no-fault and neutral position" is now hard to hold.[7] It makes more sense to see mediators as unlikely to be able to stand outside time and space and their own culturally and historically located values. As they respond to people's stories, mediators are likely to select for emphasis some perspectives over others, or to attune themselves to some people more than to others.

The idea that content and process can be separated and that the mediator is best thought of as a process facilitator who is impartial with regard to content has also been questioned. Linda Putnam has pointed out how particular conceptions of process (for example, thinking in terms of instrumental goals) influence the selection of subject matter to be discussed or emphasized. She suggests that instrumental goal-directed thinking leads to a privileging of "substantive issues over relational and identity management aims."[8] Likewise, Joseph Folger and Robert Bush have shown a "settlement orientation" to narrow the range of subject matter that a mediation conversation can address.[9]

Feminist critiques have also taken mediators to task on the issue of neutrality. They have focused their analysis on the construction of power in gender relations and on the failure of mediation to influence gendered privilege. Their accusation has been that win-win solutions frequently simply reflect the preexisting power relations between the parties and that these relations are often constructed according to patterns of privilege that are based on patriarchal assumptions of how things should be. Thus patriarchal power, unless specifically addressed in the mediation itself, gets reproduced in the outcomes that flow from a so-called neutral mediator's stance.[10] In particular, a feminist analysis has raised questions about mediators' failure to be sensitive to the effects of violence on what transpires in the mediation itself.

Mediation practice in the problem-solving model has also been found wanting by various non-European ethnic communities. For example, the emphasis on individual psychological concepts such as needs and interests does not sit well with cultural traditions that emphasize collective responsibility ahead of individual autonomy.[11] Nor does the idea of neutral facilitation of win-win solutions address situations in which the interests of one of the parties are strongly informed by racism. And culturally specific patterns of addressing conflict are not necessarily included in an approach that does not advertise its cultural origins.

These critiques point to the need for other models on which to base the practice of mediation. We think, too, that theoretical work needs to be done in the field of mediation in order to make the best sense of mediation practice and to address the problems to which these critiques point. It is our belief that social constructionism offers a useful set of ideas on which to base an approach to mediation that is both theoretically robust and intensely practical. We now outline some basic social constructionist principles before we discuss their application in practice. The narrative approach to mediation is increasingly identifying with these social constructionist principles. We also explore the possibilities arising out of the narrative metaphor itself.

## Principles of Social Constructionism

Vivien Burr has outlined seven features of social constructionist thinking in general.[12] We use these features as a base for exploring the application of social constructionist principles to the practice of mediation. For our purposes in this chapter we have collapsed her seven features into four: antiessentialism, antirealism, language as a precondition for thought, and language as a form of social action.

### Antiessentialism

Antiessentialism is the idea that people are more the products of social processes than determined by essences from the inside. Whether the so-called essences are biologically or environmentally determined, this viewpoint argues that human nature is far more fluid and unstable than has been supposed. It turns out that much of what we have been told is hardwired into our psyches is, when looked at through a social constructionist lens, mapped onto us by the social and cultural world around us.

From a theoretical point of view, this notion destabilizes the assumptions of individual psychology. It makes less reliable the concept of individual psychological needs around which people's interests are formed. This is not to imply that people's needs are not keenly felt, but it does shift the balance of the relationship between social change and personal change. From a social constructionist perspective, people's needs are not so much essential (or natural) as they are constructed in discourse or in conversation. Therefore, a different kind of conversation might potentially lead to a revision of these needs. This perspective shifts the purpose of mediation beyond the task of need fulfillment (in which the needs to be fulfilled are taken as given) and in the direction of transformation. What might be experienced keenly as a need in one context or in one formulation of an issue might change dramatically when considered in the light of a different conversation.

## Antirealism

Antirealism questions the existence of objective facts. All knowledge is derived from a perspective. Perspectives are relative to particular cultural or social versions of reality. In this sense, knowledge can never be final and is relative to time and place and to the social landscape out of which it has been produced. The position from which something is viewed is as important as the object being viewed in the construction of a particular reality. Therefore, coming to know the truth about anything is as much about coming to understand the perspective from which it appears in a certain way as it is about how the object looks. Moreover, all facts are assumed to serve particular interests as a result of the process of privileging certain perspectives as established or accepted facts.

This principle has implications for how mediators hear the stories that disputants tell them. The task of mediation is not just to help people sort out the facts from the story of the conflict, or even to establish as facts people's interests or needs. Instead, it is to deconstruct the perspectives from which such "facts" have been established and to appreciate the interests served by those perspectives. In the process, all of these things become more fluid. Another way of saying this is that from a social constructionist perspective we are not just interested in hearing the facts and establishing parties' interests in a mediation. We are also interested in the cultural and historical processes by which these facts and interests came to be.

Also implied by this principle is that theories of human need, such as those advanced by Freud and Maslow mentioned earlier, are to be considered plausible stories or metaphors produced out of cultural and historical landscapes rather than as universal truths. Similarly, theories and models of mediation can never achieve the level of certainty that transcends culture and history. Even when they have been empirically validated, they do not escape the cultural and linguistic world in which the methods of empirical validation are couched.

## Language as a Precondition for Thought

The idea that language is a precondition for thought was expounded by Austrian philosopher Ludwig Wittgenstein. According to him, the way we think and the concepts and categories we use when we think are provided for us in the language or discourse that existed before we entered into it.[13] Hence, it does not make sense to say that people have thoughts or feelings on the inside that precede their expression. It makes more sense to speak about how discourses and linguistic formulations make up our subjective experience. In other words, language, or discourse, is a precondition for thought.

Moreover, words are not simply vehicles (or neutral tools) we use to represent an event or reality. As Wittgenstein argued, words construct the event. From this viewpoint, language has meaning in its use rather than in its correspondence with events in the world. It is not merely a medium for the transmission of ideas or an instrument for unveiling consciousness. Language "speaks" us into existence and constitutes our personhood as much as we use it to communicate with others.[14]

What does this mean for mediation? This *constitutive* function of language (that is, the way it produces human experience) has major implications for how we understand the nature of conflict. It has direct relevance to mediation, which by its very nature is a meaning-making activity. If language can be understood as a meaning-making activity rather than as a passive reporting function, meaning cannot be chosen arbitrarily. Language is then seen as having the function of permitting or constraining the options that might be available to us. The significance of these ideas for mediation practice is profound. The traditional psychological separation of talk and behavior becomes irrelevant. Instead, we can think of the talk we create in mediation as actually constructing experience.

Another result of thinking about language as a precondition of thought is that it undermines hearing people's stories as expressions of underlying or preexistent need. Rather, we might hear people's stories of conflict as rhetoric, or as constructions in language that shape their experience. Our language, however, is not of our own making. We inherit much of it from the cultural world into which we are born. It is therefore not so easy from a social constructionist perspective to view individuals as prime movers in their own worlds. Thus the individualistic perspective of the liberal-humanist tradition, out of which problem-solving models emerge, can no longer be viewed as a value-free, culturally neutral perspective. We can then make room for models that build on different assumptions—for example, relational and communitarian or collectivist descriptions of what it means to be a human being. Ken Gergen, for example, invites us to think that "it is not the isolated individual who is born and who dies"; rather, a relational view of the world sees us "born into relatedness," and when we die, it is not a single individual who dies but "the pattern of relationships that perishes."[15]

## Language as a Form of Social Action

It follows that if persons are constructed in language and discourse, then everyday interactions between people, more than internal psychological phenomena such as attitudes, cognitions, or motivations and more too than social structures, are placed on center stage. In these interactions, we can imagine the world being constructed. When they talk, people are not only expressing what lies within but they are also producing their world. The world constructed includes the internal world of the individual and the supports on which social structures can be built. Thus language is *performative,* and its use is a form of social action. This contradicts the typical idea in traditional psychology that language is a passive vehicle by which thoughts and feelings are expressed and actions are described.

The implication of this view is that mediation is a site where social action is always taking place rather than just being talked about. It is where lives and relations are being produced and reproduced. It is where cultural stories are performed and enacted. It is also where social or institutional change can take place. Thought of in this way, mediation is more than just a place where particular interpersonal problems get resolved and some kind of social homeostasis gets restored. It is where we should take care to talk with an eye on the kind of world we are creating because we are always in the process of creating it.

## A Narrative View of Conflict

Our use of the narrative metaphor in mediation is strongly influenced by the postmodern philosophical movement.[16] Postmodern philosophy emphasizes the enormous variation in how people live their lives due to the quite different discursive contexts that surround them. Postmodern thinking suggests that there is no single definable reality. Rather, there is great diversity in the ways we make meaning in our lives. It is inevitable that differences will result from this diversity of meaning and that conflict will arise from time to time within or between people. Therefore, from a narrative perspective conflict is understood from the outside in as the almost inevitable by-product of diversity, rather than as the result of the expression of personal needs or interests.

Also from a narrative point of view, conflict is likely because people do not have direct access to the truth or to the facts about any situation. Rather, they always view things from a perspective, from a cultural position. Drawing on this perspective, they develop a story about what has happened and continue to act into a social situation out of the story they have created. Facts, from this perspective, are simply stories that are generally accepted. From time to time these stories lead to diametrically opposed readings of events. Again, this is not anyone's fault. It is to be expected, given the nature of human cultural interaction. Nevertheless, these stories have effects and produce realities.

Conflict is also an inevitable product of the operation of power in the modern world. Later in this chapter we present an outline of a poststructuralist analysis of modern power, but suffice it to say here that this analysis stresses contests over whose meanings get to be privileged. Such contests are central to the ongoing creation of the social world. They are also never finalized. Power and privilege are often threatened and we can expect many of the disputes that come to mediation to be sites where such contests are being worked out. For example, in the ongoing contests between men and women over gender entitlements, divorce mediations are key sites for the production or reproduction of power relations between men and women.

## Discourse

The concept of discourse is a useful metaphor in the understanding of mediation. Discourse is both the process of talk and interaction between people, and the products of that interaction. Talk tends to happen in recursive patterns within particular locales, and we can therefore speak about these patterns as particular discourses. Often just below the surface of any conversation are a set of structuring statements about how things are that give meaning to the words being exchanged. These discourses also give meaning, in the end, to social practices, personal experience, structural arrangements, and institutions. Discourses include the taken-for-granted assumptions that allow us to "know how to go on" (according to Wittgenstein) in social situations of all kinds.[17]

Discourse exploration in mediation is a useful tool for depersonalizing conflict. It helps us see how systems of meaning, or fields of knowledge and belief, shape not only people's perspectives, agendas, and desires but also the very nature of a conflict.[18] Focusing on the discursive context of a conflict is a significant move away from focusing on the individual as a unitary and contextually independent being who is the creator and cause of the conflict. The emphasis falls on the way meaning is constructed within discourse rather than on the individual as the sole producer of the discord.

People can be influenced by a number of discourses at the same time. To illustrate this situation, Michael Apple used the metaphor of hearing the sound of many radio stations being played at the same time.[19] The naming of discourses can assist the mediator to hear and name the source of the sounds being played simultaneously. In other words, the more mediators know the discourses that are significant in the dispute, the more likely they are to help identify a way forward. The less familiar that mediators are with the dominant conflicting discourses, the more difficult it will be for them to understand the complexity of the conflict.

## Deconstruction

The idea of deconstruction as we are using it in this book is that it is possible to "unpack" the taken-for-granted assumptions to which we become subject as a result of the operation of discourse.[20] In the process of deconstruction, ideas that masquerade as unquestioned truth or as inevitable realities are exposed. Deconstruction is achieved by adopting a different position in a discourse than that which is considered normal and viewing things from a new perspective. In the process, the familiar is rendered strange, the logic of dominant stories no longer appears inevitable, the gaps or inconsistencies in a story are highlighted, and the opportunities to resist an unquestioned truth are made clear. Deconstruction is less confrontational or adversarial than critique.

So how can this idea of deconstruction be useful to the practice of mediation? In brief, it is useful in that it emphasizes curious exploration rather than simple acceptance. If mediation is about creating new meanings in a dispute where existing meanings have become stale or stuck, then deconstructive listening and deconstructive questioning are useful tools in this creative task. A useful image is to think of a conflict story being told by the parties in a mediation as a suitcase into which have been thrown a collection of meanings. These are the meanings that the parties have made of the events that have transpired between them. These meanings are constructed out of the discourses to which the parties are subject in the world around them. The mediator's task is to unpack the suitcase and take out the pieces and hold them up for view by the parties. This unpacking involves adopting a naive posture and asking questions, not so much about the hidden depths of the suitcase but about the obvious and ordinary aspects of the baggage that comes with the dispute.

For example, if a person speaks about someone else behaving rudely and offensively toward them, a mediator might ask what that person means by rude and offensive behavior. This should not be a confrontational question that puts someone on the defense as much as it should be a respectful inquiry into the assumptions that go into calling someone rude and offensive. Behind such a description is a set of standards against which someone's actions are being measured. The exploration of this meaning reveals not only the facts of what transpired but also the worldview out of which these standards of judgment arise. Deconstructive inquiry renders these background assumptions visible and open to revision. When positions within discourses are named and the discourses themselves are brought into the open, they can be acted on and changed.

This approach can also allow a mediator to disassemble the parties' taken-for-granted assumptions about the nature of conflict itself. It can assist a mediator to avoid jumping too rapidly to conclusions or to accept too easily prior assumptions about the nature of the conflict or about the private experience of the individuals with whom they are working. However, this kind of inquiry requires practice in recognizing the discourses at work in a conflict situation. The powerful potential of thinking in terms of discourse is displayed when apparently intractable and debilitating patterns of interaction are deconstructed and other possibilities for discursive location are opened up.

## Multiple Subjectivity and the Nature of the Self

How mediators understand the nature of the self has a bearing on how they manage a dispute between parties. We have already discussed how problem-solving and interest-based approaches emphasize the individual as an independent, stable, unitary, self-motivating, and self-regulating identity. Such a definition of the individual accentuates searching inside the person for the causal factors of conflict. Persons engaged in the conflict can be viewed in static terms and their reluctance to resolve the conflict can be viewed as emanating from their stubborn and close-minded characters. When making meaning is located inside the individual, the need for change and adjustment is seen as being the individual's responsibility.[21] This leads to the notion that individuals are required to own their own actions and that the choice is theirs and theirs alone.

An alternative view is to look for the narrow cultural and social prescriptions that constrain people's ability to view the options available to them. Through the postmodern lens, a problem is seen not as a personal deficit of the person but as constructed within a pattern of relationships. From this perspective, the social context is the key to understanding self and identity. The self is constituted by myths, traditions, beliefs, assumptions, and values of one's particular culture, all developed within discourse. Philip Cushman captures the distinction between the social constructionist view of culture as a constitutive force and a modernist understanding: "Culture is not indigenous clothing that covers the universal human. It infuses individuals, fundamentally shaping and forming them and how they see others, how they engage in structures of mutual obligation and how they make choices in the everyday world."[22] The individual is constituted by these social practices and is forever undergoing the effects of the discursive or cultural arrangements that are present in day-to-day interactions with people. In each interaction, the individual has opportunities to recreate or reconstruct himself or herself anew. From this perspective, identity is not fixed, nor is it carried around by the individual largely unchanged from one context to another. This is a more dynamic view of the nature of the self than the humanist or modernist versions, which emphasize the need for self-volition and motivation to emerge from within.

From a postmodern perspective, it is the repetitive interactions between people rather than some built-in stable nature that provide stability and a sense of continuity. Often this stability and continuity are preferable and satisfying, because the relational patterns promote comfort and harmony. When the repetitive patterns conflict, however, these relational patterns become problematic. This is the point at which a mediator might be invited to help disrupt such interactions and create a context in which new self-descriptions can emerge.

This description of the continuity and coherence of the self as built on discourse and repetitive interactions has another corollary. It leads to an idea of self that is less stable than that postulated by modernist psychology—a self that is open to multiple influences, often from contradictory sources. The modernist position tends to emphasize the primacy of the rational mind over the body and the emotions, and the mind's capacity to integrate experience in order to take up a singular, noncontradictory position. Postmodern theorizing about the self, conversely, emphasizes the significance of the *multiply positioned subject*. People's lives are complex and composed of the multiple identifications and subject positions that are offered to them. As people take up these different identifications, it makes more sense to think of them as taking on multiple identities.[23] If taken seriously, this view undermines a linear view of growth and change, and the notion that there is a predetermined optimal state of normal integration. As a result, a mediator using a narrative frame of reference is concerned with "co-constructing a context in which a change in the set of alternatives from which choice is made becomes possible."[24]

What does this mean for mediation? The importance of these ideas is that they affect what we select for attention from what people say. They shape how we make sense of people's stories. From a social constructionist or postmodern point of view, the viewpoints people express in a conflict situation are constructed by discursive fields that produce shifting, multiple, and contradictory forms of subjectivity.[25] They are not fixed positions that spring from internal biological imperatives, even though they may be strongly held and firmly entrenched. As mediators, we might also listen for the ways in which disputants speak themselves into positions (or are allocated such positions by someone else's speaking) within a field of particular discourses.

From here we can conceive of mediation as an opportunity for participants to reconstruct their interpretation of the history of a dispute in the light of some alternative discursive positions. These positions can never be value-free, neutral, objective positions. They will always be drawn from the cultural context to which we have access. People are connected, often simultaneously, to a number of different discourses, such as those associated with their family situation, occupation, gender, ethnicity, socioeconomic positioning, religious affiliation, sexual orientation, age, ability or disability, and so on. Jeffrey Escoffier referred to the common experience of living on the boundaries of different communities of discourse and finding oneself within overlapping identities and interests or "border" identities.[26] Narrative mediation seeks to capitalize on these overlaps. The mediator strives to bring forth overlapping descriptions of the dispute (rather than settling on a singular, coherent account) in order to create space for new meanings to emerge. Each new meaning offers an opportunity for participants to reposition themselves in an alternative discourse.

For example, participants in a conflict are invited to disrupt the tendency to take up binary (either/or) subject positions in relation to the conflict. When first meeting separately with each of the parties, narrative mediators are interested in exploring more than what the parties are clear and certain about. They are also interested in the grey areas, the dilemmas and the internal conflicts people are experiencing. They avoid conveying an expectation of adherence to a unified view of the problem because they do not expect people to have a singular coherent or unified experience of life. Ambiguities, contradictions, and internal conflicts are always emerging from our exposure to the multiple and sometimes contradictory meanings of events around us.

From a narrative perspective, this complexity is an ally rather than an enemy of the mediation process. Complexity increases the range of possibilities for how things can develop. Multiple identities increase the range of resources that people can bring to bear on a situation. Conflicting discourses mean that people can always learn from looking at things from another perspective. Thus, opportunities for creative change are made possible, if only people start to look for them rather than attempt to reduce complexity. In other words, we believe there is more to be gained from celebrating the complex and contradictory nature of life than from celebrating the chimera of coherence and singularity.

## The Politics of Mediation

It is largely accepted by contemporary researchers into mediation that disputes and conflicts shape and are shaped by mediator practice in a potent and dynamic way. Mediators are not dispassionate process specialists concerned only with the implementation of unbiased techniques and practices to lead disputing parties to a resolution of their conflict. Effective mediators are fully immersed in the complex dynamics of conflict between the parties, whether they like it or not. They are forever making overt and covert judgments on how issues are to be addressed, which settlement prospects are preferred, and how diverse interests are to be attended to.

Mediators are influenced by the level of commitment of the parties, the complexity of the issues they have to address, the extent of leverage they have in shaping outcomes, and the nature of their role with less powerful participants. The moves the mediator makes influence the disputing parties' actions and reactions, ultimately shaping how the conflict is addressed.

Advocates of mediation have often downplayed the effects of the mediator's own biases, values, and viewpoints and instead have emphasized the importance of mediator neutrality and impartiality. Christopher Moore makes a distinction between neutrality and impartiality as a way of asserting the potential for mediator objectivity and evenhandedness.[27] He suggests that neutrality is possible only when the mediator has had no prior relationship with the disputing parties and would not gain any benefit or payment for mediation services from one of the disputing parties. In contrast, he describes impartiality as refraining from favoring one disputing party's interests, wishes, or proposals over another's. Moore acknowledges that the mediator may have a personal opinion about a desirable outcome but he states that the successful mediator can separate his or her personal opinion about the desired outcome from what the parties want. The test of impartiality is considered to lie ultimately with the final judgment of the conflicted parties. When all parties at the end of a mediation can testify to the evenhandedness and fairness of the mediator, only then, according to Moore, can the mediator be deemed impartial.

Advocacy for mediator neutrality and impartiality, however, is still a weak defense against those critics who suggest that mediation is a flawed instrument for handling disputes because it is so vulnerable to the intervenor's biases, prejudices, and preconceptions. Rifkin, Millen, and Cobb have described neutrality and impartiality as a folklore in mediation and have raised serious questions about the extent to which mediators can truly be neutral and thus separate from their own cultural histories.[28]

Critics of mediation are concerned about its lack of formality and structure. In the privacy of the mediation room, away from public scrutiny and any formal accountability, mediators can contribute to less powerful groups being further seriously disadvantaged. Mediators might also impose their views in the mediation process to the extent of changing the frames of reference initially decided on by the disputing parties. Folger and Bush summarize this view thus: "When conflicts are mediated, social justice issues can be suppressed, power imbalances can be ignored and outcomes can be determined by covertly imposed third-party values."[29]

However, as these authors also point out, other approaches to resolving disputes may be equally affected by the imposition of the viewpoints of any professional attempting to assist parties to resolve disputes. More widely accepted processes for dealing with disputes, such as, for example, a court hearing or a negotiation process, are so intertwined with dominant cultural practices and implicit cultural knowledge that they too are likely to reproduce social injustice.

If we accept that mediator neutrality and impartiality are attractive ideas rather than straightforward expectations, we must then grapple with the fact that mediator influence is an integral part of the mediation process. There is good reason to view mediator influence as potentially producing either just or unjust outcomes.

Some mediators suggest that their influence should be used to offset the advantages that a more powerful party may have in the mediation. Indeed, if the mediator fails to bolster the influence of the weaker party and to curb the dominating effects of the stronger party, some critics would suggest that mediation becomes an abusive activity. Take, for example, the differential levels of influence that an employer and an employee bring to a mediation, or a landlord and tenant. These positions offer different degrees of entitlement in relation to one party's ability to make decisions that affect the other party. Consider too the disparity of power and influence between a party who is educated, rich, and eloquent and one who is uneducated, poor, and inarticulate. When these degrees of variance over relational influence are present, mediators could be called unethical if they did not find some way of attending to power discrepancies.

There are problems, however, with mediators managing the differences in status, authority, and relational position between parties by shoring up the weaker party and checking the behavior of the party perceived to be dominant. This kind of analysis of the workings of conflict and how conflict can be resolved is based on some assumptions about power. One of these assumptions is that some people possess more or less power than other people. In other words, power is viewed as a commodity or property that can be possessed in finite quantities that are distributed (unevenly) among people. This view is related to a structural analysis of social hierarchies. In these hierarchies, those at the top possess the largest amount of power and have the greatest influence in a conflict.

It is presumed that the mediator also possesses a considerable amount of power by virtue of the mediator role. It makes sense, from this type of analysis, for the mediator to work at balancing out the distribution of the commodity of power, at least in the mediation. The obvious difficulty here is that the mediator will no longer be regarded as a neutral and impartial agent in the mediation process, particularly by the party originally deemed to possess the most power.

This perspective is founded on a particular metaphor, however. The commodity metaphor brings with it a set of assumptions that from a postmodern perspective are highly problematic. It is an essentialist understanding of power. Michel Foucault has extensively critiqued the use of the commodity metaphor in the conception of power.[30] He has also suggested some quite different ways of thinking about power that do not rely on a structural analysis and do not lead to static pictures of power belonging to and resting with individuals.

A narrative approach to mediation draws on this poststructuralist analysis of power. From this perspective, power does not so much adhere to structural positions in hierarchical arrangements as it operates in and through discourse. Discourses offer people positions of greater or lesser entitlement. Within particular discourses, some positions are rendered more legitimate or more visible and others are subjugated. Some voices get heard and others are silenced.

But of course discourses are products of the shifting, changing, unstable conversations that take place in communities and language worlds. As discourses shift and change, so the discursive positions of legitimacy and marginalization ebb and flow. Some people may be positioned in places of influence and privilege within a particular discourse in one context but may not necessarily carry this power with them into another context, or even into another conversation. People regularly mount challenges to these positions, too. Thus power is always unstable from a poststructuralist perspective. It is more a relational phenomenon than a commodity or quantity possessed by an individual. It is never localized here or there, never in anybody's hands, never appropriated as a piece of wealth.

Power viewed from this perspective cuts across individual lives in a variety of ways that can open up opportunities or close them down depending on the context in which individuals find themselves. This perspective does not in our view preclude the notion that power can operate systematically with a degree of consistency so as to be more oppressing to some individuals in particular contexts than to other individuals in the same contexts. These systematic effects of relational power need not be viewed as a tidy package that is owned or static. Power is everywhere and pervades the entire social body. All social life then comes to be a network of power relations, and these relations are always capable of being reviewed, not only at the level of large-scale social structures but also at very local and individual levels.[31]

When power is understood in these ways, mediators can recognize that those who belong to apparently disadvantaged groups can have access to courses of action that significantly influence a relationship. From this perspective, it makes no sense to speak of somebody as powerless in any total sense, or as having no ability to act. Also problematic is the notion of empowerment, which relies on the commodity metaphor of power.

Narrative mediators would rather talk about how people can take up opportunities to resist the operation of power in their lives. Such mediators start from the assumption that this is always possible. Equality of power may never be achievable, or even desirable, because it is a notion that brings us back into an individualistic, commodity-based reading of power relations. Rather, the power relations that exist might be viewed as the ongoing product of struggles and contests. These relations are constantly being produced and reproduced, even in the middle of a mediation. As people express resistance to a particular power relation, that relation starts to change, even in the tiniest of ways. This process of expressing resistance develops a sense of agency in people who have felt silenced and marginalized.

Viewing agency from this perspective acknowledges that there are likely to be opportunities to act in apparently powerless circumstances in a variety of settings at different times. Even the most downtrodden or defeated person can demonstrate some level of psychological resistance to an oppressive or constraining circumstance.[32] This analysis moves away from a globalized notion of powerlessness and sensitizes persons to their ability to act, even in some modest way.

# The Narrative Metaphor

The narrative metaphor itself deserves a little more explanation. We need to consider its usefulness to thinking about mediation.

As Michael White put it, "We enter into stories, we are entered into stories by others, and we live our lives through stories."[33] When we use the adjective *narrative* to describe our approach, we are referring not simply to a concern with the storytelling phase of the mediation process, in which both parties are encouraged to tell their story of the conflict. Rather, we are referring to a mode of thinking. This mode of thinking has been argued by Jerome Bruner to be particularly suitable for helping us understand complex human intentions and interactions.[34]

From Bruner's perspective, people construct their intentions and enact their "performances of meaning"[35] with the characteristics of a well-formed story in mind more than with facts, realities, or cause-and-effect logic. In mediation, therefore, we might expect to hear two conflicting narratives being played out, each with its own characterizations and thematic elements. In each of these narratives, we might expect slightly different arrangements of plot elements to have been selected for inclusion. Each selection would be made on the basis of narrative plausibility or coherence. Moreover, each arrangement of plot elements would draw forth different characterizations and construct a different account of the events of the dispute. Each account would also set in motion a different plot trajectory for the future, because one of the features of narratives is that they develop sequentially and connect events through time.

Bruner says that alongside this "landscape of action" in which people construct intentions, set goals, act, and create situations, there is a "landscape of consciousness," in which people know, think, and feel.[36] Each landscape has an impact on the other. In other words, people make meaning in story form. Then the meanings they make serve as the stage on which they enact their performances.

The point for mediation is that stories take on a life of their own. Thus, when a conflict story takes root, it generates a momentum that does not reflect the facts or realities of a situation because stories mediate our knowledge of reality. It is more accurate to talk about how stories shape and create realities as people act in response to the stories around which they are performing meaning.

It follows, then, that the success of a mediation might depend not so much on the extent to which a mediator can separate the story of the dispute from the realities or facts, but on the extent to which the mediator can work with the parties to create an alternative story. Such a story needs to be plausible and to include the significant events of the conflict story in a way that makes sense to the participants.

But a further characteristic of stories is that they are cultural creations. Indeed, a cultural world is constituted within a framework of stories. Therefore, the stories within which we live our lives always draw from the cultural stories of the world around us. Moreover, the cultural imperatives in a story can create a narrative in which the end of the story has been prefigured by an event in the beginning.[37]

Therefore, in a mediation there are likely to be a series of stories at work at different levels. There will be the conflicting stories of the dispute that each party brings. Any support persons who become involved, including lawyers, will have their own versions of these stories, too. There will be the unfolding story of the mediation itself. And there will be background stories that shape the meanings from which people draw the elements of the other stories. These background stories may include larger stories of relationship, familial stories, cultural stories, or fictional accounts (drawn from books and movies).

The task of mediation can be considered to be a teasing out of these stories in order to open up possibilities for alternative stories to gain an audience. Rather than searching for the one true story, the narrative mode of thinking welcomes the complexity of competing stories and numerous influential background stories. Out of this complexity can emerge a range of possible futures from which parties to a mediation can choose. This is the *subjunctive mood* that narrative thinking promotes.[38] It is useful for mediation because conflicts so often narrow the field of vision for protagonists. The subjunctive spirit opens people's thinking to the possibility that things can be different. In this kind of climate, substantive changes are possible.

We have outlined some general philosophical assumptions on which the narrative perspective is built. What we need to do now is describe a model of practice within which these ideas can be fleshed out. That is our task in the next chapter. Then we describe the methods and techniques that this model requires mediators to master in order to practice it well.

## Notes

1. Fisher, R., and Ury, W., *Getting to Yes: Negotiating Agreement Without Giving In* (Boston: Houghton Mifflin, 1981).
2. Menkel-Meadow, C., "Toward Another View of Legal Negotiation: The Structure of Problem Solving," *UCLA Law Review*, 1984, *31*, 794.
3. Maslow, A. H., "Self-Actualizing People: A Study of Psychological Health," in C. E. Moustakas (ed.), *The Self* (New York: HarperCollins, 1956); Freud, S., *An Outline of Psychoanalysis* (New York: Norton, 1969).
4. Goldenberg, I., and Goldenberg, H., *Family Therapy: An Overview* (Belmont, Calif.: Wadsworth, 1985).
5. Fisher and Ury, *Getting to Yes.*
6. Rifkin, J., Millen, J., and Cobb, S., "Toward a New Discourse for Mediation: A Critique of Neutrality," *Mediation Quarterly*, 1991, *9*(2), 151.
7. Burton, J., *Conflict: Resolution and Prevention* (New York: St, Martin's Press, 1990), p. 204.
8. Putman, L., "Challenging the Assumptions of Traditional Approaches to Mediation," *Negotiation Journal*, 1994, *10*(4), 339.
9. Folger, J. P., and Bush, R. A., "Ideology, Orientations to Conflict, and Mediation Discourse," in J. Folger and T. Jones (eds.), *New Directions in Mediation: Communication Research and Perspectives* (Thousand Oaks, Calif.: Sage, 1994).
10. Astor, H., and Chinkin, C. *Dispute Resolution in Australia* (Sydney, Australia: Butterworth's, 1992).
11. Relationship Services, New Zealand National Working Party on Mediation, *Guidelines for Family Mediation: Developing Services in Aotearoa* (Wellington, New Zealand: Butterworth's, 1996).
12. Burr, V., *An Introduction to Social Constructionism* (London: Routledge, 1995).
13. Wittgenstein, L., *Philosophical Investigations* (Oxford, England: Blackwell, 1958).
14. Davies, B., *Shards of Glass: Children Reading and Writing Beyond Gendered Identities* (St. Leonards, Australia: Allen & Unwin, 1993).

15. Gergen, K. J., *The Saturated Self: Dilemmas of Identity in Contemporary Life* (New York: Basic Books, 1991), p. 243.
16. Foucault, M., *The Archaeology of Knowledge* (A. Sheriden-Smith, trans.) (Oxford, England: Blackwell, 1972); Harvey, D., *The Condition of Postmodernity* (Oxford, England: Blackwell, 1989).
17. Wittgenstein, *Philosophical Investigations*.
18. Gee, J. P., *Social Linguistics and Literacies* (London: Falmer, 1990).
19. Apple, M. W., *Official Knowledge: Democratic Education in a Conservative Age* (New York: Routledge, 1993).
20. White, M., "Deconstruction and Therapy," in D. Epston and M. White (eds.), *Experience, Contradiction, Narrative and Imagination* (Adelaide, Australia: Dulwich Centre Publications, 1992).
21. McNamee, S., "Psychotherapy as a Social Construction," in H. Rosen and K. Kuehlwein (eds.), *Constructing Realities* (San Francisco: Jossey-Bass, 1996).
22. Cushman, P., "Why the Self Is Empty: Toward a Historically Situated Psychology," *American Psychologist*, 1990, *45*(5), 601.
23. Weedon, C., *Feminist Practice and Poststructuralist Theory* (Oxford, England: Blackwell, 1987).
24. Fruggeri, L., "Therapeutic Process as the Social Construction of Change," in S. McNamee and K. Gergen (eds.), *Therapy as Social Construction* (London: Sage, 1992).
25. Lather, P., "Critical Frames in Educational Research: Feminist and Poststructural Perspectives," *Theory into Practice*, 1992, *31*(2), 87–99.
26. Escoffier, J., "The Limits of Multiculturalism," *Socialist Review*, 1991, *21*(3, 4), 61–73.
27. Moore, C., *The Mediation Process: Practical Strategies for Resolving Conflict* (San Francisco: Jossey Bass, 1996).
28. Rifkin, Millen, and Cobb, "Toward a New Discourse for Mediation: A Critique of Neutrality."
29. Folger and Bush, "Ideology, Orientations to Conflict, and Mediation Discourse," p. 5.
30. Foucault, M., *Power/Knowledge* (C. Gordon, ed.; C. Gordon, L. Marshall, J. Mepham, and K. Soper, trans.) (New York: Pantheon, 1980).
31. Hartsock, N., "Foucault on Power: A Theory for Women?" in L. Nicholson (ed.), *Feminism/Postmodernism* (London: Routledge, 1990).
32. Robinson, T. L., and Ward, J. V., "A Belief in Self Far Greater than Anyone's Disbelief: Cultivating Resistance Among African American Female Adolescents," in C. Gilligan, A. G. Rogers, and D. L. Tolman (eds.), *Women, Girls, and Psychotherapy: Reframing Resistance* (New York: Haworth Press, 1991); Robinson, T. L., and Hamilton, M., "An

Afrocentric Paradigm: Foundation for a Healthy Self-Image and Healthy Interpersonal Relationships," *Journal of Mental Health Counseling,* 1994, *16,* 327–339.

33. White, M., "The Externalizing of the Problem and the Reauthoring of Lives and Relationships," in M. White, *Selected Papers* (Adelaide, Australia: Dulwich Centre Publications, 1989), p. 6.

34. Bruner, J., *Actual Minds, Possible Worlds* (Cambridge, Mass.: Harvard University Press, 1986).

35. Bruner, *Actual Minds, Possible Worlds,* p. 25.

36. Bruner, *Actual Minds, Possible Worlds,* p. 14.

37. Bateson, M., "Composing a Life," in C. Simpkinson and A. Simpkinson (eds.), *Sacred Stories* (San Francisco: Harper San Francisco, 1993).

38. Bruner, *Actual Minds, Possible Worlds,* p. 29.

# Chapter Three

# A Narrative Model of Mediation

*I repeat . . . that all power is a trust—that we are accountable for its exercise.*
(BENJAMIN DISRAELI, "VIVIAN GREY")

*In Language there are only differences.*
(FERDINAND DE SAUSSURE,
"COURSE IN GENERAL LINGUISTICS")

*A word is dead,*
*When it is said,*
*Some say.*
*I say it just,*
*Begins to live,*
*That day.*
(EMILY DICKINSON, No. 1212)

This chapter outlines a model of the narrative mediation process. We have deliberately called this approach a *process* because we think the word *process* focuses on the dynamic, shifting, and changing elements of mediation rather than on abstractions, facts, or structures. By concentrating on process, the mediator is invited to think about and work with the responses of the conflicting parties rather than follow some static, preconceived plan. Any experienced mediator knows that mediation cannot be carried out in a predictable straight line. People are not that simple. However, to describe the narrative mediation process presented in this chapter, we have organized our ideas sequentially to assist you in grasping the unique aspects of narrative mediation. It is necessary to qualify this presentation by saying that it is a teaching tool rather than a map of how mediations usually go.

## Overview of the Narrative Mediation Process

Figure 3.1 presents a diagram of the narrative mediation process we describe in detail in the rest of the book. This process has three phases—engagement, deconstructing the conflict-saturated story, and constructing the alternative story—and both the mediator and the parties in dispute are located within both dominating and alternative discourses.

### Dominant Discourse

The dominating discourses position both the mediator and the participants within a series of taken-for-granted assumptions about an issue with which they have to contend. Indeed, it is only within discourse that disputes can develop. Dominant discourses affect many aspects of how disputes take shape.[1]

For example, the language used to describe a conflict situation is not invented by the parties. They draw it from the world around them. What they draw will include certain formulas for thinking that are prefabricated in cultural patterns of exchange. Consequences follow from each word used to describe the problem. For example, the way in which everyone proceeds is affected by whether the parties and the mediator talk about a dispute to be resolved, a disagreement to be sorted out, a problem to be solved, or a fight to be refereed. Moreover, the stories that the parties tell of what has happened in the buildup of the conflict are necessarily going to be told from a discursive position, not from an objective viewpoint.

The sense of what a person is entitled to expect from another person lies in the background of any conflict situation. Although individuals often have their own slants or emphases on these expectations, the expectations are also largely built on notions accepted within the individual's cultural world. (We talk more about entitlements in Chapter Four.)

Discourses legitimate some people's positions in relation to others. For example, the discursive consensus about the relative positions of landlord and tenant culminates in laws that express a

**Figure 3.1. Construction of the Mediator-Party Relationship.**

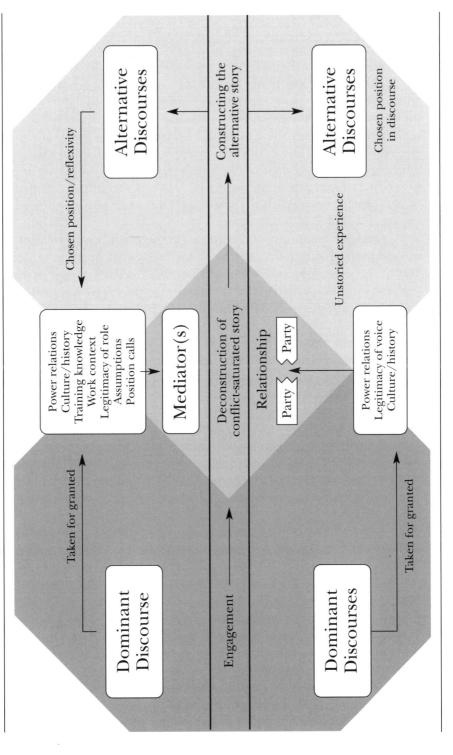

particular perspective on this relationship. As people enter into the roles of landlord and tenant, they take up the discursive positions that these roles provide and act toward each other out of these roles. Certain ways of speaking and behaving are legitimated and privileged by the dominant discourse in this relationship.

Discourses affect the extent to which a person's voice can be heard by another person. They create situations of privilege in which some voices are more likely to be heard above others. They also conversely create contexts in which people become frustrated and resentful because they cannot get the other person to hear and acknowledge their viewpoint.

As people speak, they take up discursive positions in relation to one another—for example, they may take up the position of victim of the other person's wrongdoing. As they do so, they invite others (such as the mediator and the other party) to respond to them in that position. In other words, they call each other into position in a relation.

Dominant discourses also affect what gets storied in the telling of the events of the conflict. These tellings will always be, to a greater or lesser extent, selected from all the available information. Discourses will operate in the background to shape the selection process.

In many instances, dominating discourses actually close down options for people and contribute to the growth of problems that eventually spill over into other problems. In other words, discourse has an intimate role in the construction of disputes. For example, patriarchal discourses might invite men into positions of exaggerated entitlement and women into submissive positions. Even the mediator might be influenced by these patriarchal discourses into taking for granted as normal arrangements that are patently unjust.

In some contexts, the effects of dominating discourses may be very positive. This may be true for the mediator as well as for the parties to a dispute. For the disputing parties, the dominant idea (common to various cultures) that bad feelings between people should be talked through and sorted out might assist the mediation process. Dominating discourses can also legitimate and support the role of the mediator. We would have no quarrel with a mediator who used the privilege and authority bestowed on him or her by his or her discursive position to influence the process in ways that bring about greater satisfaction and equitable arrangements for the participants in a dispute.

## Alternative Discourse

As these dominant discourses are exerting their influence, alternative ways of speaking or thinking are also finding expression in some communities of interest. These alternative discourses may be expressed in small pockets of resistance, and parties to a dispute will at least be aware of them. Wherever there is injustice or oppression there will be protest. For example, the dominant discourses that shape people's expectations of who will take up the position of major caregiver for children after a marriage separation would specify that mothers should take up this function. However, there are also many examples of fathers who take up this position or of various joint parenting arrangements. Couples who arrange things in these ways are drawing on alternative discourses to support their stance and are offering each other positions out of these discourses. For example, perhaps they are drawing from a feminist discourse, which might question the assumption that caring for children is primarily a woman's responsibility.

Mediators can also take positions in relation to alternative discourses. Indeed, we would hope that their training and ethics would often require them to do so. If, for example, a mediator takes the position of sympathetic listener to someone whose voice has not been heard within the dominating discourse, the mediator calls the other person into the position of speaker or of "having a voice" (at least temporarily). In this way, professional discourses exert influence on how each of the parties experience the dominating discourses surrounding the problem.

The alternative discourses in a conflict often emerge or become clear as a result of the deconstruction phase in the mediation process. Deconstruction often leads to more preferred options becoming available to the parties. For example, Chapter One described how Fiona produced an alternative, more positive discursive account of herself after participating in early mediation sessions. It is in the process of repositioning themselves in some alternative discourse that people find creative ways forward in conflict situations. Although these ways may at times be described as "solutions" or as "win-win" outcomes, it is our belief that an emphasis on discursive repositioning enables something far more potent than satisfying interests or meeting needs to take place. Discursive repositioning includes the conscious shaping, albeit in some small way, of the discourses out of which needs and interests are produced.[2]

This is the sense in which we argue that the discursive context shapes the conversation for all participants in the mediation, including the mediator, who is responsible for managing the mediation process through its three phases—the engagement phase, the deconstruction phase, and the reconstruction phase. We now elaborate on these three phases.

## Engagement

Figure 3.2 represents the engagement phase of mediation from a narrative perspective. In this phase, the mediator concentrates on establishing a relationship with the conflicting parties. To achieve a workable relational context, the mediator needs to attend to the physical setting in which the mediation is to take place, to the nonverbal behavior displayed by all parties in early interactions, and to the relational moves made by the mediator and the parties. Attention is also drawn in the first phase to the discursive positions that both the mediator and the parties are called into as a result of the discussion of the issues.

### Before Meeting with the Parties

Future clients might be enticed into mediation by receiving a letter of introduction to mediation with an accompanying brochure outlining its purpose. It is more likely, however, that clients will be referred to a mediator. In many instances, the referral is based on the reputation of the mediator. The content of a dispute often ensures that mediation is a personal if not an intimate encounter for participants. The disputing parties will ask themselves, "Can I trust this person with my confidential and private issues?" Because the acute concerns arising from a conflict can leave people emotionally vulnerable and shaken, the quality of the first spoken communication between the mediator and the potential client is crucial.

**Figure 3.2. Domains of Engagement.**

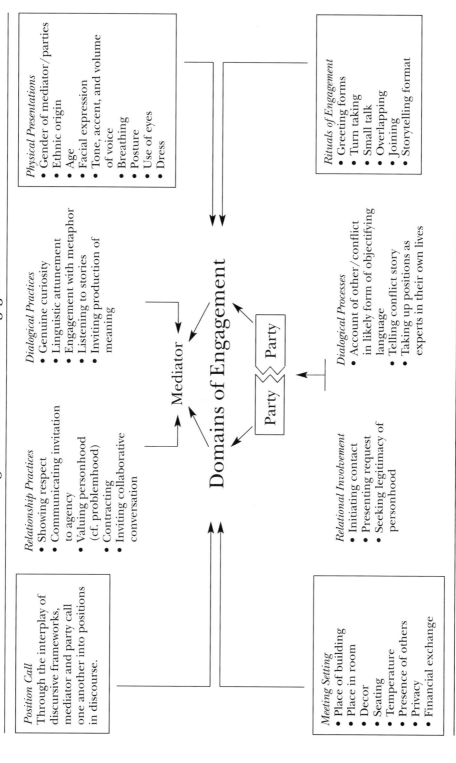

Physical Presentations
- Gender of mediator/parties
- Ethnic origin
- Age
- Facial expression
- Tone, accent, and volume of voice
- Breathing
- Posture
- Use of eyes
- Dress

Rituals of Engagement
- Greeting forms
- Turn taking
- Small talk
- Overlapping
- Joining
- Storytelling format

Dialogical Practices
- Genuine curiosity
- Linguistic attunement
- Engagement with metaphor
- Listening to stories
- Inviting production of meaning

Dialogical Processes
- Account of other/conflict in likely form of objectifying language
- Telling conflict story
- Taking up positions as experts in their own lives

Position Call
Through the interplay of discursive frameworks, mediator and party call one another into positions in discourse.

Relationship Practices
- Showing respect
- Communicating invitation to agency
- Valuing personhood (cf. problemhood)
- Contracting
- Inviting collaborative conversation

Relational Involvement
- Initiating contact
- Presenting request
- Seeking legitimacy of personhood

Meeting Setting
- Place of building
- Place in room
- Decor
- Seating
- Temperature
- Presence of others
- Privacy
- Financial exchange

Domains of Engagement

Mediator

Party

Party

The mediator needs to demonstrate that he or she understands the concerns of the client. This may be achieved by the mediator paying close attention to the timing of comments in response to information provided by the client, and by skillful use of active or reflective listening. The mediator can monitor his or her ability to understand even the most subtle concerns of the client by using paraphrasing to summarize and reflect the feelings, concerns, and issues expressed by the client. Client-centered skills, advocated by Carl Rogers some three decades ago, still have their place in building a strong connection with disputing parties.[3]

## At the First Meeting

Mediators need to be aware of the impact their physical presence may have on the parties. In the first words uttered, it will be evident to the parties in the dispute that the mediator represents a cultural history that is reflected in the mediator's vernacular patterns, vocabulary, inflection, accent, and register. Clients will already have reacted in some way to the mediator's verbal interactions on the telephone. A variety of issues might be raised for the disputing parties about whether this mediator will understand their experiences. For example, they may wonder what impact the gender of the mediator might have on the parties and on the mediation process. Will the gender of the mediator be an impediment to resolution for one or more of the parties given the issues that might arise in the presenting conflict? Will it be necessary to have a co-mediator of the opposite gender? The same principle applies in relation to the ethnic background of the mediator. If ethnic differences impinge on a conflict that has, for example, racist overtones, again the mediator may need to have a co-mediator who is of an appropriate ethnic background. Of course, the mediator may need to consider numerous other identity issues that are significant to the parties when building an effective relationship with them. For example, for some participants in the mediation, the religion, sexual orientation, age, class, or disability of the mediator may be important.

## Rituals of Engagement

The mediator must be attentive to how best to greet participants and how to engage them in relating the conflict narratives they may want to express. Greeting rituals are culturally learned. Each move the mediator makes, even in the process of greeting, is expressed in a language that shapes the relations between the participants in the mediation. The mediator must consider the cultural expectations of the participants in determining how the meeting should be conducted.

In many communities, the participants and mediator may be expected to get right down to business, not to waste time, and to start to name the problem immediately. In other communities, rituals of engagement may require the presence of a figurehead of the community, or an elder or religious person, to give their blessing prior to the commencement of the meeting. For many Maori communities in New Zealand, so important is this ritual of engagement that the absence of the appropriate protocol before the beginning of the mediation may lead directly to the mediation's failure. In some settings it may be more important to gain clarity about the familial relationships between the parties and the mediator prior to the mediation rather than launching immediately into discussion about issues concerning the conflict.

At the beginning of the mediation, consideration must be given to how structured the mediation needs to be. More structure is applicable in the early phases of the mediation. The mediator will generally strengthen the quality of engagement with the participants if she or he explains clearly the structure of the meeting and commits to ensuring that negotiated guidelines are adhered to.

Some mediators feel that separate meetings with each of the parties breeds suspicion because the disputing parties may worry that the opposing party is presenting distortions to the mediator. When a mediator chooses to meet with parties separately, this issue needs to be considered and dealt with accordingly. Other mediators may be concerned that if they do not meet with parties separately first, they may not have an opportunity to understand the parties and the issues with sufficient clarity.

In the event that the parties are met with separately, the mediator will need to make a careful decision as to which party is met with first. The mediator may need to address the problem of one of the parties presuming that his or her story is privileged over the other's because he or she has been chosen first. When the mediator begins with both parties rather than with separate meetings, however, it is important for the mediator to pay attention to who is going to speak first, because this may also have an effect on the parties. (We discuss this further in Chapter Six.)

## Mandated Clients

In some mediation settings, the parties in a dispute are mandated to attend. When parties are directed by a judicial or other organization to attend mediation, the mediator's skills of engagement take on a new significance. Early interactions with these parties often require the mediator to defuse antagonism or address other issues such as resentment about having to participate or other forms of resistance. Numerous articles and texts have discussed the issues specific to working with reluctant participants. We discuss strategies for dealing with resistance in Chapter Nine.

## Mediating with the Right Participants

At this juncture, mediators need to be sure that it is appropriate to engage the parties in the process. As mediators we must have confidence that the "right" participants are attending the proposed mediation. Often the presenting conflict produces one or more parties who are inadvertently caught up in another person's conflict. A classic example of this occurs when an employer, senior manager, or line manager invites a mediator to attend a dispute between two junior employees. In fact, the dispute was triggered by an earlier unresolved issue between, say, the junior employee and the line manager, and the conflict has been diverted into a peer working relationship. In this circumstance, it may be more useful to set up a three-way meeting rather than attempt to accomplish a mission on behalf of someone who is not present in the meeting.

## When Not to Mediate

It may be inappropriate to engage in a mediation process when there is an imminent threat of some form of violence to one party by the other party. In other instances, it may be harmful to mediate when one of the parties is going to be clearly disadvantaged or damaged by a mediation process. It is important for the mediator to identify the potential for harm as much as possible before entering into the process.[4]

For example, it would be wise to call off the mediation if one of the parties is not prepared to agree to basic procedural processes required for the mediation to take place with safety. This may occur when one party demonstrates that he or she is not seeking understanding or resolution but rather to use the forum to discredit and consistently attack the other. On such occasions, it is preferable that the mediator disengage from the process and refer the parties to other options, such as a disputes tribunal or perhaps a court of law.

Another reason not to proceed with a mediation would be the parallel pursual of some other dispute resolution method. For example, if one party is carrying on with litigation, this might undermine the efforts of the mediator to work with the parties in mediation. In this circumstance, mediation should await the completion of other methods of dispute resolution or else require that the other process be put on hold long enough to give the mediation a chance to proceed. We discuss managing tricky issues in mediation in more detail in Chapter Nine.

## Contracting

Mediators need to have an explicit written or verbal agreement with the parties about how the mediation will be conducted. Mediators should commit themselves to an ethical code of conduct and outline clear guidelines for managing the process and the protocols that need to be followed in the mediation. These guidelines should include the need for confidentiality and respectful conduct toward all participants. A fee for service needs to be negotiated. Agreements need to be reached between the mediator and the parties to safeguard against such things as litigation or a request from a client that the mediator act as a witness in a court hearing subsequent to the mediation breaking down.[5]

## Physical Setting

The cornerstone to developing an effective working relationship with the disputing parties is the extent to which the mediator demonstrates respect, understanding, and trustworthiness in the mediation process. In the beginning, the parties may feel insecure and psychologically exposed. To assist in building a strong alliance with the participants, the mediator has to satisfy himself or herself that he or she is creating a psychologically safe environment. A number of questions have to be asked and answered:

• *Is the location where the mediation is about to take place the most suitable one?* It is useful to think of physical settings as a language. Buildings and locations and decor speak to people and are products of discourse. The mediator should consider how the physical context positions the participants in relation to each other and in relation to the mediator. On some occasions, it might be appropriate to meet in the workplace because of its accessibility to the participants. However, the workplace may be inappropriate if it advantages one person in relation to the other, if it fails to provide adequate privacy, or for other reasons. People sometimes talk about neutral venues. However, from a discursive perspective, there are no neutral venues. Any venue speaks to people in some way and will be more or less conducive to meaningful conversation according to the cultural preferences of the person entering it.

• *Is the meeting place sufficiently comfortable and appropriate for the parties to feel respected?*

• *Are the building, its entranceway, and the mediation room itself welcoming, comfortable, and appropriate?*

• *Does the decor provide for a sufficiently relaxed atmosphere that is unencumbered by any covert or overt messages or undercurrents that might favor one party or the other?*

• *How is the seating arranged and is it appropriate for the nature of the meeting that is about to take place?* For example, it may be culturally appropriate to sit around a large corporate table, because this physical arrangement may be regarded as one that acknowledges the serious nature of the dispute. In another instance, it may be more appropriate for the participants to sit on comfortable chairs around a low coffee table.

• *Who else's presence would assist the parties to feel supported and comfortable?* In some instances, a spokesperson, family member, advocate, or professional person might need to be present to help the parties engage more readily in the process.

The main point here is that the parties must feel respected and comfortable in a physical setting that best reflects their cultural location. In many instances, the mediator may have to ask the disputing parties what kind of mediation venue would be appropriate to their needs.

## Relational Practices

We have a keen interest in how the discursive context and narrative content influence the moves made by all parties to a dispute, including those of the mediator. Every piece of nonverbal behavior both is shaped by and helps to shape the discursive context into which people's words will enter.

Moreover, the background assumptions and narrative accounts of the mediator are intimately related to the approach that will be taken to the mediation. As people start to speak, they continue to take up and offer each other positions in a relationship. A key question is, Whose words will come to be granted authority in this relationship? It is easy for a mediator to convey subtle disrespect for people's voices if early in the mediation process they are not treated as worthy of being heard for one reason or another.

Ideally, narrative mediation is a cocreative practice in which the parties to the dispute are viewed as partners in the mediation. They are respected from the start because they possess local knowledge and expertise that can help bring about some form of resolution. They are spoken to as if their intentions are worthy. The narrative process is concerned with unearthing the competencies and resources of the participants in a respectful manner. Of particular interest will be the relational attitudes of understanding, respect, and cooperation. Although conflicts tend to push these qualities aside, a mediator should convey early in the engagement process a desire to seek them out again and promote their expansion rather than concentrate on faultfinding.

This is not an easy or straightforward activity. It requires displaying some deliberate attitudes of respect, enthusiasm, and resilience from the start. The disputing parties need to be assured by the mediator's manner that their voice will be valued. Conveying a message of curiosity about and interest in the participants' experiences is the first step in establishing such a relationship. We say more about this kind of curious stance in Chapter Five.

Engagement is strengthened both by what we say and by how we say it. Mediators using a narrative approach pay close attention to the moment-by-moment interactions (verbal and nonverbal) of the mediator and the disputing parties. These interactions can be attended to as products of the conflict-saturated story or as metaphors that embody particular versions of experience. The mediator demonstrates his or her skill by using language to offer openings for the telling of stories and the expansion of metaphors. In the process, people are invited into a new position in relation to the content of the dispute. We say more about the particular conversational moves entailed in this repositioning in Chapters Six, Seven, and Eight. Suffice it to say here that a mediator should avoid assuming an authoritative stance that positions one or more of the participants in a correspondingly submissive or passive role, restricting their involvement to being a passenger in the process. Rather, the mediator should actively invite people into positions of partnership in the development of preferred resolutions.

## Inviting the Telling of the Story

As in other mediation approaches, it is usual to elicit the telling of the conflict story early in the process. Indeed, the narrative approach leads to a strong interest in stories. Stories are, we believe, the backbone of experience.[6] Out of the stories people construct they take up their stances of opposition and conflict. So we are very interested in hearing people's stories of what has happened. In the process, the mediator is still pursuing engagement. The engagement the mediator is seeking is with the perspective of the people involved in the problem. In other words, the mediator is interested in learning the story from which the person is operating, not just with the story the person is telling.

It is also important to be clear that from this perspective the mediator is not listening to the stories people tell with a view to sifting out the facts or the truth from among the details of what people say. Such an aim risks communicating a subtle disrespect for people's stories. It sets them up as falsehoods tainted by personal bias and implies a process of replacing people's stories with a higher truth based on a more rational objective account. From our perspective, such an account would be just another story, one reflecting the mediator's biases. It would also position the parties to the dispute as in effect knowing less than the mediator.

The alternative stance is to listen to people as experts on their own lives. This stance implies hearing their stories as constitutive of the conflict even though perhaps limited by the evolving conflict story itself. The aim of narrative engagement is to validate people's storied perspectives as a preliminary step toward expanding the possibilities that might be available in these stories beyond what the conflict story might predict. We say more in Chapters Six and Seven about how to go about this. But briefly, the narrative orientation might be described as an effort to join the parties to a dispute in an alliance against the effects of the conflict. The alliance is negotiated early on and the conflict itself becomes the opposition. Meanwhile, the parties are invited to join the mediator in a struggle to rescue a spirit of understanding and cooperation from the jaws of conflict.

Narrative mediation is very much about creating a relational climate in which this spirit is allowed to flourish, whether or not the parties are inclined to have an ongoing relationship with each other. At the engagement phase this means endeavoring right from the start to develop ways of speaking that invite relationship repairing and rebuilding, or at least promote a respectful encounter. The emphasis on relational issues is perhaps one way in which the narrative approach to mediation is distinguished from other models. We say more about this in Chapter Five.

As we described in the first chapter, narrative mediators are not merely in the business of problem solving. Of course, in the initial stages of the mediation, many parties in a dispute will not want to pay attention to how they relate to each other. Their primary interest will be to address the specific details of the problem, after which they may have no desire for further association or interaction with each other. The mediation encounters may have been so punishing for the parties in dispute that they will want to wash their hands of the other party once the problem has been solved. In these instances the mediator could be seduced into believing that the relationship between the parties is of secondary importance. Certainly when ongoing involvement between the participants is unlikely after a conflict has been settled, they may invest little in developing a respectful interaction with each other. They will want the conflict solved so that they can move on with their lives. We suggest, however, that in most cases the need for a mediator to assist with resolution of the conflict is the result of a breakdown in the relationship between the disputing parties. Had there been sufficient trust and volition to address the initial problem, of course there would have been no need for a mediator to be involved.

## Deconstructing the Conflict-Saturated Story

Figure 3.3 illustrates the next stage of the mediation process as we conceive it from a narrative perspective. This phase relies on the maintenance of the relational context that the mediator must have established by successfully engaging the participants in the process.

This phase of the process involves the mediator in doing something more than developing a supportive relationship with each of the participants and listening respectfully to their stories. At this point, the mediator begins to work actively to separate the parties from the conflict-saturated story. We refer to this work as *deconstructive* in that it gently seeks to undermine the certainties on which the conflict feeds and invites the participants to view the plot of the dispute from a different vantage point. In this way, it lays the groundwork for the construction of an alternative story.

The assumption here is that the story of what has taken place to which each party subscribes is conflict-saturated. In other words, plot elements and characterizations that are selected for emphasis support the ongoing persistence of the dispute. Elements that contradict the ongoing persistence of the dispute, such as moments of agreement, cooperation, and mutual respect, will be left out of the stories that both parties tell.

### Position Calls

Every story offers people positions to take up in relation to each other.[7] Remember that these stories and the positions they offer are constructed in discourse. They are embedded in the stuff of conversation. They therefore are sometimes not immediately obvious, usually because they are sitting right under our noses. For example, when a person complains about how someone else has treated them, the person might take the position of victim in relation to the other. At the same time, the person constructs the relational position of villain for the other person. As the person speaks from this position, the story that is told contains expressions

**Figure 3.3. Deconstruction of the Conflict-Saturated Story.**

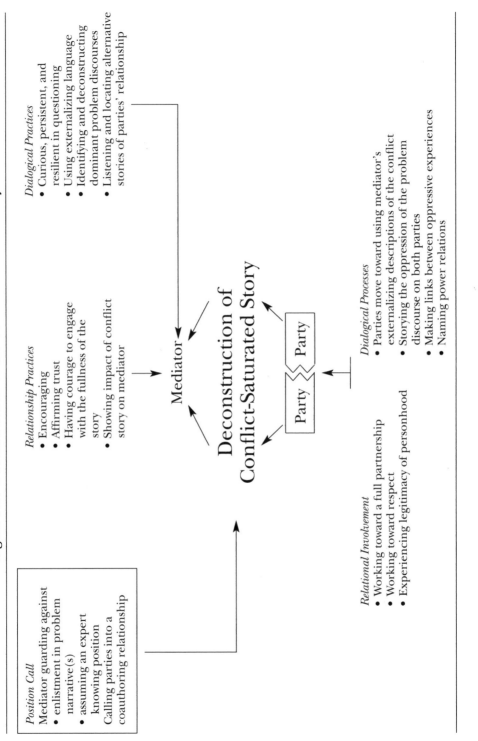

*Position Call*
Mediator guarding against
• enlistment in problem narrative(s)
• assuming an expert knowing position
Calling parties into a coauthoring relationship

*Relationship Practices*
• Encouraging
• Affirming trust
• Having courage to engage with the fullness of the story
• Showing impact of conflict story on mediator

*Dialogical Practices*
• Curious, persistent, and resilient in questioning
• Using externalizing language
• Identifying and deconstructing dominant problem discourses
• Listening and locating alternative stories of parties' relationship

**Deconstruction of Conflict-Saturated Story**

Mediator

Party Party

*Relational Involvement*
• Working toward a full partnership
• Working toward respect
• Experiencing legitimacy of personhood

*Dialogical Processes*
• Parties move toward using mediator's externalizing descriptions of the conflict
• Storying the oppression of the problem discourse on both parties
• Making links between oppressive experiences
• Naming power relations

that take for granted this relational dynamic. Each such expression calls the person hearing it into a position from which to respond (for example, oppressive villain or sympathetic ally). One can either enter into the position into which one has been called, or one can refuse to do so. This is the notion of *position calls*.

The deconstructive thrust is to make visible the relative positions that each version of the conflict story offers. This process of rendering visible does not necessarily need to be done in a critical way. It just needs to draw everyone's attention to the effects of the discursive positioning in order to make it possible for people to vary from this position when they prefer to do so. It is best done in a spirit of wondering and curiosity rather than opposition.

What also needs to be remembered is that the mediation itself is a discursive context as well. It is a site in which stories are being retold. As they are retold, they take on different forms in response to the context and in response to the mediator. The mere presence of the mediator in the conversation alters the positions of the disputing parties in the conflict story. At the very least they need to make room for a third person and offer at least two position calls in the version of the story they are telling.

But the mediation context itself can call people into positions. Relating to a professional person invites the disputing parties into a professional discourse with its own background stories. For example, one such story may feature the professional mediator as expert problem solver and the lay disputants as lacking in conflict management skills. If the mediator begins to speak from this discursive position, the parties may be called into a deficit position, one down from the mediator, and may either show deference to the mediator's knowledge or rebel against showing such deference. In this way, a power relationship may be constructed.

The mediation itself is an event in time. As it develops, it takes on the properties of a story in its own right. It has a beginning, a middle, and an end. It has a plot that features twists and turns, climaxes and low points, complications and denouements. The position calls that mediators offer to the disputing parties in each utterance they make are significant to the development of this plot.

From a narrative point of view, we urge mediators to guard against making position calls to mediation participants that assume that the mediator is in an expert knowing position (and thus call the participants into trusting the knowledgeable expert). Rather, we argue that the mediator should speak in a way that invites the production of a coauthored relationship.[8] In Chapter Five we explain more about the details of this kind of relationship.

We also urge mediators to be careful of the position calls made by disputing parties as they tell conflict-saturated stories. In the process of such tellings, participants can easily call mediators into positions within the conflict-saturated story. One such position might be that of sympathetic rescuer of a party's victimhood. It is important therefore for mediators to stay alert to the ways in which they can be enlisted into problem narratives as participants in the ongoing life of these narratives. Problem stories can sometimes overwhelm mediators and convince them that a conflict is insoluble. If this happens, the mediator will lose effectiveness, and possibly the respect of the parties in the dispute.

## Relational Practices

The relationship established with the disputing parties in the engagement phase needs to be continued in the deconstruction phase of the process. Indeed, the deconstruction phase can proceed only if the mediator is able to continue to convey respect and compassion to the disputants. If these qualities are not evident, the deconstructive questioning that we describe shortly will sound like an interrogation. An attitude of empathetic curiosity is required and the mediator's interest in each person's perspective must be genuine. Conflict is often very painful and the mediator will engender trust in the process only if he or she is not personally phased or scared by the dispute. This is the sense in which mediation requires the mediator to show courage in hearing the parties' stories in their fullness. This courage also applies to the willingness to ask the questions needed in this deconstructive phase.

If the mediator does convey this relational sincerity, compassion, and courage, the parties are likely to begin to trust the process. As they do they will become involved in it. This response appears in the diagram in Figure 3.3 as *relational involvement*. As the mediator asks questions that draw forth the parties' knowledge about how to resolve the dispute, they will start to move into partnership with the mediator. From this position, not only can a resolution to the conflict be found but also a personal experience of legitimation can be offered to each of the parties.

One more point needs to be made about the relational emphasis at this stage of the mediation. It has to do with timing. We think it is important not to ask questions about outcomes too early in the conversation because the parties may be reluctant to expose their opinions overtly before sufficient trust is built in the process. Deconstructive questioning seems more likely to develop this trust than a rush to a negotiation over outcomes. When premature outcome talk is attempted, we would expect reluctance to reach agreement to be evident and negotiations to proceed at a grudgingly slow pace.

We illustrate this phase by referring to the following scenario, which draws some distinctions between the problem-solving model and the narrative process. The scenario outlined here is based on an Australian LEADR (Lawyers Engaged in Alternatives to Dispute Resolution) training video in which a mediator grapples with a commercial dispute between a head chef and the owner of a restaurant.[9] The training video presents the different moves that a mediator using an interest-based approach would make in resolving the dispute. We use the same dispute to demonstrate the narrative approach.

### The Scenario: Loss of Respect

A restaurant owner, Penny, employs a kitchen assistant, Mark, who quickly shows talent for creating exotic dishes. Within two years, Mark is propelled to the position of head chef. With Penny's support, he gives the restaurant a new identity through a range of new dishes that are eagerly sought by the patrons. The restaurant's clientele triples. Both Mark and Penny are excited about what they have created together. Penny has provided the resources and encouragement while Mark has created a thriving trade with enticing dishes.

Mark, however, comes to feel that Penny is failing to acknowledge the contributions he is making. The overt conflict arises when Mark sets up a new restaurant down the road. Initially, he provides only lunches in his restaurant and continues to work at Penny's restaurant in the evenings. Some of the menu items are adapted from his creations at Penny's restaurant. He also creates a range of new dishes. Penny is furious that Mark has established his own restaurant and feels betrayed. Mark is outraged at Penny's interference when she places an injunction on his business, effectively closing him down. She accuses him of stealing some of her menu items and of taking clientele away from her restaurant. Mark wants to fight Penny's legal challenge. Both recognize that to fight it out in court will be hugely expensive and time-consuming and could ultimately lead to both of them losing their businesses.

In the mediation video based on this scenario, the mediator follows the interest-based model. He focuses on the underlying interests of each of the parties in a successful business and helps them step back from their polarized positions and reach an agreement. Mark and Penny do come to an agreement after a tortured set of moves and countermoves. The mediation sessions focus on what each of the parties is prepared to offer in order to invite the other party to give ground. Mark and Penny begin to offered small concessions as they are reminded of the significant costs of not resolving the problem. Each of them grudgingly offers a little territory in return for some accommodation by the other. Ultimately they decide that Mark can continue his business as long as he concentrates on lunch. In return, Mark commits to working in Penny's restaurant for a specified period and to continuing to develop the cuisine. He agrees not to offer any menu items at his restaurant that are the same or similar to those he developed in Penny's restaurant.

Although there is a resolution, Penny and Mark appear to demonstrate little trust or respect toward one another, even after the outcome has been negotiated. Both are presented in the video as smugly satisfied that they are getting what they want out of the mediation. The substantive issues are resolved but an underlying hostility remains.

We think there are problems with this mediation. Little attention is paid to Penny's experience of being betrayed by Mark. There is also no attempt to address Mark's outrage at Penny's efforts to close his business down. The conflict is represented in instrumental terms as a problem to be fixed by reaching a settlement that leaves aside relational experience and with little regard for the moral issues of justice and equity.

We predict that unless the relational issues were addressed, this resolution could unravel. We suggest that the most desirable, satisfying, and long-lasting resolutions to problems occur when the mediator pays attention to promoting respectful engagement between the parties. Of course, this respectful relationship will not emerge from the efforts of the mediator to appeal to some higher moral principles possessed by the parties. Rather, we believe that there are some specific moves the mediator can make to attend to the relational issues at hand. We return to explaining our narrative model and relate it to this scenario.

## Dialogical Practices

This is the heart of the deconstructive phase of narrative mediation. It involves the mediator asking questions that will open up space for reconsideration of the conflict-saturated story. These questions seek to reposition the parties in relation to what has happened so that the situation can appear otherwise. At first these questions might be about what has happened as each party is asked to describe the problem. However, we would also explore the discursive context from which the dispute arose. We would explore in detail how the problem began and how it unfolded. Later in the mediation process, this knowledge could be used to assist the mediator in contrasting the beginning of the problem with the problem-free period when, for example, Mark and Penny experienced great excitement working together.

*Curiosity.* Questioning is a key part of deconstructive work. Careful inquiry into the meanings of the elements of the stories that the parties tell seeks to avoid taking any particular meaning for granted. It also conveys the idea that meanings are not fixed but negotiable in conversation and related to context. Curious inquiry sometimes needs to be pursued persistently simply because discourses often work right under our noses to make the way things are seem like the only way they can be.[10] By asking questions, the mediator tries to make visible the workings of the dominant problem discourses. At the same time, he or she listens for possible alternative descriptions of the problem but does not necessarily bring these descriptions into the mediation discussion immediately. (See Chapter Five for more explanation of the spirit of inquiry referred to here.)

For example, in the dispute between Penny and Mark, the mediator might take up a curious, naive posture in wanting to understand how the conflict began in the first place. He or she might hear that Mark began to feel used or undervalued by Penny when he recognized that he was largely responsible for the enormous growth in the business. Was Penny having difficulty hearing Mark's concerns? The mediator might then invite the parties to compare individually how the quality of the conversations changed. The next inquiry could be into the quality of the working relationship before there was a sign of a problem. The purpose of this move is to identify from the outset experiences that remain outside the problem-saturated descriptions.

*Developing an externalizing conversation.* Externalization is a device used to help people separate from a story that locates the conflict in the nature of either person or to the relationship. It shifts the emphasis away from personalities, or blame, and focuses attention on the problematic features of the problem itself, which is spoken of as a third party in the dispute. (In Chapter Six, we outline in detail how to develop an externalizing conversation.)

We look now at how externalizing conversation might be used in the dispute between Penny and Mark. The mediator might look for some description of the dispute that includes both Mark's and Penny's perspectives. Such a description might need to include notions like betrayal or interference. It might even be called simply the argument. Then the mediator might speak about the argument as the cause of Mark and Penny's difficulties, rather than speaking about Mark and Penny as the cause of the argument. The argument might be thought of as having designs in their lives, intentions of its own, tricks that it plays on them, ambitions for their future, and fears that they might work together to undermine it. Such linguistic play, done skillfully, leads to a new perspective on the problem and positions the disputants as victims of the argument's actions rather than as either victim or perpetrator in each other's eyes.

Here are some typical questions that might be asked to explore the effects of the externalized problem on the lives of Mark and Penny:

- What effects would you say distrust and being taken for granted have had on your working relationship in the last few months?
- What has betrayal done to the excitement you both shared when you first started working together?

- What is the agitation doing to your creativity and business acumen?
- What effect have these consequences had on your general feelings of well-being? Your bodily health? Your mental health? Your relationships with others?

As the negative relational patterns come into greater focus, the parties will gain a clearer sense of the harm the problems have caused them. Mark and Penny might discover that there are many similarities in their experiences of what the problem has done to them.

*Deconstructing the dominant discourse.* Using curiosity and externalizing conversation, the mediator can help to deconstruct the assumptions from which the problem narratives are assembled. For example, the mediator might help the parties explore the assumptions that underpin employer-employee relations, attitudes toward business, the rights of individuals in the workplace, and the like. Out of these assumptions the parties to a dispute will have built a sense of entitlement that forms the basis of the claims they are making on each other in the conflict. A curious exploration of such entitlements is a step toward the creation of an alternative story, one that may be more inclusive of both persons' concerns.

Before asking deconstructing questions, it is helpful to ask the participants' permission to ask these questions because they could be perceived as intrusive. The mediator needs to move gently and respectfully in this area. The mediator might give a couple of examples of the questions and then let the parties decide whether they would like to answer them. Because the questions invite participants into a relatively vulnerable place as they disclose information about their privately held values, it is often preferable to ask these questions in individual sessions. People are much more willing to explore the issues raised by such questions when they are not under the scrutiny of the person with whom they are in conflict. Here are some examples of deconstructing questions that might be asked of Penny and Mark:

- Penny, as an entrepreneur, can you help me understand the significance to you of an employee of yours setting up his own business when he discovered how talented he was?

- Penny, where did you get your ability to recognize raw talent when you saw it?
- Penny, what are your ideas about how an employee should behave when you have given them a lucky break? Where did you get these ideas?
- Penny, because you feel you discovered Mark, how much do you think he needs to repay you in loyalty before he develops his creativity in other ways? Have you had any previous business experiences that give you guidance on the answer to this question?
- Penny, what are your views on rewarding employees like Mark who make major contributions to improving the turnover of your business? What business experiences have you had that have shaped your views on how to treat employees like Mark?
- Mark, what are your views about employee-employer relations in the context of running a restaurant?
- Mark, what protocols have you established in your own restaurant for rewarding employees who contribute more than other employees? What experiences have you had that have assisted you in making decisions about supporting your employees?
- Mark, what protocols do you think need to be identified to determine the level of reward offered for increasing the business turnover of your employer? How could this have been done?
- Mark, what silenced you from discussing with Penny your intention to take some entrepreneurial steps of your own?

It may well become clear that many of Penny's and Mark's taken-for-granted assumptions about employer-employee relations represent very different viewpoints. Let us say, for example, that Penny was of the view that as an employer she alone should benefit from the new business and increased profitability that Mark had attracted. She was, after all, the one who had employed him in the first place, taken the financial risks, trusted his abilities, and given him his lucky break. This discursive assumption about entitlement may lead her to believe that Mark owes her a considerable debt for having discovered him. Mark, conversely, may believe that it is he alone who has assisted Penny's business turnover to triple. As an employee, he may believe that he is entitled to be financially rewarded and acknowledged for his contribution to the business far beyond other employees' wages.

Overtly naming the discursive positions held by the parties makes it easier for the mediator to clarify exactly where the sticking points are. Bringing these discursive positions forward in the mediation can help the parties gain a clearer view of the assumptions each of them holds, and help them understand why the other party holds the views he or she does. After the parties' responses to the deconstructing questions have been discussed in the individual sessions, they can be brought into the joint sessions with the permission of both parties and clearly expressed.

Introducing a contextual element into the mediation can help the parties make more sense of the views held by the other party. The mediator may invite the parties to reflect on how the problem narrative has affected their lives up to the present. The conversation will continue to be externalized. The parties may be asked to evaluate the extent to which the problem narrative has dominated their lives, and how they would like their circumstances to be different.

Often the mediator assumes that he or she knows what outcome the parties want from the mediation process. Conflicting parties usually want their own way, and they want the conflict to stop. Sometimes, however, for whatever reason, one of the parties may not want a resolution. This view might be exposed by direct questioning. Direct questioning will also help to identify what a successful outcome might look like when the mediation is completed.

## Constructing the Alternative Story

Deconstructing the conflict in the problem-saturated story assists the mediator in opening the space necessary for alternative, conflict-free, or conflict-diminished descriptions to be entertained. In this phase of narrative mediation, the mediator is occupied with crafting alternative, more preferred story lines with people who were previously captured by a conflict-saturated relationship. Figure 3.4 represents this phase in the mediation process. This phase may lead to a resolution that takes the form of an agreement between the parties. However, this is not assumed to be the best outcome. Sometimes the development of an attitude of cooperation and respect may be more important than any substantive agreement. On other occasions the story of what has happened may be revised in ways that dissolve the conflict altogether.

**Figure 3.4. Constructing the Alternative Story.**

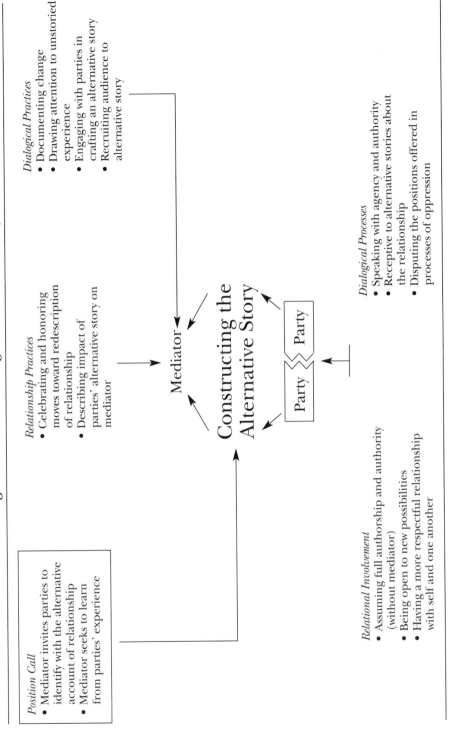

*Position Call*
• Mediator invites parties to identify with the alternative account of relationship
• Mediator seeks to learn from parties' experience

*Relationship Practices*
• Celebrating and honoring moves toward redescription of relationship
• Describing impact of parties' alternative story on mediator

*Dialogical Practices*
• Documenting change
• Drawing attention to unstoried experience
• Engaging with parties in crafting an alternative story
• Recruiting audience to alternative story

Mediator

**Constructing the Alternative Story**

Party

Party

*Relational Involvement*
• Assuming full authorship and authority (without mediator)
• Being open to new possibilities
• Having a more respectful relationship with self and one another

*Dialogical Processes*
• Speaking with agency and authority
• Receptive to alternative stories about the relationship
• Disputing the positions offered in processes of oppression

## Recovering Unstoried Experience

Because conflict tends to narrow people's focus onto things that support the ongoing life of the conflict, it is safe to assume that there will always be experience that lies outside the reach of the conflict story. These experiences will contradict, or at least not fit into, the conflict. They are rich and fertile soil for the creation of a different account of events. Out of this soil can grow new ideas for resolving the dispute. Stories are always selections from the available information strung together in a more or less coherent form. And because they are selections, elements will always be left out of them. Among what gets left out will always be material that can be employed to construct a different story. Michael White and David Epston (following Erving Goffman) have coined the term *unique outcomes* for this material.[11] These outcomes are unique because they are often isolated pieces of lived experience that are not salient in people's thinking simply because they do not fit into the dominant story. In this sense they remain experiences subjugated beneath the weight of that story. We conceive of the mediator's task in this stage of the mediation process as listening for these unique outcomes or asking questions to elicit them and then seeking to build on them a counterstory to the conflict-saturated story.

A good starting place can be coauthoring with the parties their preference for a different and conflict-free description of their relationship. Such preferences are statements of meaning. Few people want painful conflicts to continue, although many suspect that the person with whom they are in conflict does want this. Even saying out loud that you want an argument to stop contradicts the conflict story.

People seldom report that the conflict completely occupies their lives. Usually, although they might report that the conflict occupies a substantial area of their thinking, there are aspects of their lives that the conflict has not taken over. This is one opening for the mediator to explore. In these areas may lie potential resources that the parties can draw on to maintain equilibrium or moments of calmness. Sometimes a mediator might ask the parties to rate in numerical terms how much the conflict is dominating their day-to-day lives. For example, the mediator might ask Penny and Mark to rate on a scale of zero to ten how much the conflict occupies their day-to-day lives, with ten meaning "completely dominating" and zero meaning "not at all."

## Developing a New Narrative

Once a piece of information has been uncovered, the challenge for the mediator is to work with the parties to develop significance around that information. The postmodern assumption is that meaning is not essential to or inherent in a word, event, or personal characteristic. Meaning is achieved in a social context—in this case, in a conversation. If we take this idea seriously, we can set ourselves the goal of creating significance out of a piece of information where it did not previously exist. Thus, unstoried experience can be granted significance through its incorporation in a storying process.

In the example, Penny might report that Mark's betrayal has virtually used up all of her willingness to connect with him in any positive fashion. However, she might slip in a comment that while she has trouble speaking to Mark alone, she believes there are some positive features about him that give her hope that something worthwhile could come out of the mediation. The mediator could pick up on this comment and explore these features in detail, carefully relating them back to Penny's early experience of Mark, when she held a positive view of his abilities. The mediator would elicit any further positive experiences Penny has had with Mark when these same features might have been evident. Penny's experiences of Mark could thus be assembled into a narrative account. This account would not be saturated with recollections of him that feed the conflict story.

Mark could also be asked about the supportive qualities Penny exhibited that allowed him to develop his creative talents in her restaurant. Every effort would be made to story qualities that the parties could appreciate about the other. This story would be based on lived experiences or encounters from their previous working relationship. Hearing each other speak about the abilities and talents of the other can have an enormous influence on the parties' willingness to build trust. It can also provide openings for the reintroduction of a respectful quality to their interactions.

During this phase of the narrative mediation, the adeptness of the mediator is required to tease out the beginnings of a more preferred narrative from amid the problem story. Although people can usually acknowledge evidence of desirable and respectful encounters, it is challenging to maintain these alternative descriptions in the face of the current dispute. Therefore, attention must be paid to building on the potential for further alternative descriptions of the relationship. There is a tendency for the participants to become reenlisted in the problem description if the mediator does not pay attention to strengthening the emerging non-conflict-focused interactions.

At the very least, alternative story development with parties who have known each other for some time requires two or three lived experiences that testify to more respectful and favored interactions. These experiences need to be elicited and carefully marshaled together in a purposeful conversation if the conflict story is to be prevented from continuing to dominate. They are then woven into a coherent narrative with a history, a present, and a future. If the parties are continuing to interact with one another, the mediator should be persistently curious in subsequent mediation sessions to discover more examples of respectful interactions to add to the growing alternative story.

In Penny and Mark's situation, for example, the mediator could ask the parties if there have been any incidents in the last week when the conversation between them was tinged with any degree of respect. They might state that they have been avoiding each other on most occasions and staying out of each other's way because they have been distressed by the conflict. Rather than attending to the avoidance, the mediator might persist with the question about difference. Instead of saying, "Have you managed to develop a respectful way of speaking?" the mediator might ask, "Was there any occasion during the few interactions you did have when a small amount of mutual respect may have been evident?"

We call questions such as these *smalling questions*. By accessing lived experiences in small chunks, the mediator gets much more information about how to strengthen alternative story lines.[12] Penny and Mark might be invited to magnify relatively small interactions that have had positive features and incorporate them into the growing alternative account of respectful interaction.

## Types of Questions Used to Develop an Alternative Story

Here are some types of questions that can be used in the process of taking up a unique outcome and developing a story around it. This is just one way of classifying these questions.[13] We are not advocating their use in a mechanical way or suggesting that questions of each of these types should always be asked. They are listed here simply as learning tools to aid you in understanding and expanding the range of purposes to which questions can be put in the process of storybuilding.

*Unique outcome questions* are introduced to facilitate the development of personal agency. They invite people to identify actions and intentions that stand apart from the problem story. These events may have occurred before the mediation session, they may happen during the mediation itself (such as an agreement on an item of discussion in a context in which the disputants are arguing and disagreeing over nearly everything), or they may be imagined events that have not yet taken place. Here are some examples:

- How is it that conflict did not completely stop you from wanting to talk together and find your way through the present difficulties?
- Why did hurt feelings and blame not stop you from canceling this meeting?
- Do any recent occasions stand out for you in which hurt feelings and blame did not completely destroy your efforts at searching for a solution?
- Have there been any instances recently when you experienced a hint of not being defeated by hurt feelings and blame?

*Unique account questions* help people make meaning out of unique outcomes. They ask a person to make sense of an event that is an exception to the conflict story it represents. Often this contrast may not have occurred to the person. Such questions allow thematic development of the alternative story to take place. They provide people with the basis for an alternative account of their efforts to make progress with conflict issues. Here are some examples:

- How do you explain that you were able to be more in charge of blame, humiliation, hurt feelings, or injustice than you initially thought?
- When other people may have held on to hate, how did you develop the resources not to be dominated by blame and claim a sense of space for yourself?

- What do you think it means that you are agreeing about that issue?
- How significant is it to you that she is willing to cooperate on your request in this case?

*Unique redescription questions* address the narrative development of character and relationship. They invite people to reflect on themselves and on the relations between them to develop a fuller articulation of how they would like to be. They get at people's preferences for their personal development or for their relationship. Where a conflict has taken over the description of a relationship, these questions create an opportunity for a redescription to take place. Here are some examples:

- What does this tell you about yourself that you otherwise would not have known?
- What does your movement away from conflict say about your ability to resolve painful difficulties?
- Does cooperation suit you better than arguing, or not?
- If most of the time you were able to talk civilly and respectfully about things, as you have been doing today, what would your relationship be like?

*Unique possibility questions* move the focus toward the future. They encourage people to speculate about the implications of what has been talked about in the mediation and to project it forward. What gets projected forward may be plot trajectories, characterizations, or themes. Each of these would be derived from and build on the unique outcomes, unique accounts, and unique redescriptions. The mood of such questions is subjunctive and the aim is often to open up a field of wondering rather than some definitive solution. Here are some examples:

- Given your present understandings and your desire to heal the wounding effects of blame, what might be your next step?
- If you were to advance the cause of cooperation, what might you try to do in the next week?
- Now that you have noticed these chances to explore greater respect in your relationship, what difference could they make?

*Unique circulation questions* help anchor the newly developing more-preferred story through the provision of an audience. They recognize that stories are not always the property of those at the center of a dispute. Often other people are affected by the dispute. For example, in a divorce mediation children are deeply affected by the resolutions their parents create. But there are also many other people who might bear witness to what happens in a dispute, including relatives, neighbors, colleagues, friends, customers, employees, teachers, and so on. If these people are available, they can actually be asked to comment on the alternative story and give an opinion on it. If they are not present, the participants can be asked to ventriloquize their presence and imagine out loud what they would say. The aim of such questions is to locate the outcomes of a mediation back in the social, cultural, and linguistic community in which the central protagonists live. Here are some examples:

- If your children were witness to these discussions, who would be most excited about this change in direction?
- What difference would introducing more cooperation into this situation, as you have been proposing, make to your other staff or to the service you provide for your customers?
- Who will be most likely to support the continuation of these developments?

One final point is worth making in this section. Throughout the restorying phase, it is useful to check that the questions are heading in a desirable direction for the parties and are not merely satisfying the mediator's desires. For example, the following questions might be asked:

- Is this a preferable development?
- What in particular has been beneficial?

## Constructing Agreements

As the alternative story of respect grows, the parties may be ready to work through outstanding challenges. When the mediator has reached the point with Penny and Mark when a degree of goodwill and respect are present, the largest part of the mediation has been accomplished. From this point on, conversations about resolving the dispute may be much more straightforward. Only at this stage would a narrative mediator begin to problem solve with the parties. When a better relational pattern is developed, a problem-solving approach can then be effective. In our experience, when the relational issues are addressed in a positive way, many people are in a stronger position to negotiate the details about settling the dispute themselves.

Nowhere in this alternative account about managing the conflict would we focus on having either party offer a compromise, that is, give something to get something in return. In most instances, parties in conflict are in fact interested in working with the relational content of a conflict. Even in an apparently straight commercial transaction, a person's preference for relations with customers or business associates can be explored. However, in some situations where the parties are not going to have any further association, they may be reluctant to address personal relational content.

Even so, narrative mediators still work with the effects of the conflict situation in people's lives. In most instances, concentrating on the interpersonal domain still delivers effective outcomes. Moreover, in our experience, this narrative approach considerably shortens the negotiation phase of a mediation, because it engages people in negotiation from a place of greater willingness. Some mediation models privilege substantive issues while the relational issues are sidelined. Our preference is to address the relational issues in preparation for the settling of substantive issues.

## Documenting Change

The final aspect of the process of constructing an alternative story that we want to include in our model is the creation of a written record of the content of the mediation. This record may include notes of meetings to be kept on file, written agreements arising out of the mediation, letters written by a mediator to other participants, reports to third parties about the mediation, or any other kind of document that arises from the specific nature of the mediation.

The narrative perspective on the drawing up of written documents is concerned with the politics of their authorship. They should first of all be collaboratively written rather than appear as judgments or pronouncements from a position of expertise. The narrative perspective also alerts us to the possibilities that such documents offer. We view them as opportunities for developing further the narrative that has been advanced in the meeting. They can strengthen unique outcomes and alternative stories that took a tentative hold in the meeting. Because dominant stories can be expected to reassert themselves after a meeting with the mediator is over, such strengthening may often be crucial to the survival of a new perspective.

Therefore, in narrative mediation the creation of written documents is part of the mediation process, not just a functional record of the process. If we take this perspective, we are also interested in people's ongoing responses to what gets written. The written record does not just represent what happened in the mediation. It also gets mixed up in it at a particular time. And people will do things with what they read. Most likely there will be ongoing reflections on the written record, and new, sometimes unexpected, developments will follow from the reading of them. In Chapter Ten we explore some of the possibilities that written documents, particularly letters to clients, can offer the mediation process.

This, then, is an overview of the mediation model we are keen to advance. It has three phases: engagement, deconstruction of the conflict-saturated story, and construction of an alternative story. Lest this summary sound too linear and simplistic, let us stress again that these are not discrete stages. They do not always follow one after the other in tidy sequences. At times a mediation may move back and forth between these stages in a seemingly haphazard manner. Nor are we advocating the structuring of the mediation for participants in these three stages. Rather, these stages are like background organizing frameworks for mediators to use to guide their thinking. We expect mediators to concentrate early in the process on building engagement with the parties to the dispute, although there may be early opportunities for asking deconstructive questions or for pursuing some opening to an alternative story. Similarly, toward the end of the mediation process, if it has been making progress, we would expect to be focusing more on the future than on the past. We would hope to be discussing mostly the elaboration of an alternative story, even though there will still be a need for asking occasional deconstructive questions and for continuing to attend to everyone's continued engagement with the process.

In Chapter One we told a story to illustrate a narrative approach. In Chapter Two, we distinguished the narrative approach from the problem-solving approach and laid out the theoretical ground for a narrative model. In this chapter we have outlined the overall model. Before we go on to look more closely at each of the stages of the model, we want to address a particular issue that strikes at the heart of how we think about how conflict develops. The issue is *entitlement*. It is the focus of Chapter Four.

## Notes

1. Mills, S., *Discourse* (New York: Routledge, 1997).
2. Winslade, J., and Cotter, A., "Moving from Problem-Solving to Narrative Approaches in Mediation," in G. Monk, J. Winslade, K. Crocket, and D. Epston (eds.), *Narrative Therapy in Practice: The Archaeology of Hope* (San Francisco: Jossey-Bass, 1997); Winslade, J., Monk, G., and Cotter, A. "A Narrative Approach to the Practice of Mediation," *Negotiation Journal*, 1998, *14*(1), 21–42.
3. Rogers, C., "The Interpersonal Relationship: The Core of Guidance," in J. Hansen (ed.), *Counseling Process and Proceedings* (New York: Macmillan, 1962).
4. Chandler, D., "Violence, Fear, and Communication: The Variable Impact of Domestic Violence on Mediation," *Mediation Quarterly*, 1990, *7*(4), 331–346; Davies, B., Ralph, S., Hawton, M., and Craig, L., "A Study of Client Satisfaction with Family Court Counseling in Cases Involving Domestic Violence," *Family and Conciliation Courts Review*, 1995, *33*, 324–341; Ellis, D., and Stuckless, N., "Preseparation Abuse: Marital Conflict Mediation and Postseparation Abuse," *Mediation Quarterly*, 1992, *9*(3), 205–225; Girdner, L., "Mediation Triage: Screening for Spouse Abuse in Divorce Mediation," *Mediation Quarterly*, 1990, *7*(4), 365–376.
5. Moore, C., *The Mediation Process: Practical Strategies for Resolving Conflict* (San Francisco: Jossey Bass, 1996).
6. White, M., and Epston, D., *Narrative Means to Therapeutic Ends* (New York: Norton, 1991); Monk, G., Winslade, J., Crocket, K., and Epston, D., *Narrative Therapy in Practice: The Archaeology of Hope* (San Francisco: Jossey-Bass, 1997); Freedman, J., and Combs, G., *Narrative Therapy: The Social Construction of Preferred Realities* (New York: Norton, 1996);

Dickerson, V., and Zimmerman, J., *If Problems Talked: Narrative Therapy in Action* (New York: Guilford Press, 1996).

7. Drewery, W., Winslade, J., and Monk, G., "Resisting the Dominant Story: Toward a Deeper Understanding of Narrative Therapy," in J. Raskin and R. Neimeyer (eds.), *Constructions of Disorder* (Washington, D.C.: American Psychological Association, forthcoming).

8. Monk, Winslade, Crocket, and Epston, *Narrative Therapy in Practice.*

9. Lawyers Engaged in Alternatives to Dispute Resolution, *Sous Chef or Sue Chef?* (Sydney, Australia: Cynthia Palmer Productions, 1997), video.

10. Geertz, C., *Local Knowledge: Further Essays in Interpretive Anthropology* (New York: Basic Books, 1983).

11. White, M., "The Externalizing of the Problem," *Dulwich Centre Newsletter,* special edition, 1989, pp. 3–21.

12. Monk, Winslade, Crocket, and Epston, *Narrative Therapy in Practice.*

13. White, M., "The Process of Questioning: A Therapy of Literary Merit?" in M. White, *Selected Papers* (Adelaide, Australia: Dulwich Centre Publications, 1989).

# Chapter Four

# Entitlement

*He has but one eye, and the popular prejudice runs in
favour of two.*
(Charles Dickens, "Nicholas Nickelby")

*It's them that take advantage that get advantage i' this
world.*
(George Eliot, "Adam Bede")

In this chapter we examine the effects of entitlement and exaggerated entitlement on the creation of conflict, and the subsequent implications for managing the mediation process. We show how entitlement is constructed within a cultural context and shapes human needs and interests diversely. In the remainder of the chapter, we demonstrate how narrative mediation can be used to deconstruct entitlements in an attempt to assist people to build more equitable relations when conflict is being addressed.

Patterns of entitlement emerge from within a complex network of power relations and societal narratives. Although entitlements often arise from dominant discourses that are present in the community, they sometimes emanate from alternative discursive content. Take, for example, the emergence of the civil rights movement in the United States. In the 1960s, African Americans in Alabama were required to give up their seats on buses to white people. An African American seamstress named Rosa Parks decided she would hold on to her seat. The bus driver stopped the bus and had Rosa arrested. In that one act of claiming the entitlement of staying in her seat, Rosa challenged the exaggerated status and entitlement of white Americans in the South. That act began one of the most successful civil rights movements of the twentieth century. African Americans and other groups took a stand against racist and other socially unjust laws operating in North America. These groups felt entitled to take a stand against what they recognized as a gross form of injustice. Rosa Parks's decision to claim her seat was not made alone. This act of entitlement rose out of a readiness within the African American community to challenge racism through civil disobedience. This readiness had a history that dated back to much earlier periods when African slaves engaged in acts of defiance of slavery. Thus, an alternative discursive context was emerging in contrast to the dominant racist one. We think this understanding of entitlement has merit in helping us to appreciate how conflict is produced. It points to conflict as a contest over entitlements rather than over interests or needs.

Other forms of entitlement are perhaps more familiar. People often find themselves believing that others should treat them well and look after their needs. They are particularly sensitive to being treated unfairly when they have contributed to another person's well-being and their actions have not been reciprocated. Furthermore, it is not uncommon for one party to believe that he or she deserves to be treated in a favored manner, that is, that he or she is entitled, even though he or she has done nothing to deserve any special favors. When one party experiences a discrepancy between what he or she believes is deserved (based on a notion of entitlement) and the favors he or she actually received, a strong negative response may be produced. This is a common phenomenon and is featured in many human interactions.

As we noted in Chapter Two, conventional approaches to mediation focus on how people have unmet needs that must be satisfied if a conflict is to be settled. Interest-based or problem-solving models address the issues that conflicting parties feel are unfair or unjust by seeking out possible compatible interests and needs in an attempt to help defuse the conflict. It is argued that if the disputing parties are able to recognize that they can both have their needs met in resolving the conflict, they will become motivated to work at finding a solution. Need, from this perspective, is viewed as a fundamental characteristic of being human and arises naturally. From a liberal-humanist viewpoint, human need is inherent and preexistent. We disagree. Although we cannot deny that all human beings share the need for food and protection from a hostile physical environment, we argue that the majority of people's psychological, social, and emotional human needs are constructed within the sociopolitical landscape.

## Types of Entitlement

We suggest that human need is discursively constructed. There is something about the dominant description of need that appears nonnegotiable and taken-for-granted. It invites us to accept that need must be catered to because everyone has it. However, we find it more useful to work with the concept of entitlement rather than need. Entitlements lend themselves more readily to close scrutiny, debate, and challenge. When we talk about an individual having a need, there is less opportunity to examine the nature and legitimacy of that need because it is seen as preexisting. Entitlement, conversely, is seen as linked with an intention or a desire that has been constructed. The mediation process can therefore be viewed as addressing the contest over differing notions of entitlement rather than as a process that sets out to meet people's needs.

Patterns of entitlement often form around specific groups or identities in a community. Societal discourse constructs patterns of entitlement that privilege the concerns of one individual or group of people over those of another. From this perspective, conflict can be understood as a clash of entitlements that occurs between individuals or groups in overt or covert ways on a day-to-day basis.

### Gender Entitlement

Historically, gender entitlement has been strongly linked to discourses of patriarchy, which tend to privilege the interests of men over the interests of women. The exaggerated entitlement that many males assume in comparison to the diminished entitlement that women obtain in the majority of cultures has existed for so long that it is difficult to ascertain where these entitlements originated.

There is nothing inherent in being male to justify these entitlements. One could target the greater physical prowess of the male over the female in early human evolution or the superior religious construction of the male as depicted in the oral and written traditions of many ancient religions. In the last few hundred years, the discourses of science have often privileged patriarchal practices over alternative descriptions while claiming the status of objective research. Whatever explanation is used to account for conflict between men and women, the distorted sense of male entitlement continues to be featured in many domestic conflicts.

Overall, men continue to earn on average a much higher income than women, they are promoted more rapidly to senior positions, and they often gain more kudos and support for doing so. In many communities, women contribute more to unreciprocated social-emotional care of their partners in relationships. Women tend to be burdened with the role of primary caregiver to children and to have greater domestic demands placed on them than men do. This often occurs in a climate where women's contributions to these activities are devalued while men's contributions to assisting with child care duties and domestic tasks tend to receive attention and praise. In cultures all over the globe there are countless examples of gender entitlement ranging from the privileging of patriarchal history to the value placed on male sporting achievements.

## Race Entitlement

Dominant societal discourse produces entitlements with phenotypical (skin coloring, facial features, body shape) or racial characteristics. In the West these entitlements are linked historically to the colonizing activities of Western Europe in the eighteenth and nineteenth centuries. In the dominant colonizing discourse, the colonized emerge as the image of everything the colonizers are not. The colonized are positioned as lazy, wicked, backward, and in important ways not fully human. This discourse places the colonizers as the entitled party who are served by the colonized. Racism, as we know it today, or the practice of one group viewing itself as superior to another, has emerged from the colonizing practices of the nineteenth century. This colonizing pattern typically occurs when a technologically advanced country's cultural accouterments are imposed on a communal and collective societal structure. Western colonizing practices continue today in the form of entitlements constructed by ethnic and phenotypical characteristics. For example, in Western communities white skin and Caucasian features, such as a narrow, pointed nose, small nostrils, thin lips, and wavy or straight hair, are deemed to be more attractive than black skin, a broad nose with flared nostrils, full lips, and kinky hair. In a rather provocative manner, Iris Young discusses how patterns of ethnic entitlement get built into the minutiae of interaction:

> White people tend to be nervous around black people. . . . In social interaction, the socially superior group avoids being close to the lower status group, avoids eye contact and does not keep the body open. . . . Members of oppressed groups frequently experience such avoidance, aversion, expressions of nervousness, condescension, and stereotyping. For them such behavior, indeed, the whole encounter, often painfully fills their discursive consciousness. Such behavior throws them back on to their group identity, making them feel noticed, marked, or conversely invisible, not taken seriously, or worse, demeaned.[1]

Furthermore, the phenotypical features of individuals are influential in determining the level of access they will have to certain resources in the community. Although there have been major changes in recent years, the Western majority culture is still responsible for producing inequalities in the availability of resources, such as good quality housing and employment, for individuals who do not fit into the dominant race.

## Other Identity Entitlements

While there are significant discrepancies in the levels of entitlement between groups, there is also wide variation in access to entitlement and resources within groups. While gender and ethnic and racial identities stand out as significant domains in which entitlement is legitimated or denied, a complex array of other discursive contexts also permit or legitimate entitlement. The following are examples of factors that affect the entitlement of individuals within dominant Western groupings:

- Being young is deemed to be more desirable than being old.
- Having physical or intellectual ability is prized over physical or intellectual disability.

- Being heterosexual is still regarded as normal and desirable by the majority culture while being homosexual or gay is viewed as abnormal.
- Certain religious affiliations are viewed by the majority culture as more acceptable than others.
- Affluent individuals are often treated with more respect than the poor, and individuals who are highly educated have access to more abundant community resources than those who are poorly educated.

We hope we have said enough to demonstrate that any community legitimates entitlement along a variety of identity dimensions. We want to make clear the extent to which discourses offer, regulate, and preclude particular forms of identity. The picture is complex because different discursive contexts call forth and favor one identity over another. Although systematic cultural patterns legitimate different levels of entitlement, it is too simple to say, for example, that whites are *always* privileged over blacks, or men over women. People are made up of multiple identities that are legitimated to various degrees. For example, in most communities a young, well-educated, middle-class African American woman in a high income bracket has access to greater entitlements than an older, white, lower-class, uneducated man with few financial resources. Cultural context introduces and creates further complexity in the way entitlement is legitimated. For example, a white, heterosexual, able-bodied man working in settings that privilege nonwhite, disabled, homosexual identities may find his access to an entitled position seriously diminished compared to his access in a Western majority cultural setting where his dominant identities were legitimated. We argue that identity and entitlement are fundamentally linked, each defining and being defined by the other.

## Entitlement and Agency

We think that there are distinct advantages to mediators' viewing the parties as representing a multitude of identities, each of which promotes or diminishes the level of entitlement permitted by the discursive context. Just as we have remarked on the dynamic relationship between identity and entitlement, we also think it is helpful to introduce the term *agency* into the discussion to push the narrative mediation theory further.

Arising out of the social constructionist literature, agency is the act of diminishing the extent to which the discursive context can capture and control a person's activities. It follows that entitlement is expressed by a person's agency in his or her interactions with others. A conflict might gather momentum when the parties are reluctant to abandon their positions of agency. What is far more likely, however, is that a conflict occurs because people think they have no agency at all.

It is helpful to recognize that there is enormous variation in the extent to which people are constrained or encouraged by discursive placement. It makes no sense to speak of somebody as completely powerless or having no ability to act. Viewing agency from this perspective acknowledges that there are opportunities to act in apparently powerless circumstances in a variety of settings at different times. Moving away from viewing oppression and marginalization in global terms sensitizes the mediator to notice how a person has the capacity to act, albeit in some modest way.

## The Implications of Entitlement

Entitlement is a new concept in the mediation literature. We believe that introducing this idea into mediation offers the mediator a more sophisticated analysis of power relations in the mediation process. It invites the mediator to consider how the multitude of competing entitlements ebb and flow within the mediation conversation while also alerting the practitioner to systematic patterns of marginalization and legitimation that are featured within a conflicted interaction.

The mediator can either promote social justice and attend to equity and fairness, or reinforce unjust dominant cultural practices. We argue that the mediator needs to take an overt position in challenging and addressing some of the exaggerated entitlements that arise for individuals because of the discursive positions into which the conflicting parties are called. The mediator in this situation is hardly neutral. One of the strong threads in this book is our emphasis on how the mediator's own discursive position has a bearing on the mediation process. Narrative mediators may state openly their opposition to violence, racism, and sexism. They may open to question what is considered the norm because the norm is a cultural product that privileges some groups of people. To be neutral and not challenge the norm may serve to support privilege. This is a very different approach in comparison to traditional methods of mediation that emphasize the importance of mediator neutrality.

Exaggerated entitlement contributes to a large number of conflicts within families and in the workplace. It is helpful for the mediator to register when a party has a private set of assumptions about an injustice that is based on unearned privilege claimed at the expense of the other party. By being attentive to how systematic patterns of entitlement are featured in conflict, the mediator can make efforts to assist those whose voices are often silenced or marginalized. This assistance needs to be approached by the mediator in a manner that does not alienate the party who appears to be the most advantaged as the mediation begins.

## Mediating Patriarchal Entitlement

Some of the most difficult family mediations arise when one party, coming from a position of fixed entitlement, has an uncompromising view about what is required to solve the dispute. Following is an illustration of a dispute that has been constructed to a large extent on patriarchal entitlement. Although this dispute was not resolved in mediation, it is an excellent example of the contribution that patriarchal entitlement can make to a family conflict.

*An Explosive Scenario*

Juliet and Thomas were having a dispute about access arrangements. Thomas was seeking to spend more time with his son, Henry. Juliet and Thomas had been married for five years and had subsequently been living apart for three years. Thomas left Juliet just after she conceived Henry. Juliet had no support from Thomas during her pregnancy, although Thomas did contribute financially to Henry's upbringing after he was born. Thomas remarried, and then wanted Henry to become part of his new family. He stopped his financial contribution to Juliet for Henry's care.

Juliet reluctantly came to the mediation. In three sessions, Juliet and Thomas agreed to an elaborate arrangement whereby Thomas would see Henry two

days a week and most of the summer holidays. The mediator was ready to for-
malize all of the agreements about Thomas's access to his son when Thomas
said, "Oh, there is just one more thing I want to add. I want to be sure that my
child will be addressed publicly using my surname." (Henry had his father's
surname but Juliet wanted to change it.) "Furthermore," he said, "I have
asked my friends to check and tell me whether his last name is used at school
and at church." From this moment on the mediated agreement unraveled,
leading to Juliet requesting that all the understandings reached up to that
point be rescinded. Thomas replied, "If Henry is not going to keep my surname, you can count on me leaving his life forever. If you won't use his
correct name, then I will not see him."

"Good!" replied Juliet. Both parties said they had had enough and would not
be returning to mediation. They left the room.

This scenario clearly illustrates how entitlements can be legitimized by the social worlds we inhabit while at the same time contributing to the construction of unjust situations. Let us explain
further. From one perspective, it is legitimate for a father to expect
his son to be called by his father's surname. This practice conforms
to dominant cultural conventions in the West. From another perspective, however, the mother has a right to have her son take on
her family name, because the father has had only a peripheral role
in his son's life. Thomas's view was that as a matter of right his son
would be named after him. For him, this was a statement to the
world that his son was his. This is perhaps not a surprising conclusion for Thomas to reach given the prevalence of the liberal discourses of ownership in the West. Perhaps Thomas viewed Henry
keeping his surname as representative of a "title of possession" over
his son.

The mediator asked Thomas why it was so important to him that Henry should
keep his surname. Thomas reemphasized that he had provided financial assistance to his son up until he remarried. That his son would take on the surname of his mother was perceived by Thomas to be the greatest insult. Thomas
felt that his friends, colleagues, and church acquaintances, who would be influenced by the same discourse of entitlement, would look down on him for
not being a proper father, reflected by the change in his son's name. Thomas's
perception was that such a change in name would be symbolic of his failure to
contribute to his son's life, and his failure to have a moral and educational influence over Henry.

It appeared that Thomas, in the grip of the patriarchal discourse, positioned himself as the head of the household, presiding over all significant decisions, including matters related to the child's well-being. If he was to be regarded as a man who had failed to assert his authority over the woman who was the mother of his child, it seemed preferable for him to withdraw completely from any role with his son. Clearly his status was on the line and the discursive hangovers of patriarchal practices had greater impact on his attitudes, reactions, and decisions than the discourses that invited him to stay connected to his son. On this occasion, the patriarchal discourses of entitlement persuaded this father, who had been so close to stepping more fully into his son's life, to exit completely from all contact with his child. It is hard to know whether this departure will be permanent. The strength of reaction made it highly conceivable that he was disengaging for good.

## Learning from Failure

It is worth exploring the possible discursive implications that contributed to Juliet assisting in derailing the mediation. If Juliet were to accept the position offered to her by the patriarchal discourses, she would have consented to Thomas's wishes. However, for Juliet there was more at stake. It was not lost on Juliet that renaming her son with her own surname could unsettle the fragile agreement she and Thomas had reached at their previous session. Juliet believed, however, that Thomas had exploited her. He had barely had a parenting role at all, and soon after he remarried, he had ceased financial contributions to Henry's upkeep and all contact with Juliet. Only in the weeks prior to the mediation did Thomas want to reassert what he felt was his rightful place as Henry's father by seeing his son on regular occasions. Juliet, in the meantime, had met a new partner and wanted Thomas to play a relatively minor role in Henry's life. To some extent, Juliet had used the potency of the patriarchal discourse as a way of manipulating the extent to which Thomas would be involved in Henry's life. She called his bluff and he subsequently withdrew.

From another perspective, however, Juliet was experiencing herself as a woman entitled to assert her own wishes. This assertiveness was based on a sense of entitlement that had its origins in a discourse that spoke of women's rights as individuals free from patriarchal domination. The process had been costly, however. She was left thoroughly frazzled by the mediation and emotionally raw. She had had enough and did not want to pursue any further discussion about parenting arrangements. This, then, was a contest over differing entitlements. In this case, there was no resolution.

Unsuccessful mediations provide numerous opportunities, however, for mediators to reflect on their work. Other strategies, such as considering the issues of entitlement, could have been employed by the mediator to address the conflict in the situation just described.

Because of the speed and intensity with which Thomas's and Juliet's negative reactions to one another arose, it may not have been possible to renegotiate a further mediation session to address the highly charged issues. It is not uncommon in the heat of the moment for one or both parties to walk out on mediation. In a highly volatile mediation session, it is sometimes helpful for the mediator to call a break in the proceedings before one or both of the parties gets so overcome by intense emotion that the mediation is brought to a premature end. Time-out can let the parties calm down enough to enable them to continue to explore the issues.

Alternatively, the mediator might request a meeting with one of the parties to discuss an entitlement issue. In an attempt to address the conflict about changing Henry's surname, the mediator could have scheduled an individual session with Thomas to deconstruct the significance of Henry's change of surname. Attempting to deconstruct Thomas's feelings of entitlement over his son's surname in the presence of Juliet would not have been helpful. It would have been too humiliating for Thomas.

Substantial progress had been made on the specific details of the caregiving plan for Henry at earlier mediation sessions. However, the one unresolved dispute about Henry's surname was sufficiently fierce to undo all of the previous understandings. The mediator in this conflict was using a jigsaw puzzle or building block approach to resolve the conflict. In such an approach, the disputing parties are encouraged to work first with the issues that are perceived to be most resolvable. The pieces of the conflict that are more difficult to solve are left until last.

Our view, however, is that unless competing notions of entitlement are addressed early on, agreement on specific issues is often vulnerable to being tossed aside in the heat of the moment. There is merit in meeting with one of the parties in an effort to deconstruct exaggerated notions of entitlement before moving into a joint session. The following example illustrates in more detail some of the techniques that narrative mediators can use to deconstruct discourses of entitlement.

### Challenging Entitlement in a Narrative Mediation

Discourses of ownership were evident in mediation between a husband and wife, Bruce and Mary, who were considering divorce. They had a specific issue that required attention. The couple was having a dispute about whether an affair had occurred between Mary and a visitor to their home. The couple decided that if they could resolve the dispute over the alleged affair, they would most likely remain married.

Bruce was adamant that the affair had occurred and Mary was equally adamant that it had not. This unresolved dispute was threatening to end their ten-year relationship. The conflict was also distressing the rest of family. The three children in the home were caught up in the endless arguments raging between their parents. Both Mary and Bruce sought mediation. They needed to find some way out of their awful mess.

Bruce believed that Mary had had sex with a male visitor who had stayed with the family for a week. Bruce stated that Mary and the visitor had stayed up late a couple of nights and he was sure he heard them having sex. He described seeing evidence of sex on a bathroom towel. He would not elaborate on what he meant by this. He also accused his wife of not being in bed when he woke up early one morning. Mary was highly distressed by Bruce's accusations. The serious breach of trust in their relationship was having a devastating effect.

Mary admitted that she had been attracted to the visitor, but that was all. She also admitted to staying up late for two nights and having long conversations with the male visitor. On one occasion she agreed that she had stayed up until 1:00 A.M. However, she was outraged that Bruce had accused her of having an affair. Having sex with a man outside of marriage was for Mary completely taboo. She thought it was ridiculous for Bruce to draw any conclusions about her having sex with the visitor based on marks on a bathroom towel.

Irene, the mediator, thought that it was a bad idea to get caught up in acting as a judge or arbitrator of Bruce and Mary's dispute. Using some narrative techniques, the mediator explored the effects on the couple of "believing that this event happened." The mediator asked Bruce and Mary to come up with a name for this issue that had created so much havoc. They thought that calling it "the affair question" was fine. Irene used externalizing language to begin to undermine the level of blame and guilt featured in the conflict. It was by mapping the effects of the issue that it became clear that the discourses of entitlement were present. Bruce had begun to monitor Mary's movements. He would call her three times a day to check on where she was. At the worst stage, Bruce would take time off from work to enable him to better check on Mary. During the night he would wake up and check that Mary was in bed.

Further questioning made it clear that Bruce was exhausted from monitoring Mary's movements. In the meantime, Mary felt like a caged animal and was aware that she was always being monitored.

This is an extreme example of a situation that was strongly influenced by entitlement discourses produced from a history of patriarchy. When mediators are confronted with a scenario like this it is easy to blame one of the parties for reprehensible conduct. The party could then pick up on negative judgment exhibited by the mediator, and resolving the dispute would become more difficult.

## Understanding the Discursive Pattern

We have found that to avoid judging or blaming a party for unjust behavior, it is helpful to focus on how discourses of entitlement restrain a person's ability to demonstrate fairness and equity in dealing with another person. This framework enables the mediator to look at the background influences that are shaping the present conflict. As we described in the last chapter, the mediator should be interested in deconstructing the discourses that are helping to produce the conflict. Before a mediator can do this and thus render problematic discourses less influential in a client's life, he or she must be familiar with the discursive patterns that accompany the kinds of injustices that are contributing to the conflict. Irene (the mediator) was familiar with some of the traditional patriarchal discourses that are often played out in family, community, and even business mediations. She knew the negative effects of patriarchal discourses of exaggerated entitlement from her own experience growing up in her family. She had also studied a feminist analysis of Western sociocultural history and had gathered many insights into the subtleties of patriarchal interactions and the regulating effects of patriarchal discourses on men and women in relationships.[2] The conflict between Mary and Bruce was only one more example of a conflict she understood all too well. It is one thing to understand patriarchal discursive patterns, but it is quite another to know how to address the impact of their effects in order to create more respectful encounters.

We have found Alan Jenkins's book *Invitations to Responsibility* particularly helpful in addressing the exaggerated entitlement often exhibited by men toward women in home and work relationships.[3] Jenkins suggests that exploitation of another person occurs when a sense of entitlement overrides the person's social-emotional responsibility. When one of the parties has an exaggerated sense of entitlement, the attribution of responsibility for abusive behavior is often directed to an innocent other. The monitoring and controlling behaviors exhibited by Bruce toward Mary, based on Bruce's beliefs in Mary's affair, is an example of what exaggerated entitlement can lead to.

The extreme effects of patriarchal entitlement invite the belief that men have a right to be the head of the household and that women can be possessed or owned by men. Bruce felt that he had the right to take charge of his wife. He was convinced that Mary had breached the rules of the marriage by having an affair and that he had the right to ensure that she did not do so again. In addition, as husband, he assumed he had the right to censure her activities and punish her for her serious discretion. As a result, Mary felt like a prisoner in her own house. The discourses of entitlement had also affected the kinds of responses that Mary could legitimately express. Patriarchal discourses can foster female submissiveness and deference. Many women positioned by patriarchal practices take up a sense of responsibility for the creation and maintenance of the social-emotional climate in the marriage.

Although Mary expressed outrage at Bruce's behavior, she did not feel she could leave Bruce. She told herself that she had committed herself to him when she had married him and to leave Bruce would be a breach of her marriage vows. Mary was devoted to raising the children and supporting her husband and had put her paramedic career on hold. In the presence of an exaggerated sense of entitlement by men, some women hold themselves responsible for causing their male partners to behave the way they do. Privately, Mary blamed herself for the problem erupting and felt guilty about her feelings of attraction for the visitor. Besides, if she was to leave Bruce, Mary did not think she could support herself financially. She also believed she would be blamed for the separation if she were to part from Bruce. Thus, the idea of leaving Bruce with the three children and setting up her life apart from them was unthinkable.

Clearly, Bruce's behavior is supported by patriarchal patterns of entitlement. These discursive features position Bruce as someone who believes he is entitled to a certain authority and control over his spouse. Mary, conversely, is called into a discursive position of deference and submissiveness. These specific patterns can be deconstructed in a variety of ways.

## Models of Relationship

We have found it useful for the mediator to help the person who is captured by exaggerated entitlement to imagine that he is someone who, in his own better judgement, would not want to abuse or hurt another person. Generally, when you ask someone whether they want to be in charge or in control of their partner or in an equal relationship that involves respect and care, they opt for the latter. Thus, when individuals are behaving abusively, the mediator might take the stance that the exaggerated entitlement or patriarchal views exhibited by one party are restraining that party's ability to engage respectfully with the other party. One approach used by our colleagues Wally McKenzie and Rosemary Smart to address this circumstance is to ask the couple caught in an abusive situation to consider on which of the following four models of relationship they would like to base their lives.

*The equal relationship.* The intersecting circles in Figure 4.1 represent a couple who have what could be described as a partnership or equal relationship. The intersection of the two circles represents shared intimacies, interests, responsibilities, and duties, and activities that the couple enjoy doing together. The parts of the circle that do not intersect represent the couple's activities that fall outside their common interests. This relationship is depicted as equal because there is both space for the couple to explore their own interests as well as space to share equally in the tasks of living a life together.

*The roommate relationship.* Figure 4.2 contains two circles of the same size, side by side but not intersecting. This model illustrates equality but not intimacy. The couple does not share a close association; alternatively, they pursue their own interests in an equal, open fashion. This relationship is characterized as a roommate relationship.

*The traditional relationship.* Figure 4.3 contains one large circle encapsulating a small circle. The large circle demonstrates that the entitlements of one party are bigger than the entitlements of the other. The first party is in a dominant position in most interactions and tends to assert a controlling influence on the other party. The small circle inside the large one shows that the dominated party

**Figure 4.1. The Equal Relationship.**

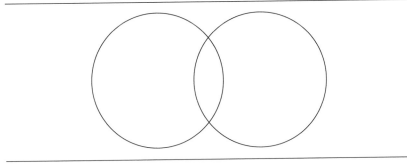

**Figure 4.2. The Roommate Relationship.**

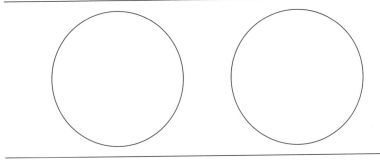

has fewer rights in the relationship. The party represented by the small circle has no independent interests. The dominant other subsumes this person's life. The person represented by the small circle is said to live their life for and through the person represented by the large circle.

*The emergent relationship.* The relationship represented in Figure 4.4 is similar to the one described in Figure 4.3 except the person represented by the small circle is beginning to emerge from the confines of the large circle. The person represented by the small circle is beginning to experience a small degree of independence and freedom. Although strongly bound to the identity of the person in the large circle, this person is able to express some disagreement on some subjects.

**Figure 4.3. The Traditional Relationship.**

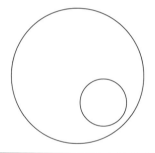

**Figure 4.4. The Emergent Relationship.**

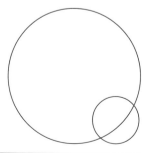

After the mediator illustrates these four relationship models, he or she asks each party which model they prefer. We have used this approach on numerous occasions and have found that in virtually every instance, the disputing couple identifies the equal relationship (Figure 4.1) as most desirable. The couple can then be asked why they have chosen this model. This is often an invitation for one or both parties to discuss the type of relationship they presently have. One of the parties might comment on how dissatisfied they are with their present living arrangements and give numerous examples of why the relationship is not equal. This sets the stage for a conversation that deconstructs the dominant discourses that accompany an exaggerated sense of entitlement that one of the parties may hold.

## Deconstructing the Dominant Discourse

We return now to Bruce and Mary. Bruce acknowledged that he wanted an equal relationship. The mediator asked a series of questions to invite Bruce to change his view of his behavior in significant ways. This approach to dealing with exaggerated versions of entitlement invites the parties to engage in discussion about the issues without becoming overly defensive or losing face. Here are some examples of questions the mediator might ask:

- Do you want a marriage within which you can respect each other?
- Do you want a marriage that will enable you to enjoy each other's company or tolerate each other's company?
- How important is it for you to have a marriage based on genuine respect and trust?

Bruce wanted to stop the monitoring and stalking behavior. He wanted to be free of the controlling behavior he had been demonstrating. He did want a relationship based on respect and trust. In the spirit of respectful persistence and curiosity, Bruce was asked to identify how he had come to the decision to abandon his controlling behavior. He recognized that despite what he believed about the affair, he was being disrespectful and abusive toward

Mary. The mediator recognized that the desire for things to be different was not enough to help facilitate a change in Bruce and Mary's pattern of engagement. Jenkins suggests that it is necessary to assist many men to distinguish between their desire to give up controlling behavior and their plan for bringing an abusive pattern to a halt. The mediator could discuss the plans Bruce has made to guard against being enlisted in further monitoring behavior. For example, the mediator could ask Bruce, If Mary was to do something again that was in your view detrimental to the relationship, how would you guard against enlisting an abusive, violent, or controlling response? Such a question invites the individual to argue against patriarchal patterns of entitlement. Jenkins's approach invites engagement with the issues while circumventing the need for defensiveness and potential loss of face.

## Collapsing Time

Introducing the concept of time into the discussion made it easier for Bruce to come to grips with how his relationship with Mary was suffering. The mediator asked Bruce whether Mary was likely to be feeling more respected or less respected by him over time. He was also asked how his attempts to talk Mary into agreeing that the affair had actually occurred were likely to affect her over time. Michael White uses a technique called *collapsing time* to intensify the direction of the story line.[4] Collapsing time is a useful technique for determining the trend of a relational pattern. A common question in this technique is, What will happen if the issue is continued over the next three months, six months, one year, two years, five years?

In Bruce and Mary's situation, the mediator became focused on assisting Bruce to develop a greater degree of understanding of and empathy with Mary's experience of his behavior. The mediator asked Bruce to describe some of the effects of his controlling behavior on Mary by asking the following questions:

- What effect has your controlling behavior had on your marriage and on your respect and trust of Mary?
- What effect has this behavior had on you and how you feel about yourself, that is, on your feelings of self-respect and confidence?

This technique utilizes the principle of *news of difference* to examine the effects of exaggerated entitlement. Gregory Bateson, anthropologist and psychologist, noted that learning takes place when people can detect new information as a result of comparing one set of events with another.[5] When individuals are bolstered by an exaggerated sense of entitlement, it is difficult for them to see the extent to which their entitlement has a negative effect on the disadvantaged party. By drawing the attention of the disputing parties to the subtle negative changes that can accompany an escalation in the conflict, a clearer strategy for addressing their concerns can be achieved.

The series of questions just listed provided Bruce with the opportunity to begin to understand and appreciate the effects of the problem story on Mary's life and on his own life. He realized that not only had his trust of Mary diminished because of the affair he suspected, but his subsequent behavior had seriously jeopardized the degree to which Mary could trust him. It was deeply disturbing to him when he realized that Mary had become frightened of his behavior and that she had significant fears about what he might do next. He became acquainted with how vulnerable he felt at the prospect of Mary leaving and how this had affected his confidence.

To deconstruct the effects of Bruce's exaggerated entitlement in the form of his controlling behavior on Mary, the mediator proceeded to ask him the following questions:

- Do you want Mary to stay with you because she wants to out of love and respect, or because she feels she has to?
- Do you want Mary to be her own person with her own ideas, or your person with your ideas?
- If Mary were doing as she is told, would she be more likely to give out of love and desire, or out of duty?

Bruce recognized that he could not have a positive relationship with Mary if she felt obligated to do what he said. Once it was established that Bruce was seeking a more respectful and caring relationship, he was asked whether it would be helpful to understand what had stopped him from achieving these goals for his relationship. He was then asked to identify what had thwarted him from achieving these goals with his partner. Bruce reported that worry about losing Mary had led to his controlling and monitoring behavior. He said he did not know how he would manage if Mary were to leave him. He also became aware that his way of showing love to Mary was misinformed and harmful and that it came from a place of desperation.

## Addressing Entitlement
## Using Alternative Story Development

By the third mediation session, Bruce reported that he had stopped checking up on Mary's movements. Mary endorsed this and stated that there had been a significant positive shift in Bruce's behavior. Using unique outcome questions (introduced in Chapter Three and explained further in Chapter Eight), the mediator asked Bruce whether there were other occasions when he had stood up to the old-fashioned style of relationship (referring to his controlling behavior). Bruce commented that he was putting more effort into his work and becoming less preoccupied with the "affair issue." In fact, he didn't refer to this issue any more in conversation with Mary. In addition, he described how he was standing up to the insecure feelings he had previously experienced when he felt he was going to lose Mary.

The mediator concentrated on identifying other examples supplied by Bruce and confirmed by Mary that challenged the problem-saturated story of being in control.

Bruce could now label this behavior more accurately as abuse. The few occasions that Bruce identified as examples of challenging the prevalence of the exaggerated entitlement story in his life were not, on their own, enough to ensure that a respectful mode of relating would last. The mediator sought to assist Bruce to story these new developments in his life by inviting him to discuss periods in his life when he had treated Mary with great respect and had related to her as an equal. The mediator then used a range of narrative questions to assist Bruce to give an account of himself as a man who worked at building respectful relationships with women. Mary, too, had a role to play in renegotiating a more respectful relationship with her husband. She needed to stop looking after Bruce's feelings by constantly reassuring him that everything was alright. She was taking more risks and speaking her mind to Bruce about subjects she had previously avoided. These conversations acted as challenges to Bruce's ability to hold to an equitable relationship with Mary.

In this chapter we have discussed the value of entitlement as a conceptual tool for understanding conflict. We think that the focus on entitlement and its relationship to identity and agency provides the mediator with some refreshing new ways of understanding conflict, as well as new possibilities for practice. We have commented on the challenges that mediators face when people in conflict have an overdeveloped sense of entitlement that translates into what they regard as their inalienable rights and needs. We have made the case that promoting shared understandings and meanings between disputing parties is, to a large extent, achieved by unpacking and deconstructing the ways in which human entitlements are constructed in ongoing disputes.

**Notes**

1. Young, I., *Justice and the Politics of Difference* (Princeton, N.J.: Princeton University Press, 1990), pp. 133–134.
2. Marecek, J., "Gender, Politics and Psychologies of Ways of Knowing," *American Psychologist,* 1995, *50*(3), 162–163.
3. Jenkins, A., *Invitations to Responsibility* (Adelaide, Australia: Dulwich Centre Publications, 1990).
4. White, M., "Negative Explanation, Restraint and Double Description: A Template for Family Therapy," in M. White, *Selected Papers* (Adelaide, Australia: Dulwich Centre Publications, 1989).
5. Bateson, G., *Steps to an Ecology of Mind* (New York: Ballentine Books, 1972); Bateson, G., *Mind and Nature: A Necessary Unity* (New York: Bantam Books, 1980).

# Chapter Five

# The Relational Context of Narrative Mediation

*Seal up the mouth of outrage for a while,*
*Till we can clear these ambiguities*
*And know their spring, their head, their true descent.*
*And then will I be general of your woes*
*And lead you, even to death. Meantime forbear,*
*And let mischance be slave to patience,*
*Bring forth the parties of suspicion . . .*
(WILLIAM SHAKESPEARE, "ROMEO AND JULIET")

Now that we have laid out the theoretical territory, it is time for us to approach the tasks that the mediator must perform. We have already pointed to the value of thinking in terms of a discursive framework. But we have been referring mainly to the background thinking that mediators working in a narrative frame need to bring into the room with them. We now show how to use these notions in the practice of mediation.

## Trust

One of the first requirements for a successful meeting is for the mediator to establish a relationship of trust and respect with the parties. Typically, trust is one of the casualties of conflict. Therefore, there is not a lot of trust in many of the situations that are placed in front of a mediator. Perhaps the parties' willingness to trust another person has been badly hurt by the experiences the dispute has put them through.

Conversely, the mediator can capitalize on a number of advantages. One of these is the professional role that the parties implicitly expect the mediator to play. General discourses of professional relationships position people in a place of trust with regard to professionals. If I go to a doctor or a lawyer, I expect them to represent the standards of trust that are enshrined in the traditions and ethical codes of their professions. This is also true with mediators. Of course mediation is by no means a profession with the standing and history of the medical or legal professions. It is often performed by someone who has a different professional allegiance (such as a counselor, lawyer, manager, or social worker). However, mediation is still cast in the shadow of all general professional discourse, which creates an expectation of trustworthiness.

Expectations can be dangerous, however. They can lead to assumptions that are unwarranted. They can lead a person in the client role to trust the mediator without thinking about whether his or her interactions with the professional are proving worthy of that trust. This puts the mediator in a position of advantage. One might even say that it puts the mediator in a position of power—a power constructed according to the nature of the relationship between client and professional. Everything the mediator does is affected by this power relation. Her words are likely to echo with the authority of professional power. Her assumptions are implicitly less open to challenge. Her suggestions sound more like instructions. Her attitudes have a persuasive influence. Such is the nature of privilege, and mediators, we believe, need to understand that their position, from the moment they start to interact with the disputing parties, is one of privilege. Of course there are many other relational patterns out of which different kinds of privilege are constructed, and these too might be present in the mediation meeting. Privilege may be constructed out of gendered patterns of relation, out of the cultural positions people bring into the room, out of the economic resources at their disposal, and out of a host of other sources of legitimization or meaning. So, privilege is a complex phenomenon, never unidimensional, and constructed out of the many interlocking patterns of relationship.

If we think of power as a commodity that is bought or exchanged or fought over like a favorite toy, then this analysis of privilege becomes problematic.[1] Sometimes people think that the way

to handle power relations is to seek to efface the power, to equal-
ize the power or empower the client, or even to claim that mediation is not possible because of the existence of a power relation.
We think that this problem shifts in nature once we step out of the
idea of power as a commodity. If power inheres in a relation rather
than existing as a commodity, then we cannot avoid it or do away
with it. According to Michel Foucault's analysis,[2] power is present
in every utterance in every relation. It is constantly shifting and
fluctuating as we offer each other positions within a variety of discourses and supplement the positions offered to us by others in return. Therefore, the positions offered by traditional professional
discourses are not to be ignored, but rather than thinking of them
as fixed structural arrangements, they should be thought of as invitations to a particular conversational pattern. Once we develop
the discursive awareness to take cognizance of these patterns and
include this awareness in our conversational responses, then the
power relation (including some of its structural features) has already shifted and changed. We can ensure that we are doing this
by calling into a position of privilege the voice of the other, and by
being willing to accommodate to that position rather than ex-
pecting the other person to accommodate to us.

The question of building trust therefore becomes an ethical
question, not just a technical one. How do we, as mediators, respond to the position in which we are placed by clients who implicitly expect us to be trustworthy? One option is just to accept the
privileges of the position we are offered and make the most of it.
We can assume that if people want the services of a mediator, they
should be grateful for our expertise and allow us to do our job without offering much resistance. We can just assume the right to ask
anything we like, and we can instruct people to act in response to
our suggestions. We can use the trust we are offered (even if cau-
tiously and reluctantly at times) as leverage to get the problem resolved. We can focus on the desired outcome of the mediation and
treat the means of achieving it as automatically justified by that end.

The narrative perspective, however, asks us to take more seriously the ethics of the professional relationship. We believe that in
a professional relationship, trust is actually enhanced by being
more openly cautious about acting on the privilege that inheres in
a professional role.[3] Whereas professional discourse would position

us in a place of being trusted automatically, we would argue for making that expectation explicit, and even for raising that place as questionable. What we need to do, then, is outline a stance (in the end, it is an ethical stance) that builds on this perspective of professional privilege and uses it to enhance the trust that can be constructed in the mediator-client relationship.

One of the first steps is to begin to think of trust as an achievement rather than as a given. Trust is achieved in social interaction, even if it is built on apparently structural arrangements such as power differentials. The difference in power that accrues from professional privilege, for example, is substantial only to the extent that the people in a professional relation embody it in their interactions. Even hierarchical relations are underpinned, we would argue, by a network of interactions that give them apparent substance, rather than being the essences of social structures. In other words, there is nothing in the relationship between the mediator and the client that makes the privileged position of the mediator essential other than the stances that the people involved take in relation to each other. Privileged positions and the expectations we build on the basis of them are fluid rather than fixed, constantly shifting and changing rather than predetermined.[4] This perspective opens up the possibility of altering the relationship between the mediator and the parties by changing the stances they take.

In this way, trust can perhaps be understood as an expectation that accrues from other professional interactions that have influenced the parties to a dispute. But it is also primarily an achievement, or a moment-by-moment series of little achievements. The mediator achieves trust by adopting a stance that proves trustworthy to the parties, and by the disputing parties choosing to engage with that stance. This stance is always subject to subtle (or not so subtle) moves to renegotiate or revise it.

The ethical question, then, in building a relationship of trust is, How do we understand and handle the privilege and power that the professional relationship grants us? and How do we understand and handle privileges granted to us on the basis of other discursive positions that intersect with the mediation relationship? For example, if a male mediator works with one male disputing party and one female disputing party, the possibility of developing trust during the mediation process may depend on how the mediator handles the privileges that are constructed out of patriarchal gendered assumptions.

## Reflexivity

The relational dimension that enables people to be accountable for positions of privilege has been described in various ways. The term that we choose to describe it here is *reflexivity*.[5] A reflexive practice of mediation, we believe, builds a trustworthy process for both the mediator and the disputing parties. This practice needs to be distinguished from the *reflective practice* advocated by Donald Schön and others.[6] The idea of the reflective practice is not inconsistent with that of the reflexive practice, but the emphasis is slightly different. This difference lies mainly in the reflective practice of handling privilege and power in ways that demonstrate the principle of accountability.

Reflection suggests a personal approach. It refers to the individual's thinking back over her or his experience and learning from it. Reflexivity may include reflection, but we use the term *reflexivity* to refer to a more dialogical or conversational process, one that involves people calibrating their actions with each other. This form of accountability involves taking account of and reflecting on the impacts one has on the other. It contrasts with the more common form of accountability, which is focused upward toward employers or funders rather than being concerned with the views of clients.

The concept of reflexive practice has often been talked about in relation to research methods, where it has been used to distinguish research that objectifies and exploits its subjects from research that respects its subjects as coparticipants in the research process. In such research, the researcher includes himself or herself as a participant whose actions in asking the research questions are constructed not as neutral or objective but as situated and interpretative. These actions are always open to alternative interpretation as well, especially in light of the contributions of the coparticipants in the research task.

Similarly, in fields of professional practice, such as mediation, a reflexive approach opens to view the positions from which people relate to each other. It makes privilege and power subjects for discussion and deconstruction. This process of opening to view is not a neutral activity, however. Reflexive moves that would make relational positions evident begin in themselves to shift or transform these positions. From a social constructionist perspective, they are constructive of the social conditions of our lives. We shape these social conditions even as we are shaped by them. Thus the social world out of which we act is the product of the discursive exchanges into which we speak and act. Most of the time, this activity takes place without our conscious intent. Reflexive practices help to make what we are barely aware of more obvious, and therefore more available to our conscious efforts to change. In this sense, such practices are very relevant to what mediation is about.

Reflexivity in the sense we are referring to pertains not merely to talk. Working reflexively is about making shifts and creating spaces that have material consequences in people's lives. For this reason, we prefer to speak about reflexivity using spatial metaphors that refer to shifts in and movements of bodies rather than visual metaphors that refer to seeing things differently, such as through another's eyes or insights.

The central metaphor we are exploring is that of *positioning*. In each utterance we make in a conversation, we offer others positions from which they may relate to us. We issue them position calls (as discussed in Chapter Three). Each response in a conversation is to some extent shaped by the utterance that has preceded it. We can think of these positions as participants' physical orientations to each other that express relational influence; that authorize the other to speak or not to speak, or to speak only in certain terms; that allow what we say to count or not count; or that limit or widen our possibilities for acting in our own worlds. This is the sense in which language, as Bronwyn Davies suggests, speaks us into existence and constitutes our personhood, as we use it to communicate with others.[7]

Reflexive practice, then, is about how we make ourselves accountable for the position calls we offer our clients. It is about how we take up positions in relation to the position calls they offer us. It is about how we offer them space or crowd them out. It is about how we handle authority, that is, the right to be an author in others' life stories. Professional and academic discourse grants this authority to the mediator and privileges the mediator's position ahead of that of the client. Clients are typically rendered as recipients of (or subject to) the authority of the mediator. The position of client, or "case," can objectify a person in a way that to a large extent removes opportunities for the client to have a legitimate voice in the process of mediation, except in relation to the content of mediation conversations.

Reflexive practice is about the mediator opening up his or her position in relation to his or her work in order to accomplish the following:

- To understand the constitutive effects of mediation on both the mediator and the clients
- To make transparent the position calls that the mediator sends to clients
- To invite clients to reposition themselves in relation to the mediator and in relation to their own life projects
- To invite clients to respond to the mediator's positioning of himself or herself in relation to the clients
- To shift the mediator's position to accommodate a subjective stance by a client
- To invite the client into a position of commenting, theorizing, or editorializing
- To prepare the mediator to be surprised rather than to seek to confirm what he or she suspects or knows
- To refuse to colonize the client by assimilating the client's knowledge into the mediator's
- To adapt the mediator's knowledge to include what he or she has learned from the client

Implicit in this definition is an interest in the micropolitics of the mediation relationship. It is an attempt to avoid the assumptions involved in "practicing down" just as researchers have "researched down."[8] Practicing down is usually achieved by professionals laying their theoretical knowledge over the client's experience. Reflexive practices are those that render transparent the practices of power in the mediation relationship and leave space for clients to alter the configuration of these practices.

Implicit, too, is the assumption that the relationship is a dialogical process rather than simply personal reflection.[9] Reflexivity is more than individual navel gazing. Rather, interpretations of experience are made in conversation by at least two people. The intention of this stance is that in a genuine conversation each participant should come out of the process a little changed. The mediator's thinking is brought out from under the cloak of objectivity. Clients are treated as persons with something to say about the process and as psychological theorists in relation to their own lives.

Following are some ways in which a mediator can embody such reflexivity in his or her practice:

- Ask the parties' permission to take initiatives in the conversation (such as asking further questions on a particular subject) rather than assuming the right to do so on the basis of professional privilege.
- Speak or write reports about clients only in ways that you would be happy for them to overhear or read.
- Inquire from time to time whether the mediation conversation is going in the direction the clients wish it to go or whether it is covering the topics they wish it to cover.
- Treat the parties as people from whom you can learn at every step of the way. This may include inviting them to comment on or theorize about their own experience, the mediation process, or what may be helpful to do next.
- Treat all documents or recordings that come from the mediation process as being coauthored with the clients rather than as belonging exclusively to the professional. Make it clear that access to files and notes is open to clients.

## Curiosity

Narrative mediation is built on a postmodern ethic of curiosity. The theoretical basis for this ethic of practice is the premise that there is no privileged viewpoint from which mediators can understand the realities of the world in which we live. Empirical observational methods grant us a valid perspective from which to inform ourselves about the world, but not a perspective that deserves to be privileged above or that excludes all other perspectives. Indeed, there is much to be gained from seeking out the increased possibilities for living that arise from widening the perspectives from which we view the world.[10] Thus, for example, women's ways of knowing, diverse cultural traditions of knowledge, and local, vernacular, or situated perspectives of many other kinds offer us valid perspectives from which to understand things.[11] From the accessing of multiple perspectives comes a potentially richer vein of opportunity to be mined than we get from seeking out the singular truth as it is defined by scientific canons of knowledge.[12]

Mediators have long known this in practice, of course, even when they have not taken it into account in their theories. Mediators have always credited clients with credibility for their own thoughts and feelings and have sought to enter into the clients' phenomenological worlds. They have rejected the idea that one party's account of a dispute can ever be the truth. But when mediators work from the assumption that there is (in theory at least) a single truth, an uncomplicated reality, or a set of facts that can be discovered or deduced from the stories the parties offer, then they are making an accommodation with the modernist, scientific viewpoint that reduces the value of the disputing parties' stories. This use of the word *story* is almost pejorative. A story has a lower status than a "fact" or "reality."

Postmodernism takes the idea of phenomenological perspective one step further. It seeks to unseat the grand narratives of science from their pedestals and to render all forms of knowledge as cultural products, produced in discourse and constructed in complex webs of conversation, rather than seeing them as representations, however approximate, of reality. Note that this is different from saying that all realities are relative, as some have claimed. We are not suggesting that reality does not exist; rather, we are simply saying that people's processes of knowing construct the versions of reality they come to experience and that these are all they have to go by. Moreover, the assumption of privilege for perspectives based on ideals of objectivity and neutrality is not justified from a postmodern viewpoint.[13]

From a narrative perspective, people who present their problems to a mediator do so within an epistemological framework. They speak their problems into existence through the narratives they tell about them. They construct their stories out of the discourse that circulates in the conversational contexts of their lives, and they construct their disputes out of the elements of these stories. This does not make their problems unreal. Discourses, from a social constructionist perspective, have very real consequences. What this idea does suggest, though, is that we should pay more attention in mediation to the meanings that are created within such discourses. The postmodern turn is a turn to meaning. Rather than searching for resolution through the expression of "true" feelings or by addressing essential interests or by meeting unmet needs, the postmodern agenda is about opening up previously unavailable worlds of meaning. If something is a problem within the dominant narratives with which the parties to a dispute are making sense of things, the challenge becomes to deconstruct the narrative itself, to see it as a framework of meaning rather than as an essential and enduring truth, and to open space for a different story to be told and for the performance of different meanings.

One of the first tools mediators need to bring to this task, then, is an attitude of wonder or curiosity. Empathy is not enough, because although it helps mediators enter into the client's experience, it does not achieve the space for thinking about how things might be otherwise. We are not speaking against empathy, which is still important in understanding problematic experiences, but we are suggesting that mediators need to value curiosity more highly than has been the case.

The expression of such curiosity requires mediators to ask questions in a certain spirit. There is a problem here, however, for people seeking to learn to work in a narrative way. Asking questions has a particular history within modernist traditions that needs to be distinguished from what we are advocating here. Asking questions is often spoken about as data collecting. This usage draws on the modernist scientific model of the scientist-practitioner who asks questions in order to learn from the client details, or "facts," that can then be interpreted within the framework of the professional's expert knowledge.[14] In a relationship between a mediator and the parties to a dispute that is produced out of such assumptions, the client's role is reduced to that of reporting, and the major initiative, the interpretive or diagnostic work, is concentrated in the person of the mediator.

This spirit of asking questions to collect data is not the kind of curiosity we are advocating. Data collection can too easily turn into an interrogation or cross-examination. Such curiosity is chiefly confirmatory rather than exploratory. Confirming hunches or hypotheses becomes the goal of the questioner in a data-gathering approach. The person answering the questions is objectified, or called into the position of assistant to the main protagonist in the drama—the mediator who generates the hunches.

What we are advocating is a spirit of questioning that calls the parties into a much more "agentic" position.[15] The voice into which the client is invited needs to include the position of making the interpretations or meanings rather than just furnishing the mediator with the information out of which the meaning of events will be made. The mediator needs to be genuinely interested in learning about what the client thinks rather than seeking to confirm hunches. The mediator's questions are more likely to be focused on eliciting stories rather than facts. Facts always assume a system of meaning in which they are elements. Stories create meaningful coherence around elements of a plot.

Some family therapists have described using a "not-knowing" stance or "deliberate ignorance" to keep the spirit of curiosity alive.[16] To achieve this stance, mediators need to be constantly willing to be informed by what their clients are saying, and they must never assume that they understand the meaning of an action, an event, or a word. From a postmodern perspective, meanings are never finalized but are always contextual and open to revision. Such inquiry should persist so that the parties to the dispute learn something themselves about what they have been saying. From this perspective, questions are understood as productive or generative of experience rather than as reports of experience.

The asking of questions in this way can also be described as *deconstructive*. Deconstruction, as we have explained (see Chapter Two), is about coming to understand how things are by unpacking the background contextual assumptions against which things make sense. In the process, the grip of an established knowledge is loosened in the hope of opening up the possibility that things can be otherwise. Asking naive or obvious questions can help this task. Examples might be the following:

- When you use an expression such as "This is not just a matter of money, it's the principle of the thing!" what principle do you have in mind?

- Can you help me understand how you came to consider this principle so important?
- So what exactly do you mean by honesty?
- What does it look like in practice?
- What have been the influences on that strong value for you?

In the process of asking and answering such questions, a conversation can develop that begins to unravel a tightly coiled, taken-for-granted reality. As the assumptions that lie behind a particular viewpoint are brought to light, the viewpoint itself comes to look like an option or preference rather than a compulsory or unassailable truth. The grip of a problematic story starts to loosen as it becomes subject to curious questioning. But the questioning must proceed from an attitude of genuine interest rather than from a technical focus.

Table 5.1 demonstrates the spirit in which we advocate that mediators should ask questions and contrasts it with a different spirit. The right column represents the idea of curiosity that is supported within the modernist agenda. The left column lists descriptions that fit into the postmodern spirit of inquiry. This spirit involves an ethical stance toward the client that is based on a different epistemological foundation and a different view of knowledge and the role of the professional.

An example of the value of such curiosity is warranted at this point.

### Curiosity: An Example

John was involved as a mediator in a dispute between a storage company and a person who had stored some household effects. Water damage and theft had led to some of the effects being either missing or damaged when they were reclaimed by the owner. There was considerable disagreement over the extent of the damage and the value of the items stored, and a protracted battle had developed that eventually involved the courts in this issue.

When the matter came to mediation, in an attempt to sort it out, it looked like a disagreement over a monetary amount. John could have proceeded in a factual way and endeavored to seek a settlement based on the monetary and legal responsibilities. Instead, he asked each of the parties a few curious questions about the meaning of the dispute to each of them. The responses were

## Table 5.1. Curiosity: Two Ways of Asking Questions.

| Asking questions in a postmodern frame | Asking questions in a modernist frame |
|---|---|
| Privileges the coherence of stories | Privileges the establishment of facts |
| Shows a desire to respect the client's truth | Shows a desire to match the client's experience to established truths |
| Seeks out the client's expertise and competence | Demonstrates the mediator's expertise and competence |
| Asks out of what the mediator doesn't know | Asks out of what the mediator knows and wants to confirm |
| Invites the client into a position of knower (subject) | Invites the client into a position of the one known (object) |
| Values a spirit of wonder and ambiguity | Values certainty (or its approximation) |
| Is naive inquiry | Is diagnostic matching |
| Is deconstructive | Is analytical |
| Explores and opens up possible meanings | Narrows down possibilities to more precise or correct meanings |
| Explores the client's meaning system | Interprets the client's words in the light of established, true meanings |
| Emphasizes particular, poetic, or local knowledge | Emphasizes generalizations based on validated knowledge or grand narratives |
| Exoticizes the domestic | Domesticates the exotic |
| Welcomes indeterminacy | Isolates determinants |
| Requires the mediator to develop the skills of respectful inquiry | Requires the mediator to develop familiarity with established knowledge |

completely surprising. John has come to trust this sense of surprise (which suggests that he is learning something) as an indicator that he is not just being curious about something about which he already knows.

The woman who had stored the household effects spoke about how the dispute was not just a matter of money to her. It was a matter of principle. She was a secretary who for many years had been called on to execute other people's business—principally her boss's. What this dispute represented, she said, was her desire to be treated as a person in her own right. These were her possessions and she was not wealthy. She resented being taken to be a person "of no account," which is how she made sense of the company's response.

What she wanted, more than the money, was to be taken seriously by the owner of the company, to be of some account. It was a personal statement of her own worth that she was fighting for.

When John asked the owner of the company (it was a small company and the owner was young and had not been in business for long) what the dispute meant to him, he also came up with a surprising answer. He said that this matter was a horrible experience that did not represent how he wanted to do business. He said he wanted his customers to feel happy with his service, he felt ashamed of how this dispute had happened, and he had been avoiding dealing with it for some time.

The honesty of both people was disarming and it provided a basis for proceeding to discuss how they might resolve the issues at hand. It provided an opportunity to ask the company's owner whether he wanted to do something to restore his business reputation in her eyes, and to ask the woman (within the owner's hearing) what would constitute for her being taken "to be of some account." In other words, the problem could then be discussed in terms that had meaning to each of the parties, rather than in the neutral but disembodied terms that discussions about money represented. In fact, the discussion in these more idiosyncratic terms was more real, more practical, and more precise than any hard-nosed brokering interaction between lawyers could have been.

The resolution was not all plain sailing by any means and there was a lot more to the dispute than what we have mentioned here. The point that warrants attention, however, was the valuable shift yielded by the mediator expressing simple curiosity about what the matters at issue meant to both of the parties. It might have seemed obvious to assume that the matter that lay between them could be described in terms of money only. Money is after all only a language by which we ascribe value or meaning to things. The parties certainly had no need to remain in ongoing contact with each other in any other way. But each of them chose to describe the meaning of the issue between them in a different currency. Asking about the seemingly obvious was what opened up the opportunity to develop a conversation about meanings. Such a conversation allowed the development of a different frame of meaning for the events that had occurred. Once each person had heard the other speak about the meaning of the dispute, the dispute had irrevocably changed in nature.

## Respect

As we have talked about the elements of trust that need to develop in the relations between a mediator and the disputing parties, we hope that a particular ethic has emerged. This ethic is expressed in the reflexive stance and in the curiosity we have been speaking about, but it deserves to be more explicitly named as *respect*. It also deserves to be explained and explored further so that it takes on a particular character and does not remain trite. Few would take issue with respect as an abstraction, but not everyone would embody the idea in the performances of meaning that we are advocating.

Central to this understanding of respect is a conception of what in another person we should respect. Our understanding here is based in a poststructuralist analysis of social relations, particularly of power relations. From this perspective, subjectivity, or the grammatical position of being a moral agent in one's own life, is not taken for granted. It is circumscribed by many discursive practices that limit opportunities for taking in a relationship the grammatical position that is offered to a noun in the grammar of a sentence. In various discursive formations, systematic exclusions often operate against the possibility of a person taking a subjective position in a particular context on the basis of, for example, race, gender, or social class.[17]

A subjective position is frequently the subject of contest, and we often experience ourselves being called into position by others as particular subjects in a sentence not of our preference. But there is a position as a subject that people can and do win for themselves (even temporarily) and out of which they can express their preferences for how they want to relate to others.

We do not mean to imply that such a position is constant, or that when it is achieved it remains, like a state of enlightenment, never to be lost again. Our sense is that discursive positioning is always being reproduced in ever-changing contexts and that there are always contests and challenges to be met, not all of which we can take on at a given moment. In other words, we are always being subjected by the discourses that swirl around us. Conversely, we are always participating in the production or reproduction of discourse, every time we open our mouths or take an action.[18]

The respect we want to embody as mediators is for people as moral agents, as producers of discourse, not just as subjugated subjects of it. So what does this entail? First, it involves listening discursively, or listening to how discourse operates on people, and also listening to their desires and preferences to contest these operations on their own or others' behalf.

Next, it entails seeking out opportunities in the mediation itself for the expression of voice. Discourses often grant privilege to certain voices over others or allow people to speak only within a narrow frame of reference. Heartfelt concerns about the particular effects of racism or sexism, for example, can be effectively sidelined if they are heard only as "political correctness." What needs to be remembered, though, is that a mediation is itself a site of discursive production, and one in which the mediator has considerable influence in shaping what can be talked about, who can talk about it, and in what terms. The ethical responsibility of the mediator is to use professional privilege in a way that grants people the right to have a voice, especially in situations where the dispute arises out of systematic exclusion of people's voices.

The respect we are speaking about also entails listening to people without allowing them to become confused by the dispute. In Chapter Six we speak more about this issue as we discuss the narrative conversational patterns of speech in which this ethic gets embodied. But it has been summarized by Michael White in the aphorism, "The person is not the problem; the problem is the problem."[19] This statement sounds so straightforward that it may seem obvious. However, it needs to be understood in the context of many habits of speech (as common in professional discourse as in lay discourse) in which people are described in terms that seek to sum up their essential being or totalize them on the basis of a narrow range of experience. This happens whenever someone is described in a conflict situation as though they are a particular characteristic, for example, aggressive, weak, a liar, difficult to deal with, stubborn, bad tempered, unreasonable, arrogant, or the like. In professional psychological discourse, the same process can happen and deficit labels of psychological diagnosis can be applied in a totalizing way. A person can be described as overreacting, emotionally disturbed, passive-aggressive, and so on.

It is very common in conflict situations for one party's descriptions of the other party to narrow considerably. Whereas the two parties may have previously had all sorts of experiences of each other, under the influence of a dispute the experiences of the other person that fit into that person's participation in the dispute tend to get selected for remembering. The complexity of experience tends to get reduced to a small range of words that are applied to the exclusion of other possibilities. They come to represent the totality of that person.

A common description of conflict situations is to call them *personality clashes*. Such a description privileges the essential individual qualities that we call personality. The assumption of personality is that individuals carry around with them some kind of stable personhood that is context free. However, people are far more complex than any description. Relationships cannot be reduced to simple summaries without distortion. There are always exceptions to any description. Contradictions are normal.[20]

What is implied in the type of respect we are advocating is a conscious effort not to see people as essentially anything, to refuse to sum people up. It implies a willingness to look for contradictions and to celebrate them as indicative of the range of possibilities that anyone has at their disposal. The value of this stance for mediation is that it helps mediators avoid getting trapped by the terms in which a dispute has people talking about each other. It is respectful because it encourages mediators to see people as more than their actions in the conflict situation. Most people appreciate being seen from this enlarged viewpoint rather than being summed up and boxed in.

The respect we are talking about also means always speaking to a person as if they are agents in the construction of their world. This statement needs to be distinguished from a humanistic emphasis on personal responsibility. We do not believe that people are responsible for all the things that happen to them or even always for their own thoughts and feelings. Many of our subjective experiences are given to us out of discourse. We are positioned subtly in every exchange by the discursive practices of others, and we have no control over that. But people can and do achieve a consciousness and understanding of such processes. Finding a linguistic frame in which to embody a particular understanding of an experience often goes a long way toward making this understanding real (in the sense of being able to act out of it). Moreover, people do protest and challenge the discursive positions into which they are called. They do seek to reposition themselves in a relationship, or in a conversation. They refuse to occupy or be constrained by a narrow little place given by a dispute, or sometimes they simply have the desire or intention to refuse this place, even if they have never put that thought into words within another person's hearing.

A useful illustration, and one that may come to a mediator's attention in an employment setting, might be sexual harassment. Before the term *sexual harassment* was invented (which was not so long ago), a person who was being subjected to unwelcome sexual attention might have felt very uncomfortable about it and done her best to defend herself against the unwelcome attention. The development of the term *sexual harassment,* however, made possible a linguistic change that has enabled people to take a different position in relation to the same behavior and to have that stance of protest legitimated in official employment discourse. If the unwelcome attention is now labeled sexual harassment, the recipient may still feel discomfort but she might also feel more entitled to be angry. In this way, a linguistic or discursive shift has created the opportunity for a different subjective experience. On this basis, the responses that become available can be thought of in terms of political protest rather than simply in terms of personal relations. As a result, the protestations that the recipient makes are legitimated (even when the legitimacy is contested). This gives the person the sense of being a social and moral agent, and the process of being legitimized has more than a little to do with the chances of a person acting successfully on his or her own behalf.

In a mediation, what we wish to convey to both parties is the kind of respect that serves such a purpose of legitimating their desires to become producers of discourse rather than just objects of the operation of discourse. We want to convey an assumption that there are places from which it is possible to act to bring about change, or it is possible to refuse to be positioned in places of limitation or diminishment. The changes sought may be local and particular, or they may be in relation to a wider social discourse that is shaping the available range of responses in a dispute. Ideally, such changes involve both parties reaching an agreement to work together against, say, racism, and developing a resolution to the dispute that embodies this commitment. On the basis of this assumption, a mediator working from a narrative perspective needs to be on the lookout for opportunities to celebrate, appreciate, and build on every little opportunity for clients to step into such a position of agency.

To be avoided are the assumptions of limitation that would undermine such an intention—assumptions such as those that ascribe deficits to individuals, those that claim that a person can be summed up in any single description, or those grounded in the belief that a relationship that is in a state of dispute can be defined by that state. Instead, the narrative mediator is always on the lookout for possibilities that lie beyond the realistic or the known, always seeing the potential for people to step into neglected knowledges or understandings, and seeking to capitalize on such potentials.[21]

In this chapter we have talked in terms of attitudes and relational principles. In the next chapter we lay out some of the methods by which these principles can be practiced and realized. We do not provide a prescriptive list of instructions but rather a set of working guidelines that we have found useful as templates. Others may well take these same principles and embody them in quite different ways. That is as it should be.

## Notes

1. Foucault, M., *Power/Knowledge* (C. Gordon, ed.; C. Gordon, L. Marshall, J. Mepham, and K. Soper, trans.) (New York: Pantheon, 1980).
2. Foucault, M., *Power/Knowledge.*

3. Fraser, N., *Unruly Practices: Power, Discourse and Gender in Contemporary Social Theory* (Cambridge, England: Polity Press, 1989); Shotter, J., "Social Accountability and the Social Construction of 'You,'" in J. Shotter and K. Gergen (eds.), *Texts of Identity* (London: Sage, 1989); Monk, G., and Drewery, W., "The Impact of Social Constructionist Thinking on Eclecticism in Counselor Education: Some Personal Thoughts," *New Zealand Journal of Counselling,* 1994, *16*(1), 5–14.

4. Davies, B., and Harre, R., "Positioning: The Discursive Production of Selves," *Journal for the Theory of Social Behavior,* 1990, *20*(1), 43–63.

5. Gouldner, A. W., *The Coming Crisis of Western Sociology* (London: Heinemann, 1970); Lather, P., *Getting Smart: Feminist Research and Pedagogy Within the Postmodern* (New York: Routledge, 1991); Lather, P., "Critical Frames in Educational Research: Feminist and Poststructural Perspectives," *Theory into Practice,* 1992, *31*(2), 87–99; Henwood, K. L., and Pigeon, N. F., "Qualitative Research and Psychological Theorising," *British Journal of Psychology,* 1992, *83,* 97–111; Lax, W. D., "Postmodern Thinking in a Clinical Practice," in J. Shotter and K. Gergen (eds.), *Texts of Identity* (London: Sage, 1989).

6. Schön, D. A., *The Reflective Practitioner: How Professionals Think in Action* (New York: Basic Books, 1983).

7. Davies, B., *Shards of Glass: Children Reading and Writing Beyond Gendered Identities* (St. Leonards, Australia: Allen & Unwin, 1993).

8. Hoffman, L., "A Reflexive Stance for Family Therapy," in S. McNamee and K. Gergen (eds.), *Therapy as Social Construction* (Thousand Oaks, Calif.: Sage, 1992).

9. Bakhtin, M., *The Dialogic Imagination* (C. Emerson and M. Holquist, trans.) (Austin: University of Texas Press, 1981); Morson, G. S., and Emerson, C., *Mikhail Bakhtin* (Stanford, Calif.: Stanford University Press, 1990).

10. Harvey, D., *The Condition of Postmodernity* (Oxford, England: Blackwell, 1989).

11. Gilligan, C., *In a Different Voice* (Cambridge, Mass.: Harvard University Press, 1982); Hare-Mustin, R. T., and Marecek, J., "Asking the Right Questions: Feminist Psychology and Sex Differences," *Feminism and Psychology,* 1994, *4,* 531–537; Kahn, A. S., and Yoder, J. D., "The Psychology of Women and Conservatism," *Psychology of Women Quarterly,* 1989, *13,* 417–432.

12. Hoshmand, L. T., and Polkinghorne, D. E., "Redefining the Science-Practice Relationship in Professional Training," *American Psychologist,* 1992, *47*(1), 55–66; Bernstein, R., *Beyond Objectivism and Relativism: Science, Hermeneutics and Praxis* (Philadelphia: University of Pennsylvania Press, 1983).

13. Olssen, M., "Producing the Truth About People," in J. Morss and T. Linzey (eds.), *Growing Up: The Politics of Human Learning* (Auckland, New Zealand: Longman Paul, 1991); Rosaldo, R., *Culture and Truth: The Remaking of Social Analysis* (Boston: Beacon Press, 1993).

14. Hoshmand, L. T., and Polkinghorne, D. E., "Redefining the Science-Practice Relationship in Professional Training," *American Psychologist,* 1992, *47*(1), 55–66.

15. Davies, B., "The Concept of Agency: A Feminist Poststructural Analysis," *Social Analysis,* 1991, *30*, 42–53.

16. Amunsden, J., Stewart, K., and Valentine, L., "Temptations of Power and Certainty," *Journal of Marital and Family Therapy,* 1993, *19*(2), 111–123; Hoffman, L., "A Reflexive Stance for Family Therapy," in S. McNamee and K. Gergen (eds.), *Therapy as Social Construction* (Thousand Oaks, Calif.: Sage, 1992); Anderson, H., and Goolishian, H., "The Client Is the Expert: A Not-Knowing Approach to Therapy," in S. McNamee and K. Gergen (eds.), *Therapy as Social Construction* (Thousand Oaks, Calif.: Sage, 1992).

17. Davies, B., & Harre, R., "Positioning: The Discursive Production of Selves," *Journal for the Theory of Social Behavior,* 1990, *20*(1), 43–63.

18. Mills, S., *Discourse* (New York: Routledge, 1997).

19. White, M., "The Externalizing of the Problem and the Re-authoring of Lives and Relationships," in M. White, *Selected Papers* (Adelaide, Australia: Dulwich Centre Publications, 1989).

20. Gergen, K. J., *The Saturated Self: Dilemmas of Identity in Contemporary Life* (New York: Basic Books, 1991).

21. Bruner, E., "Ethnography as Narrative," in V. Turner and E. Bruner (eds.), *The Anthropology of Experience* (Chicago: University of Illinois Press, 1986).

---
Chapter Six
---

# Disarming the Conflict

*Curiouser and curiouser!*
(LEWIS CARROLL, "ALICE IN WONDERLAND")

*If a man will begin with certainties, he shall end in
doubts, but if he will be content to begin with doubts,
he shall end in certainties.*
(FRANCIS BACON, "THE ADVANCEMENT OF LEARNING")

One of the first steps we prefer to take in a mediation is to meet with each of the parties separately. This is often discussed in the mediation literature as *caucusing*. We prefer not to use this term because it sometimes makes it sound as though the mediation proper happens only when the mediator meets with both parties together, and that the separate meetings have a specific but less important purpose. In our experience, it is in these separate meetings that a lot of the major work of the mediation is done. In these meetings, the mediator works carefully with each of the parties to construct a frame of meaning around the problem issue. This affects in a major way what happens when the parties are brought together. Therefore, the separate meetings are a venue for significant developments in the mediation as a whole, not an optional adjunct to the process, to be used only when things are getting sticky. In our approach, they are central to what gets achieved.

This is not to say that separate meetings are essential or appropriate in every situation. We are thinking mainly of situations in which there are entrenched disputes that make it difficult for the parties to talk freely in front of each other. Sometimes, perhaps when a mediator is called in earlier in the development of a dispute, the conflicting parties are happy to talk freely in front of each other and there is no need for separate meetings. In such a context, the work of the separate meetings can be done in front of the other person.

The situation of which Sara Cobb speaks is relevant to this issue.[1] In discussing the narrative effects of each person's story on the other person, Cobb notes that the first person to tell his or her story in a mediation has a shaping effect on what the other person can speak about. In the terms we have been using, the first speaker's utterance calls the other person into position in response. One of the effects that Sara Cobb is concerned about is the possible limitation on what the second speaker can say if the first speaker has already laid out the ground. We agree with this notion, although we would add that this effect is ongoing. Cobb is referring to the initial telling of a story in mediation. We argue that every utterance in a mediation, not just the initial telling of the story, operates in the same way. It is not just a matter of who tells the story first. Each speech act constitutes the speaker as the first speaker for the person who speaks next. Each speech act calls the other person into position in some way.[2]

It is important to preserve an assumption of agency here, however. Although the act of speaking first can be understood in these terms as an act of power, of which mediators had best be aware, the operation of such power can also be refused.[3] People can choose simply not to respond to what the first speaker has said but to choose their own narrative trajectory. If the act of speaking is an act of construction in a power relation, then it is not the structural position of speaking first that makes speaking powerful but the way people operate on each other all the time in conversation, of which speaking first is but one example.

The act of being an audience to someone else's speaking as a part of the process of constructing meaning should also not be underestimated. The listener should not be construed as passive while only the speaker is seen as active. When we speak, we all choose our words according to our judgment of the discursive audience to which we are speaking. Speakers always anticipate to some extent how what they say will be received, and they construct their speaking in relation to that expected reception. Through nonverbal feedback, interruptions, frowns, seating orientation, and many other forms of language that do not require the speaking of words, listeners are constantly exerting a shaping influence on the first speaker. In this way, the second speaker can be said to exert power from the very beginning in the construction of what the first speaker says.

What is more, mediators can always facilitate the response of the second speaker in a way that assists that speaker in telling his or her story in his or her own terms rather than in the terms proposed by the first speaker. There are various methods by which this purpose can be achieved. One thing the mediator can do is deliberately ask the second speaker the same opening question that was asked of the first speaker. The second speaker can actually be invited to ignore momentarily what the first speaker has said and go back to the beginning and tell the story from his or her own perspective, rather than just respond to what the first speaker has said. In other words, parties to a mediation can be brought into the loop of understanding the problem of the power of the first speaker, and they can be offered the chance to make their own decisions about how they will respond to this issue. The problem does not have to remain one that mediators alone have to worry about.

There will still, however, be many instances in which the memory of what the first speaker has said will call the second speaker into selecting for emphasis aspects of his or her own story that either harmonize with or serve as a counterpoint to what the first speaker has said. This result is another reason for holding separate meetings with each party before the first joint meeting takes place. In separate meetings, each participant in the mediation has the chance to tell the mediator the first version of his or her own story without being conscious of the other party listening and without being influenced by what the other party has said. In the separate meetings, each person gets to be the first speaker. In other words, each person is called into position as a subject in the grammar of the mediation from the start.

There are many other advantages of these separate meetings. One is that the mediator can concentrate on building relationship and trust with each person separately, without having to be conscious of keeping the other person waiting. The balancing of this task in a joint meeting with both parties can be delicate, and there always exists the risk of losing contact with one person while talking to the other. The stronger the conflict, the greater this risk is. Meeting with each party separately first helps to ensure that the relationship with the mediator is established on good footing from the start. Another advantage is that the participants in the mediation can feel free to say things to the mediator that they would not say in front of the other person. One person laughingly told one of us in a mediation recently that she would like to buy the other party in a dispute a one-way ticket to another (faraway) country. This was a way of communicating her frustration about how the conflict was affecting her. We laughed and joked about this idea for a minute or two, and it served to lighten the conversation in an otherwise tense situation. Such an exchange would not have been possible in front of the other party.

## Discursive Listening

The next step in the process of disarming the conflict is for the mediator to invite the telling of the conflict-saturated story.[4] Each party has an opportunity to give an account of what has happened to bring matters to the point of conflict that led to mediation being sought. From a narrative perspective, mediators hear this story as a version or construction of events rather than as a set of facts. The teller of the story always selects from the myriad events that could be included and marshals these selections into some form of coherent story. Exactly how events are made coherent has a lot to do with the background discourses that operate on the selection of what counts as important for the person telling the story. Careful listening involves hearing not just what has happened but also what necessary constructs are at work in this particular account to make sense of what has happened. This is what we call *discursive listening*, or listening to the discourses at work in a particular account and to the position calls that are issued within each discourse.

These discourses are at work on the mediator as well. They shape what the mediator chooses to hear. What the mediator hears is also a construction of events and cannot be assumed to be the same as that constructed by the teller of the story. For starters, the mediator's assumptions about conflict and about mediation shape what he or she listens for. The problem-solving method might have the mediator listening for a definable problem, some facts that form the basis of that problem, and the underlying interests of the parties that are being expressed in the problem. However, the narrative perspective has the mediator listening for the intersection of narratives in a discursive context. Each narrative propels the mediator along trajectories, and sometimes these trajectories differ from those that are propelling others who are featured as characters in the mediator's story. Conflict, from this perspective, is somewhat inevitable from time to time. It is about difference rather than about failure. Conflict does not necessarily mean "problem to be solved."

*Curious questioning* of the kind described in the previous chapter is crucial to the process of disarming the conflict. The aim of such questioning is to break up our sense of certainty that we know all that can be known about what we mean, or even more dangerously, that we know what someone else means. So if a person speaks about not trusting another person as a result of what has happened in the story of the conflict, it might be productive to inquire about the word *trust* and what it means rather than to assume we know what is being referred to. This inquiry might seek to establish the contextual significance of the word. Its context can be considered in a historical sense. The mediator might ask, "When did this idea of not being able to trust first come into your consciousness? What was happening at that time?" Or the question might have a geographical reference point: "Where in your life is not trusting played out? In what circumstances?" Or the person might hold particular personal meanings for the word *trust:* "People mean all sorts of different things when they use a word like *trust.* What does it mean to you?" or "So when you refer to not trusting him, it sounds like you mean something like wanting greater information from him about what is going on and refusing to agree to do things for him until you get that information. Is that right?"

Moreover, our words mean things in the sense that they are acts perpetrated on the world, as Wittgenstein argued.[5] They shape, and even limit, our experience. We can therefore invite people to reflect on their words as actions in their worlds. We can ask:

- What's it like, this not trusting?
- When you use that expression, what difference does it make to what happens between you?
- What does not trusting lead to?
- What does it look like in practice?

Although the focus of these questions might often be on the poetic or idiosyncratic aspects of meaning making, we cannot just create our personal meanings out of nothing. We are limited by the available discourses that are extant in our language community. Even as we form our personal meanings, we construct ourselves in relation to these discourses and in small ways reproduce or influence the ongoing shape of these discourses. Therefore, as we listen deconstructively to problematic stories in mediation, we can start to hear those discourses at work and direct our curiosity to their operation. For example, we can ask such questions as:

- As you speak about trust, I wonder what has influenced your thinking on this issue?
- What background stories have you drawn on in saying that?
- Have there been special people in your history who have taught you the meaning of trust?
- How does this theme fit into your own cultural background?
- Given the work you do, does trust have any special meanings that it would be good for us to be aware of?
- As you think about trust, what voices echo in your head that speak to you about this theme?
- Is there a gendered aspect to this idea of trust? Would it take on a different shape if you were a different gender?

A particular aspect of the discursive background to the conflict situation may be a sense of entitlement that has been hurt in the development of the conflict. This, too, can be listened for and inquired about. Questions can be asked to bring this sense of entitlement out of the background and into the foreground. In the process, its discursive supports can be noticed and explored. Some examples of such questions are:

- If you are feeling that your trust has been violated, on the basis of what principles do you make that judgment?
- Over what boundaries should someone not go if they want to maintain a feeling of trust, in your opinion?
- What ideas do you have about the origins of those boundaries? Do the same circumstances still apply as when those boundaries were first put in place?

The object of all these forms of inquiry is that the familiar taken-for-granted aspects of experience should become subjects of interest. The questions asked should not take on the spirit of interrogation. Their aim is not to challenge or confront but to open to view the discursive landscape. If the questions are handled well, the parties to the mediation often hear themselves saying things and wondering about things in novel ways. Therefore, new information or new considerations are often introduced into the story of the conflict at this point. Ordinary, everyday words or meanings are rendered strange or exotic in the process. An attitude of wonder and exploration can prevail over a sense of certainty. It is in the interests of disarming conflicts, we would argue, that the spirit of certainty that accompanies people knowing that they are right (and that someone else is wrong) is loosened a little.

## Externalizing Conversation

The next step in the disarming of conflict is laying the groundwork for a separation of the conflict-saturated story and the persons who have become caught up in it. Toward this end we advocate employing the rhetorical move of generating externalizing conversations, developed by Michael White and David Epston.[6] Early in the development of the idea of externalizing, White and Epston suggested a simple description of "externalizing the problem." This description has developed into the more sophisticated notion of externalizing conversation. The difference lies in the assumption that there is not simply one problem that can be spoken of in an externalizing way but rather a series of descriptions that evolve through time. Externalizing descriptions help to extract people from an internalizing logic and from a close attachment to the conflict as an expression of who they are.

So what do we mean by externalizing? The spirit of it lies in the aphorism mentioned in Chapter Five, "The person is not the problem; the problem is the problem."[7]

This is not just a gimmicky statement. It implies a belief about the nature of human problems that is different from the one that dominates most psychological, legal, and lay discourses. If we understand such problems as arising from discourse rather than from the expression of individual human needs, then we are led into a different way of speaking. From this perspective, the way to bring about change lies not in the assumption of individual responsibility for unmet needs so much as in the assignment of responsibility where it belongs, to the discursive conditions out of which the conflict has arisen. The use of externalizing rhetoric is one such move.

Speaking in an externalizing way means speaking about the conflict as if it were separate from the two parties in a mediation, even at times as if it were a third party to the dispute. For example, there is a subtle difference in asking, "So, how did this argument catch you both in its clutches?" and asking, "How did you both allow yourselves to start arguing like this?" In the second question, the parties to the dispute are made the objects of the implied message of responsibility, if not blame, by the mediator. In the first question, the problem itself is made the object of such blame and the two persons involved are given a different position. They are the recipients of the problem's malevolent designs rather than the originators of its operations.

What is often noticeable in this approach is that the sense of blame is reduced in the equation. In mediation contexts, this is potentially a powerful difference because blame is often not far from the lips of people in a conflict. Moreover, sensitivity to blame from the other party is also not far from consciousness. The mediator's speaking in an externalizing way is often experienced as a relief by the parties in a mediation, as a lightening of the heaviness of the usual ways of speaking. Blame and its counterpart, guilt, are burdens that can best be thought of as hindrances to the task of finding a constructive way forward in conflict situations. The humanistic assumption that this can be achieved by the individual taking responsibility for his or her part in producing the conflict fails, in our experience, to obviate this heaviness. The lightening embodied in an externalizing way of speaking can rapidly give the parties a different experience of the problem they have been living with.

By contrast, the metaphorical externalized description of the problem can be loaded with blame. It can be personified as a third person in the relationship, given a personality, and ascribed all sorts of malicious designs against the two parties. It can be granted motives, feelings, and plans. All the terrible effects of the conflict can be laid at its door. This can be a playful way of speaking about quite painful events and it is often a way that people are happy to enter into because it is preferable to their more usual experiences of either taking on or defending themselves against blame and guilt.

So, we now give some examples of how externalizing conversations can be developed. The trick is to change the usual ways of speaking that mediators have often learned as a result of dominant humanistic discourse.

Avoid phrasing a question like, "How do you feel about what happened?" This grammatical structure serves an internalizing purpose. It constructs experience in a way that takes the problem inward. Instead, a mediator speaking in an externalizing way can say, "How does what happened invite you to feel?" It is important to notice what is happening here. The person is still being asked to speak about the emotional impact that events had on him or her. However, this impact is not implied to be inevitable. The automatic link between events and responses to these events is loosened.

Take another example. A mediator says, "What did this argument get you thinking about the other party?" Notice that the argument has been turned into a noun and objectified. The person has been left in the more free position of responding to the invitations of this imagined being, the argument. He or she is not assumed to be the prime mover in the subjective action of thinking—a recognition of the extent to which thoughts are constructed within the discourse of the social contexts in which we live. This is a metaphorical way of speaking that looks odd to those who assume that facts are more solid than metaphors. However, we would argue that the alternative ways of speaking are also metaphorical, including those that refer to facts (which are metaphors in themselves).

In the process of stating things in this way, a subtle point is communicated. If the argument "got me thinking" in a certain way, then maybe another way of thinking is possible. Externalizing conversations open possibilities for new ways of thinking about a problem. At the same time the person is not blamed for narrowness of thinking. The usual narrowing of perspective that we find accompanies the development of an argument is assigned to the argument itself rather than to some failure in the person. In this way, the assumption of a personal deficit is avoided.

The classic openings of client-centered active listening are also altered by the use of externalizing conversations. Rather than communicating constructions built on the "You feel . . . because . . ."

formula,[8] a mediator using an externalizing conversation listens actively in a different grammatical way. The process of checking out assumptions may use a different form of paraphrase, such as, "So, the problem invited you to feel . . . because. . . ." If a person tells a mediator in a separate session that he or she has come to hate the other party intensely, the mediator might respond, "So the conflict has gotten you to feel a very strong feeling like hatred. How did it manage to take over your feelings in such a strong way?"

The strong feelings are acknowledged by such a response, but a close and inevitable identification with these feelings is not assumed. Rather, the assumption communicated is that things have not always been this way and they might also change again. However, the change process relied on is not based on entering more strongly into feelings and venting them in a cathartic way. Such an approach is a classic assumption of much therapeutic discourse and it is present in the mediation literature as well. The narrative perspective, conversely, is that change is possible through the construction of alterations to stories, that is, at the discursive level, and is more efficient than individual cathartic expression of feelings or needs.

The grammatical constructions of externalizing conversations can even be useful for discussing subjects that people already consider external to themselves. Take, for example, a mediation between a tenant and a landlord over rent in arrears. If the unpaid rent is spoken about in an externalizing way, both parties can be asked about the personal effects. For example, the mediator might ask the tenant, "How have your rent arrears changed how you have been acting toward your landlord?" and the mediator might ask the landlord, "What has been the effect of the rent arrears on you?"

These questions can bring out responses that tell the story of the relationship as it has been affected by the overdue rent from two perspectives. They make possible a richer description of events than a conversation in which the mediator and the landlord join to address the tenant in a blaming way, possibly inducing a defensive response.

Blame itself can often be spoken about usefully in an externalizing manner. Guilt can also be addressed in the same way. Blame and guilt often work together in cyclical fashion to block the possibility of goodwill and understanding in a conflict situation. The act of externalizing blame or guilt reverses the internalizing logic by which this occurs and can therefore open up a search for new ways of handling the conflict. Examples of appropriate questions are as follows:

- What would be your guess about how much blame is in charge of your views of each other?
- To what extent is blame stopping you from resolving your differences?
- How much are you in charge rather than letting blame have things its own way?

## Naming the Problem

Another step in the process of developing an externalizing conversation is the ritual of naming. Early on in such a conversation it is best for the mediator to keep the externalized descriptions of a problem somewhat loose. The problem may be referred to as "it" or "the problem" or described with a variety of different expressions. As time goes by, however, it can become clear that an agreed-upon set of events can be grouped together and classed as the problem in more specific terms. In order to cement the process of separating the person from the problem, the problem can be officially named at this point.

This naming process is best not finalized until the mediation is in a joint session and both parties get to participate in the naming. To work, the name needs to include both parties' perspectives on the problem. The mediator can ask each party a question such as:

- We've talked about all these things that have happened and if you could sum them up, I'm just wondering what you would call this whole thing?
- If we were to think of a name to describe this problem that's got you at each other's throats, what would you call it?

Agreement on a name for the problem that satisfies both parties can constitute a significant step in undermining the power of the problem. For starters, a subtle realignment has taken place in the process. At the beginning of a mediation, the two parties are often squared off against each other in a stance of opposition or confrontation. If the mediator has worked carefully to develop an externalizing conversation and has reached the point of securing a name for the problem that everyone can agree on, the two parties may now be standing side by side, squared off against the problem. The linguistic shift needs to be followed through assiduously, however, in order for it to be become a permanent feature of the relationship.

Another aspect of the naming ritual is that it seeks out a little agreement between the two parties on an apparently small issue. However, considerable significance may be built around this agreement. In a situation of great antagonism, this may be the first time in a long time that an agreement on anything has been possible. After a time, a series of agreements can be built into a story of agreements and change.

Often the step of naming the problem can be achieved by tracing and summarizing a sequence of events that have transpired over time. This sequence may include one person taking an action and the other person responding. Each action becomes the context for the other person's response and calls the other into a particular form of response. In return, each response supplements the other person's position call and at the same time issues a call to the next response.[9] After a while, it is hard to determine where it all started. If this sequence of events is traced backward and forward for a while, the mediator can then comment on it and seek to summarize it in a single chunk. The cyclic or recursive nature of these interactions can be mapped (perhaps on a whiteboard or piece of paper for all to see). Once chunked together, the whole sequence of events can be named. Here are some steps that can be followed to elicit this chain of events and externalize them.

The mediator can ask the following questions:

• How did this conflict develop? What sequence of events took place?
• When he or she did that, what did the conflict invite you to do in response?
• So what would you call this whole cycle of events that has gone back and forth between you two? What name could we agree on?

Then the mediator can engage the parties in a deconstructive discussion about how this vicious cycle started to take over, how it caught them both in its patterns against their better judgment, or how they got swept along in its wake. In the process, blame can be detached from either party and ascribed to the vicious cycle itself. At such a time the mediator might comment:

- So it sounds like this whole cycle of events started to take over and just got you feeling madder and madder at each other.
- I'm wondering how far this cycle can go. Has it done its worst yet or could it get worse? Has it pushed you as far as you both are prepared to go or are you still willing to let it speak for you?
- Would you like to continue this cycle or would you prefer it to stop?

## Historicizing the Problem

Once an externalizing conversation has been opened up and the first moves have been made to separate the persons from the problem, the momentum developed has to be maintained. A lapse back into internalizing ways of speaking can quickly undo the advantages of speaking in an externalizing way. The task of telling the story of the problem can be developed within the externalizing frame of reference by historicizing the externalized problem.[10] This effort can be elicited by asking questions such as the following:

- How long has this dispute been in your lives?
- When did these effects of the problem first become noticeable to you?
- What's the history of the problem that is doing this to you?
- Was there a time when things were different, before this problem came along and took charge?

The purpose of such questions is to locate the problem in a time context. Rather than existing in a vacuum, the conflict is storied in a way that gives it an origin and a process of development and therefore, potentially, a conclusion. However, it is not just the conflict that becomes historicized in this process; the relationship between the two parties becomes historicized as well. Historicizing the problem creates a context for the relationship in reference to a time when the conflict did not exist. This time can be explored with some questions that express curiosity about the relationship between the two parties at that time. The relational qualities that were once present can be brought to the fore in a way that rescues them from the dustbin to which they have been consigned by the dominance of the current conflict. This exercise can significantly advance the story of difference, particularly if the qualities identified are those that both parties would prefer to reactivate.

## Relative Influence Questioning

Michael White has outlined a process of asking questions that helps develop an externalizing conversation further. He calls this process *relative influence questioning.*[11] It is a two-step process in which the participants in the mediation are asked two different sets of questions. The first step involves questions about how the conflict has influenced the parties. The second set asks questions about how the parties have exerted an influence back on the conflict. The first step fits with what most people expect mediation to be about, even if it is couched in the slightly unusual constructions of an externalizing conversation. The second step, however, often strikes people in an arresting way. The questions asked in this step are out of the ordinary and they invite the parties to take up a new stance that they may not have thought of before. These questions therefore require more explanation, some of which continues in the next chapter. But first, we outline here the first step in the process of asking questions to map the influence of the conflict.

## Mapping the Influence of the Problem on the Person

Now that the mediation process has reached the stage of using an externalizing description of the conflict, the challenge is to continue to separate the persons from the problem. This applies first in the separate sessions with each party to the mediation, but it takes place again when the two parties are together. The difference on this second occasion is that the story of the conflict from each person's perspective is being heard by the other person. Because audiences always exert an influence on the performance of meaning by a speaker, the telling of the story the second time will be different from the version told without the other party present.

The central organizing question that assists mediators to map the influence of the conflict on the parties is, What effect or effects has this conflict (or whatever other name has been developed to describe it) had on you?

A number of avenues may be explored in response to this question. These include the areas of life that may be indicated by the particular problem. Obviously, in a commercial mediation there will be fewer questions about the more personal aspects of the problem's influence, although it can be very significant even in such contexts for some personal statements to be made. In one organizational mediation between two groups of people whose overlapping work had them in conflict with each other it was hugely significant for all of the parties to be given a chance to say how the work issues were affecting them personally. People spoke frankly about taking the stress from the work conflict home with them, experiencing disturbances in their sleep at night, being preoccupied by the conflict at home and being less available for their families, being worried about their employment future, and so on. Because people on both sides of the conflict were experiencing quite similar personal effects, the airing of these statements, even briefly, led to an affirmation of everyone's desire to change the course of events that the conflict had launched.

Some mediators worry that asking such questions will take the conversation into a therapeutic realm rather than into a conflict resolution process. Mediators need to be conscious of this issue. It is clearly not appropriate to the purpose of mediation to engage in therapeutic conversations with either party in front of the other. However, people are not robots and they often do appreciate opportunities to express the personal impact the conflict has had on them and to have that impact acknowledged. An intransigent task focus, with no room for a personal dimension, can be experienced as impersonal, dehumanizing, slightly dissatisfying, or even insulting. It is particularly appropriate for this kind of talk to take place in the separate meetings with either party, but it can also make a big difference in the joint meetings.

To get back to the task of mapping the influence of the conflict, however, a number of areas can be explored. The aim of the exploration at this point is to map the territory in sufficient detail so that small holes in the sway of the conflict can start to be explored. This detail can be found in the triple dimensions of breadth, length, and depth. We examine each of these in turn.

*Breadth* refers to the spread of the influence of the conflict into areas of a person's life. Here are some questions that might open up such territory:

- In what ways has this conflict affected you?
- Has it had an impact on your personal life, your business, your relationships, your performance of your role, your rest and relaxation, your confidence, your attitudes, your beliefs, your bank balance, your future employment prospects, and so on?
- How has it affected each of these areas?
- Are there any ways in which this conflict has gotten you to act out of character?
- What has this argument cost you?
- What has the upset deprived you of?
- Who else has been affected by this problem, to your knowledge?

An important follow-up question for maximizing the breadth of the exploration sparked by any of these questions is a simple "What else?"

*Length* refers to the history of the conflict and has been covered already in relation to the historicizing of the conflict. But the time dimension also includes the future. Here are some questions that might generate an inquiry into the influence of the conflict over time:

- When did the dispute first rear its head?
- On what key occasions did the severity of its impact increase?
- If things keep going as they have been, where will this conflict end up?
- What future do you think the conflict has planned for both of you? For your relationship?
- Considering the way things have been escalating, what would you guess this argument will have you doing in another six months?

Again, the question "What else?" helps to extend the comprehensiveness of these inquiries.

*Depth* refers to the intensity of the impact that the dispute is having in any of the areas mentioned. Here are some questions that explore the depth of the influence of the conflict:

- How much has this problem gotten to you?
- On a scale of one to one hundred, with one hundred being the maximum, how seriously has this problem turned out to be for you?
- How stressful is all of this?
- Could you tell me a story that would help me understand how far this dispute has gone in undermining you?

## Mapping the Influence of the Persons on the Problem

The second stage of the process of influence questioning reverses the direction of the influence. This time the questions are about the influence of the persons on the problem.[12] At issue are the often overlooked efforts of people to make a dent in the problem's influence on them. They may have endeavored to resist its influence. They may have limited the dominance of the dispute or prevented it from damaging some areas of their relationship. They may even have had considerable success in overcoming the conflict on some occasions without due credit being given to these achievements. They may have knowledge of how to deal with the conflict that deserves to see the light of day but is currently being kept in the shadows because the argument is dominating the foreground.

These exceptions to the dominance of the conflict are called *unique outcomes* in Michael White's taxonomy.[13] They may not easily come to light without some probing questions being asked. The task of the mediator is to listen carefully for such gems in the course of being told the story of the conflict. These outcomes will often pop up unexpectedly and yet be given little weight by the protagonists. In order for them to assume significance, they need to be brought into the force field of the conversation by some deliberate and sometimes persistent questioning.

Let us look at some examples of what we mean by these exceptions. Imagine a divorcing couple who are at loggerheads over matrimonial property but are still managing to work well together in making arrangements for the children. For another couple, the dispute may be over custody and access but they may manage to put the dispute to one side when one of their children is sick. In a landlord-tenant dispute over property damage, there may be a history of good relations over a two-year period before the dispute arose. In an organizational dispute, angry exchanges may have dominated recent relations between the two protagonists, but both may still retain a grudging respect for each other's talents and contributions over the years. These are all little nuggets of relational gold that can be polished and refined so that they stand in contrast and contradiction to the conflict-saturated story.

Now we need to think about some of the questions that can be asked to elicit these exceptions or unique outcomes. As we have already mentioned, these exceptions can be mentioned voluntarily by the parties. If this happens, the task of the mediator is to increase their significance and therefore increase their relative influence. This can be done by exploring the knowledge, competencies, or relationship qualities they represent but that may have been forgotten.

If the parties are not so forthcoming, it falls to the mediator to ask for these exceptions. This requires the mediator to be confident that such resources are indeed available somewhere in the relationship between the two parties. This confidence can be founded on the mediator's understanding of the complexity of human experience, which makes it likely that even amid complete antagonism there is always some contradiction and we can find it if we only search hard enough. The need to search hard enough is a key point for mediators seeking to implement a narrative approach in their work. It is sometimes tempting to give up too soon. We therefore encourage people to be persistent and curious in this search and not to give up at the first refusal.

Here are some examples of questions that can be asked to elicit unique outcomes. Of course these examples are generic; the questions asked would take a different format in relation to the details of the conflict situation.

- What actions have you taken to try to diminish the power of this conflict?
- What is the history of your relationship before this dispute? What difference does it make to recall those times?

- Have there been times in this dispute when you have allowed yourselves not to be so much under the influence of the angry cycle?
- Do you consider yourself a reasonable person? How have you tried to show this in this matter?
- Have there been any occasions in recent months when each of you has made a real effort to be fair to the other? How did you do that?
- Even if you have not done any of these things, have you ever thought about doing them? Intended to do things differently? Planned a different response? Expressed a desire for change? Wished that you could turn the clock back?

## Evaluating the Desirability of the Conflict-Saturated Story

Another key step in the development of the separation of the problem from the persons is to ask the parties to make a judgment. This judgment relates to their commitment to the presence of the dispute in their lives. It may seem an obvious, even seemingly redundant question to ask, yet in our experience it can be powerfully important. This question needs to be asked after some relative influence questioning has taken place and a sense of the toll that the conflict has exacted on both parties has been made explicit. Here is an example of what can be asked:

> We have been talking for a little while about the effects of this dispute on both of you, and even a little about the dents you have managed to make in it so far. I was wondering, though, what you are thinking about where this is taking you. Do you want a future in which this dispute continues to exert this influence, or would you prefer to change the way things are going?

This question may seem somewhat trivial. Few people actually enjoy being in conflict and seek it out. It is an uncomfortable space in which to live. It is our experience, however, that asking this somewhat obvious question makes quite a difference. First, it invites an overview of the whole of the conflict story. Then, it brings into the light in a particular way all of the effects of the dispute on both parties. It is very hard to answer this question without saying that you do not want the conflict to continue. Making this statement explicitly and in front of the mediator and the other party, even if it has been thought about privately many times, makes a difference. It constitutes a first step toward changing the way things have been going. At times it may also feel like making a commitment.

Moreover, for each party to hear the other party make this statement can also make a difference in the significance of the conflict in the relationship. Under the reign of the conflict-saturated story, it is often hard to imagine the other party wanting to end the conflict. The other party often gets storied in our minds as at least maliciously wanting the conflict always to get worse.

If both parties answer the question with a statement of intention that they do not want the conflict to continue but actually want things to be resolved, then we have a situation of agreement. The alignment of both parties side by side and squared off against the problem is complete at this moment, even if it slips back again later. This agreement is also a unique outcome. It would not be predicted under the influence of the conflict story. The mediator can dwell on this moment for a moment or two. It is also possible to ask each of the parties about the significance of this agreement for them. That helps the moment to reverberate in importance. In the process, motivation to bring about resolution is enhanced. As a result, it is all the more likely to happen.

In this chapter, we have outlined the central process for setting up a narrative conversation in a mediation. The key to this process is the development of a particular rhetorical move known as an externalizing conversation. In this conversational style, people are given the opportunity to separate from themselves and from the other party the problem that has led to the conflict. This is a temporary space out of which can grow a desire for the development of an alternative story. If this alternative story were to feature agreements, new understandings, a spirit of cooperation, and a sense of resolution, it would be characteristic of what a narrative mediation aims to make possible. In the next chapter we outline more fully some of the ways in which an alternative story can be brought forth.

## Notes

1. Cobb, S., "A Narrative Perspective on Mediation," in J. P. Folger and T. S. Jones (eds.), *New Directions in Mediation: Communication Research and Perspectives* (Thousand Oaks, Calif.: Sage, 1994).
2. Davies, B., and Harre, R., "Positioning: The Discursive Production of Selves," *Journal for the Theory of Social Behavior,* 1990, *20*(1), 43–63.
3. Davies, B., "The Concept of Agency: A Feminist Poststructural Analysis," *Social Analysis,* 1991, *30,* 42–53.
4. White, M., and Epston, D., *Narrative Means to Therapeutic Ends* (New York: Norton, 1991); Monk, G., Winslade, J., Crocket, K., and Epston, D., *Narrative Therapy in Practice: The Archaeology of Hope* (San Francisco: Jossey-Bass, 1997); Freedman, J., and Combs, G., *Narrative Therapy: The Social Construction of Preferred Realities* (New York: Norton, 1996).
5. Wittgenstein L., *Philosophical Investigations* (Oxford, England: Blackwell, 1958).
6. White and Epston, *Narrative Means to Therapeutic Ends.*
7. White, M., "The Externalizing of the Problem," in M. White, *Selected Papers* (Adelaide, Australia: Dulwich Centre Publications, 1989).
8. Egan, G., *The Skilled Helper: A Systematic Approach to Effective Helping* (4th ed.) (Pacific Grove, Calif.: Brooks/Cole, 1990).
9. Gergen, K. J., *Realities and Relationships: Soundings in Social Constructionism* (Cambridge, Mass.: Harvard University Press, 1994).
10. White, M., "The Process of Questioning: A Therapy of Literary Merit?" in M. White, *Selected Papers* (Adelaide, Australia: Dulwich Centre Publications, 1989).
11. White, "The Process of Questioning."
12. White, "The Process of Questioning."
13. White and Epston, *Narrative Means to Therapeutic Ends;* Monk, Winslade, Crocket, and Epston, *Narrative Therapy in Practice;* Freedman and Combs, *Narrative Therapy;* Dickerson, V., and Zimmerman, J., *If Problems Talked: Narrative Therapy in Action* (New York: Guilford Press, 1996).

# Chapter Seven

# Opening Space

*There is in this story abundance of delightful incidents,
and all of them usefully applied. There is an agreeable
turn artfully given them in the relating, that naturally
instructs the reader, one way or another.*
(DANIEL DEFOE, "MOLL FLANDERS")

*Good things lost amid a wilderness of weeds, to be sure,
whose rankness far over-topped their neglected growth; yet,
notwithstanding evidence of a wealthy soil, that might
yield luxuriant crops under other and favourable
circumstances.*
(EMILY BRONTË, "WUTHERING HEIGHTS")

In the previous chapter we explored naming the problem that brings people to mediation in a way that starts to disarm the conflict. In a narrative conversation, rather than two people (or two groups of people) treating each other as objects under the influence of a conflict-saturated story, the problem itself is objectified and the people are approached as subjects.[1] In this idea of subjectivity, the parties are like the subject of the verb in a sentence. The subject drives the engine of the sentence, which is the verb. The spirit of the narrative mediation style is embodied in always speaking to people as if they are subjects, or active rather than passive, or creators of meaning rather than just recipients or objects of it. This is a deeply respectful way of speaking. In this chapter we show how this spirit of conversation can be a starting point for the creation of change. It opens space, which in our experience people are often more than willing to enter.

# Inviting the Parties to Judge the Problem

One of the first steps in the development of a subjective position is to invite the parties in a dispute to make a judgment. This invitation treats people as subjects with opinions worthy of being voiced. To illustrate this, let us return to the second stage of the relative influence questioning mentioned in the last chapter. The problem story has been told, an externalizing conversation has been developed, and a degree of linguistic separation of the persons from the problem has been achieved. The mediator has asked both parties in front of each other about the effects of the problem on each of them. The questions have shifted to asking about the parties' influence on the problem. Imagine the conversation at such a point. The mediator begins by summarizing what has happened immediately before:

*Mediator:* So, we have talked about how this argument has knocked you both around, and you've said that it has destroyed what used to be a good working relationship, even a friendship, and it's set you up almost to hate each other and wish that each other would leave the firm. It's kept you awake at night and it's even appeared in your dreams. Philip, you've said that it started to get your wife annoyed with you, and Moira, you said that it would most likely ruin your chances of promotion if it went on much further. You are both worried about how the argument is affecting your reputation with others in the firm. Would you agree that this argument is exacting quite a high price from you both?

*Philip:* Well, when you put it like that—yes.

*Mediator:* How about you, Moira?

*Moira:* Yes, it's been awful. I just want it to end.

*Mediator:* Well, is this high price acceptable to you both? Are you willing to pay it? [*Silence.*] Or if you could have your way, would you rather dislodge this argument from its place of power in your lives and relationship?

*Moira:* Well, I just said that I want it to end. I don't feel proud of what has happened and that is why I am here, to find a way out of this mess.

*Mediator:* Yes? So you clearly don't want to continue to pay the price this argument demands, is that right?

*Moira:* That's right.

*Mediator:* How about you, Philip?

*Philip:* Well, of course I don't want it to go on anymore.

*Mediator:* I understand that, but I just wanted to check that out rather than take it for granted. It might be that you want this to keep going, but I hear you saying that you would prefer things to change. Is that right, Philip?

*Philip:* Sure.

*Mediator:* So, we have some agreement on this. Is that right? What does it mean to hear Philip say he wants to end this dispute, Moira?

*Moira:* Well, if he means it, then that's a great relief. I was thinking that he just wanted to keep going until I was forced to leave.

*Mediator:* So it makes a difference to hear him say that he wants the argument to end?

*Moira:* Yes.

*Mediator:* What difference do you think that makes exactly?

*Moira:* Well, it gives me some hope. I still don't know how it can change, given what has happened, but I need some shred of hope if we're going to keep on talking here.

*Mediator:* OK. What about you, Philip? What does it mean to you to hear Moira speak about wanting to dislodge the argument from its controlling place?

*Philip:* Well, it's a good start, I suppose.

*Mediator:* What do you suppose it could be the start of?

*Philip:* Not arguing.

*Mediator:* Could you turn that around the other way? Like, if you were not arguing, what would you be doing differently that this could be the start of?

*Philip:* Well, getting on with things without getting on each other's nerves.

*Mediator:* Getting on with things without getting on each other's nerves. Is that what you would prefer?

*Philip:* Yes.

*Mediator:* What does that sound like to you, Moira? Does the picture of how Philip would prefer things to be appeal to you, too?

*Moira:* Yes, it fits with what I said before.

*Mediator:* So, is it significant, do you think, that you are in agreement on this? I wonder what the agreement means? Like, what does it make possible?

## A Unique Outcome

Let us pause at this point and examine what has happened. The mediator has asked each person in turn to make a statement about the acceptability of the problem and its effects. This statement may seem obvious, as Philip suggests (few people enjoy being in conflict situations), but its value lies in the significance that gets built on it. First, the statement is in itself a negation of the effects of the problem. Saying that one has had enough of the argument and wants it to stop stands in contrast to the conflict-saturated story. It would not be predicted by the argument. It is therefore a *unique outcome,* to use Michael White and David Epston's term, or an *exception,* according to Steve de Shazer's description.[2]

If we take seriously the social constructionist idea that we speak ourselves into existence, then chances are that speaking out loud the desire to end the argument opens the door for that to happen.[3] Both Philip and Moira hear themselves say this and they know that they have been heard to say it. They have also both heard the other person say it. This gives them the chance to make meaning about the other person that may not have been possible under the influence of the conflict story.

## Soliciting the Making of Meaning

Notice, however, the role the mediator plays in this example. She does not just allow such meaning making to happen but actually solicits it by asking direct questions. These questions are often kept small (Is that what you would prefer?) so as not to require too big a step toward change. That would feel too risky at this stage. The questions are also sometimes closed, requiring just a yes or no answer. Although closed questions have had bad press, in this circumstance they are used for a specific purpose. They create the easiest possible entry point to a relational stance that is different from the stance that has dominated the recent relations between the two parties. The closed question can be followed with a more open-ended one that gives the person who has already made a simple little commitment by saying yes or no the chance to elaborate. For example:

*Mediator:*   Does it make a difference to hear that?
    *Party:*   Yes.
*Mediator:*   So, what difference does it make, do you think?

The word *yes* can be thought of as a unique outcome in relation to the conflict story. It is a step out of the rut created by the conflict. The next question invites the taking of another step, this time a slightly bigger one, but one that capitalizes on the momentum of the smaller step. The difference that gets spoken about in response to such a question is being brought into existence as it is being spoken. It did not exist previously. It too can be referred back to the other person, who can make meaning of it, and thereby expanded further. All of these steps are building blocks of change.

## Highlighting Agreement

In the example, the mediator deliberately used the word *agreement* twice. Agreements are not on the conflict's agenda. The aim of a conflict is not to get people to agree but to keep them differing. Often the goal of conflict's scheming seems to be the achievement of polarized relationships. So, when people agree on something, they momentarily step out of the clutches of a dispute. This move constitutes another unique outcome. The mediator marks its significance by naming it and then building on it.

Moreover, if one of the aims of the mediation process is to make possible the creation of a settlement or agreement that serves as a map to guide the parties forward, then such an agreement needs to be crafted in the detail of the conversation all along the way. From a narrative perspective, we are interested not only in an agreement as an outcome but also in a story of agreement (provided that this is what the parties want).

If there is to be an agreement at the end of the mediation process, then it needs to be built on a story of many little agreements along the way. The final agreement then takes on the character of a denouement to a plot that has been built out of many significant plot events. This is the counterplot to the plot that the conflict would write on the parties' behalf.[4]

If the mediator takes care to seek out and name these moments as they happen (without being overly Pollyannaish in the process), then a coherent and credible story of willingness to make agreements can be crafted. This helps set the stage for reaching more significant and long-lasting agreements at a later stage in the process. It smooths the way and avoids the sense that the brainstorming of solutions comes somewhat out of the blue after the telling of the conflict story, a sense we often find in the problem-solving approach to mediation.

## The Landscape of Action and the Landscape of Meaning

The narrative perspective, as well as plot and character elements, also suggests an emphasis on thematic considerations. It is in this context that Jerome Bruner's reference to the twin landscapes on which narrative accounts can work is useful.[5] Bruner referred to these landscapes as a *landscape of action* and a *landscape of consciousness.* Michael White picked up these terms and introduced them into discussions of narrative therapy.[6] White's description of a *landscape of meaning,* an alternative description of the landscape of consciousness and slightly more accessible, appeals to us because it suggests an important conversational move that mediators can make. Let us explain these terms and then demonstrate the usefulness of them to the process of opening space for the development of alternative stories in a mediation.

### The Landscape of Action

This is the plane on which plot events take place. In a conflict-saturated story, the behaviors, actions, or practices that have embodied the conflict can be said to have happened on the landscape of action. What the parties to the dispute have said and done and had done to them are the elements of the story. When people tell conflict stories, these are the elements on which they are likely to elaborate. They give the story dramatic force and they propel the protagonists on a trajectory through time.

## The Landscape of Meaning

Human beings, however, are meaning-making creatures. They dwell on, think about, interpret, reach conclusions about, have emotional responses to, develop attitudes toward and positions about, and react against many of the plot events. All of these responses take place on the landscape of meaning. In these responses, they construct and express their sense of entitlement in relation to the issues of the mediation. All of these meaning-making responses are shaped by the available discourses within which meanings can be made. Sometimes there will be competing discourses that engage the parties in contests over the meaning of events. Sometimes such contests result from the different positions available to people within the same discourse. For example, dominant discourses about gender relations might call males and females into distinctly different positions around the care of children in a divorce mediation.

## Weaving a Story Between the Twin Landscapes

Of course the distinction between these twin landscapes is an artificial one. There is no real structural boundary. Any thought is an event and any action is an embodiment of meaning. The usefulness of this distinction lies in the application to conversation that it offers, particularly in the task of opening space for an alternative story. If we think of people as constantly creating meanings around events and then acting out of those meanings to create a story of further events, then we are thinking explicitly in narrative terms. We can start to construct questions designed to open the space for an alternative story and then carefully elaborate it by weaving back and forth between these two landscapes. When a new plot event emerges, we can ask questions designed to explore its significance for the landscape of meaning. When a new meaning emerges, we can ask questions to link it to perhaps previously overlooked, or unstoried, plot events. Or we can ask about possible plot developments that might be expected to follow from such a meaning in the future.

We return to the earlier conversation for an example. The mediator picks up on the statements made by both parties that they would prefer the conflict to end. She refers to these statements as an agreement. In other words, each party has stated what the current situation means to them (the landscape of meaning). But the coincidence of them both saying this at the same time is constructed by the mediator as a significant plot event (the landscape of action). The mediator then asks Moira whether it makes a difference to hear Philip say what he has said, and when she says yes, the mediator inquires about what difference it makes. This takes Moira back to a thematic search for significance (the landscape of meaning). Philip is asked a similar question, and both of their responses throw up opportunities for exploring possible future plot events. Philip's description of "getting on with things without getting on each other's nerves" may well serve as an opening to a discussion about future actions that each party could take to make this idea materialize (the landscape of action). Both parties could then be asked what it would mean to them if such actions were to happen (the landscape of meaning).

In the process, the mediator is helping the parties to develop a story. It is a story that has no existence outside the present conversation. However, by carefully weaving back and forth between an emphasis on the landscape of action and an emphasis on the landscape of meaning, a story of some substance, and hopefully therefore of some viability, is being opened up. It is a story that is more than fantasy because it is rooted in events that are unfolding in the moment. It is also more than just a series of chance events, because the significance of each event is being storied as meaningful. There is no separation of behaviors or facts on the one hand and opinions, thoughts, or feelings on the other. They are constantly being woven together in a coherent pattern.

## Seeking Unique Outcomes

So far in this chapter we have been talking about opening space for an alternative story in relation to a specific unique outcome. In this instance, the unique outcome arose in response to some questions about the acceptability to the parties of the effects of the problem. This is, however, only one instance of what we would call unique outcomes. Many other instances can be noticed as they arise or can be deliberately sought out with direct questions.

Remember that the second stage of relative influence questioning aims to map the influence of the persons on the problem. The conflict-saturated story has mapped out a trajectory for the parties, into which can be fitted an assortment of plot events and thematic interpretations about their significance. These are what keep a dispute going. However, human beings are complex creatures and there are so many complexities to human relations that we have found it always safe to rely on the assumption that there are always events that do not fit into this story. Complexity throws up so many possibilities in life that no single story can ever encapsulate them all. Therefore, while a conflict story narrows the focus of those involved in it and foregrounds the conflict story in their angle of vision, there will always be places on the edge of the story that do not fit into it. Rather, they speak of a different pattern of relationship that is possible if they are allowed any significance. It is one of the narrative mediator's tasks to bring these discrepancies out of the shadows and into the spotlight. This can be achieved by asking questions that redirect the parties' focus.

## Historical Unique Outcomes

We now explore some possibly fruitful avenues to venture down in search of these unique outcomes. One of these avenues is history. Just as the first stage of relative influence questioning traces the history of the problem story, so the history of satisfactory relationship can also be explored. The question, "When did this conflict begin?" can lead to a discussion of what things were like between the parties *before* the conflict began just as easily as it can lead to a discussion of what happened *after* the development of the conflict. This question can be followed with other questions, such as the following:

- So, what was it like when you were getting along better?
- Would you prefer to return to that state of affairs?
- Were there some qualities to your relationship then that have been sidelined by the argument since?

- If you could rescue some things that have been damaged by the conflict, what would they be?
- What were you doing differently back then that you are not doing so much now?

The aim of such questions is to establish contrast. Seeing the contrast between then and now reminds the parties that things can be different. It establishes the newsworthiness of the relational qualities that were in evidence at a previous time, especially if those qualities constitute a contrast with the qualities that are in evidence through the conflict story. News of difference, in Gregory Bateson's epistemological argument, is a precondition for learning or change.[7] Once such qualities are discovered, they can be explored and described in some detail. Instances of these qualities can be sought and exhibited. The mediator can inquire into the knowledge that fed into such ways of relating. Then, once again, as details are remembered or stories told, the mediator can lead the parties to reflect on the significance of each quality on the landscape of meaning. Here are some sample questions that might be asked:

- Can you tell me a story that would illustrate the difference between things as they were then and as they are now?
- You say that you used to be much more respectful of each other. How exactly did you show that? How would I recognize that respectful behavior if I were to come across it?
- Where did you learn those skills? Do they come naturally to you or have you studied them and practiced them?
- Are there some principles on which you based those practices?
- What did it mean back then that you were able to relate in this way?
- Is there anything from back then that can give us hope that you will be able to find a way out of the current difficulties?

## Being Present at the Mediation as a Unique Outcome

Given the course that the conflict story has taken and the influence it has had in the lives of the parties, even attending the mediation itself may well be a statement about a desire to create a different future. After the history of the problem has been mapped, or even right at the start of the joint meeting, it is possible to draw attention to the fact that both parties have agreed to come and discuss the situation with a view to settlement. It can be well worth asking what has brought them there. A way to do this that does not lead immediately back into the dispute is to ask about the hopes that each person has for the outcome of the meeting. Someone who had no hope for something different would be unlikely to attend the mediation. The articulation of such hopes within the hearing of the other party can make a difference to the meaning of the conflict for both people right from the start.

Both parties can in principle be in agreement on the story of hope, even if they are not in a position yet to see how it can be fully embodied. It is our bias to regard such hopes as just as solid as any of the "facts" of the conflict story. These hopes can be taken seriously by the mediator by being written down and referred to at frequent intervals during the conversation. They can be linked to other unique outcomes as these arise in the course of conversation. They can be referred back to later as a point of reference against which to measure change. Are the parties' hopes being fulfilled or is the mediation taking them in directions in which they prefer not to go?

## Other Relationships as Resources for News of Difference

Conflict stories, especially if prolonged, can undermine people's belief in their relational competencies. Confidence and self-belief are often delicate qualities that do not flourish in the unfavorable climate that ongoing conflict produces. Anger, hurt, and defensiveness can feed off each other and starve out kindness, respect, and generosity of spirit, relational qualities that foster the flowering of self-belief. This might be expected to apply especially in intimate relationships or in other complex relationships where people are in close proximity or together over a period of time. These effects of conflict are therefore most likely to surface in divorce mediation or in organizational disputes between colleagues who work closely together.

In such circumstances, it can be especially useful to invoke alternative stories, sourced from other relationships, as counterstories to the effects of a conflict. This may best be done in separate sessions if a person is feeling any distress or is in a weakened place

where they cannot face the other party with any confidence. Some
time may be needed to help the person activate other knowledge
about themselves based on other experiences of relationship, perhaps with friends. Here are some sample questions that might be
used in such an inquiry:

- So it sounds like the separation process has knocked you
  around and undermined your confidence. I was wondering
  if you could recall other experiences that are worth hanging
  onto because they are a better basis for confidence?
- Who in your life would be most supportive of your growth in
  confidence?
- What have you learned about yourself in other relationships
  that may be useful to keep in mind while struggling with this
  problem?

It is important to remember that a mediation is different from
personal therapy and not to allow such personal inquiries to develop into a therapeutic interview. Such questions would obviously
not be appropriate in many mediation contexts anyway. However,
in some situations a brief exchange in response to such questions
may be enough to ease the conversation forward by opening space
for a different story to emerge.

Even when the dispute does not touch on such personal areas,
space can still be opened for an alternative story by asking the parties about experiences in other relationships. In a commercial dispute, for example, a representative for a firm can be asked to speak
about the firm's preferred experiences of settling disagreements,
or to tell a story of when the firm's policy for handling disagreements with customers has worked well.

### Contradictory Events Within the Conflict Story

A separated couple who were engaged in a protracted dispute about arrangements for the care of their children also mentioned in passing that there had
been a time when one of their children was quite ill and was hospitalized. During this time, while the child was in the hospital for two weeks, they had put
their dispute to one side and had cooperated in supporting her. They had
agreed on patterns of visiting so that the child had at least one parent there

much of the time. They had attended consultations with doctors together and had made the child their primary focus. As the child had returned to health, they had resumed their respective positions in the dispute.

From the perspective of the conflict story, this episode was an aberration. It was put down to exceptional circumstances and the couple's interactions under the influence of the conflict story remained more real in their thinking. Easy cooperation between them to meet the children's needs was not considered an inherent feature of their relationship.

However, the mediator asked them more about this exceptional experience. He refused to allow it to remain insignificant. Instead, he was curious about how this had happened. What had the couple done differently on this occasion? What had this crisis brought to the surface from the hidden depths of their resourcefulness? He engaged them in a conversation that made meaning of these events in terms of knowledge about cooperation, and then wondered whether that spirit of cooperation appealed to them as one they would like to feature more in their family interactions.

Several things are worth noting in this example. One is that the story of conflict was not in complete control of the couple's interactions. In our experience, it seldom is. Even when noncooperation was dominating the relationship, instances of its opposite could be found. To be sure, it took a crisis to shake them loose, but there are always moments of cooperation in a story of noncooperation. However, as in this situation, such moments are very likely to be disregarded by the protagonists and treated as insignificant. This is because significance does not lie in the essential character of an event but in the process of storying that encapsulates the event. What the mediator was trying to do was encapsulate these events differently, as more significant than exceptions, as openings to a different kind of relationship story. Note also that this effort sometimes requires a persistence of questioning about a subject that does not at first appear to the protagonists to hold much interest, simply because it is exceptional and the story of conflict is more familiar.

Another point of note is that this exceptional event was mentioned by the two parties almost in passing, as if to dismiss its significance. In our experience, unique outcomes are often referred to in this way. Mediators need to remain alert to comments dropped into the corners of a conversation, in case they can be mined for news of difference. Remaining alert like this takes practice because dominant stories of conflict are likely to exert enough influence to draw mediators into their sway along with the protagonists. It is necessary for the mediator to develop confidence that exceptions will always appear, and to be constantly on the lookout for them.

Often, however, such exceptions are not dropped into the conversation, as this one was. If they are not, it is always possible for the mediator to ask about them. Again, the curiosity we have spoken of before becomes useful at this point. Here are some questions that can be asked to yield this kind of information:

- Have there been any times when this dispute has let up and allowed you to cooperate more, even for brief periods?
- Have you ever had a break from the argument and tried anything different in the way you relate?
- It sounds like the conflict has led you into saying and doing things that have been quite painful. I was wondering about how you have handled these issues in your best moments?
- Have you made any attempts to step out of the argument? To free yourself from its clutches? To work things out in a different way?
- Have you experienced any lulls in the dispute when things have gone better for a time?

## Areas of Relationship That Remain Unaffected by the Problem

Sometimes conflict seems to loom so large that it blocks from view the areas of a relationship that remain functional, resilient, and intact. Participants in the relationship can fail to notice that there are still many things that work quite satisfactorily. Television news bulletins seldom feature the many aspects of life that continue to function well from day to day. They are not considered newsworthy. So it is in relationships. Seldom do the news bulletins that are circulated in conversations about a conflicted relationship include matters for which "Work in Progress as Normal" would be the appropriate headline. As a result, these matters are not held up to the light and the resourcefulness that can be drawn from them is not as available as it could be.

A useful way to conceive of the mediator, therefore, is as an investigative reporter hunting out snippets of news that can be built into a story.[8] Of particular value is the kind of story that may be considered a scoop by editors wishing to headline positive relational values like understanding, cooperation, or respect rather than conflict, drama, and confrontation. The mediator should therefore be on the lookout for positive leads, especially where the tabloid hack reporters and paparazzi would seldom think to look.

A little training in seeking out such stories can yield surprising results. For example, cub reporters, doubling as mediators, soon discover from their informants in divorce situations that couples who are at war over the care of children may have satisfactory working agreements over matrimonial property or schooling options. Or landlords and tenants who are in disagreement over responsibility for repairs to a house can be quite happy with the payment of rent over a considerable period. Inexperienced reporters may be inclined to attribute to chance the outbreak of equitable agreements and cooperation and overlook the possibilities for a good story about the relational qualities exhibited by the parties. More earnest investigative news sleuths are not so hasty. They want to probe into the shadows of such apparently minor success stories and blow them up into major headlines, milking their informants for every tidbit of information about how such successes were accomplished. They do not pass up opportunities to ask questions such as the following:

- What do you think it means that you are able to cooperate in this area?
- What skills did you have to use to prevent this area of your relationship from being dragged into the conflict?
- Which do you prefer: the cooperation you have demonstrated in this area or the arguing and bickering you have been doing over these other matters?
- How exactly did you work out this issue so easily? Are there some principles that might be drawn from this experience that can be used to address these other, more sticky issues?

## Unique Outcomes on the Landscape of Meaning

Unique outcomes do not have to be events that have happened on the landscape of action. Sometimes they can be ideas or ideals that do not fit into the conflict story. Take, for example, a dispute between two business partners who are also friends. In the course of the mediation, both of them mention their disappointment that the friendship has been damaged by the dispute over the business. "That's not the way friends should behave toward each other!" one of them complains.

The mediator can take this opportunity to explore the background system of meaning against which such a complaint is made. This would be a *deconstructive inquiry*.[9] The idea of friendship can take many different forms and it is not safe to assume that the mediator or the parties share exactly the same understanding of what friendship is about. So the mediator might ask the person who made this complaint to explain her ideal of friendship. Curious questioning can then draw out this definition until it has developed a personal meaning. This meaning will likely be historically situated in the speaker's life. The mediator can also ask the person to situate this meaning in the history of the relationship with the other party:

- What's been the history of this kind of friendship between you two?
- What influences have there been on your ideas of friendship?
- How has this idea of friendship been manifested in your business partnership in the past?
- Has the hope for this ideal of friendship been completely extinguished by the dispute, or do you still have some hope for it to be expressed in your business partnership?
- Have there been any occasions in recent times when this ideal of friendship has been evident even for a brief moment in your partnership?

These questions focus deliberately on ideal notions (the landscape of meaning) and then refer them back to the landscape of action. It does not matter if the ideals mentioned seem to bear little relationship to the events that have transpired or if people seem hypocritical in espousing them. The narrative assumption is that change can be constructed from anywhere. Even castles in the air are useful starting points. The task for the mediator becomes one of anchoring these castles to events on the ground, or even soliciting actions that can serve this purpose.

## Thoughts or Intentions as Unique Outcomes

Sometimes a unique outcome may not have happened as an event in the relationship. It may be a stray thought by one of the parties that they have held privately but not previously voiced to the other party; it may be an intention that has not yet been acted on; or it may be an example of an understanding of the other's position that has not been expressed before. From our perspective, such thoughts are events on the landscape of action. A story that involves the elaboration of meaning can therefore be built around them.

For example, a participant may say something like one of the following statements:

- I haven't ever said this before but I have been wanting for some time to say that I'm sorry things have gotten this bad and I'd like them to improve.
- I intended weeks ago to phone you and sort things out but something stopped me and I never did.
- I have been wanting to apologize for what I said. I was ashamed of that immediately after I said it.
- One idea I've had but have never mentioned was that I could offer to let you have the kids full-time for a month each year.
- I've never said it before but I do understand how you must have been hurt by what I did.

In other words, parties to a dispute often have secret thoughts that the dispute itself does not allow to be spoken. If the right climate is created in the mediation, these kinds of statements can start to see the light of day. They are unique outcomes because they do not further the story of conflict. Rather, they open the parties to a different reality than the one that projects itself from the conflict story.

Such expressions can remain insignificant, however, if not responded to carefully. Under the influence of the conflict story, the other party may hear these statements as too little, too late; as empty words or mere intentions that don't matter much; or as insignificant because actions speak louder than words. If these statements remain isolated expressions, such predictions can easily be borne out.

The job of the mediator is to build significance around such expressions so they start to take root and eventually blossom into further actions that do make a difference. In an externalizing conversation, the failure of good intentions to materialize can be ascribed to the dominance of the externalized problem. The good intentions can then be constructed as the more authentic but subjugated desires of the person who utters them. Once voiced and heard as such, inquiry can be developed as to how they can be activated further in the future. Another way to say this is that such thoughts or intentions can be spoken of as exceptions to a more likely scenario, or they can be framed as possible openings to a new story that deserves to be constructed, sometimes against considerable odds. The latter approach is not realistic (by any objective account) but it is about the creation of new realities out of what at first appears to be only an insubstantial possibility. The substance of the statement can be carded and spun and woven in the magic of a creative conversation.

## Unique Outcomes in the Actions of the Other

The advantage of working with more than one person in a mediation context is that the resourcefulness that can be brought into play by the process can draw on the contributions of both parties. There is a sense in which two people make up more than the sum of two individual minds. As well as developing their own thoughts and actions, they are also always responding to the other's thoughts and actions. Even when one person runs dry and cannot think of a way forward, there is always the chance that he or she can respond to something the other person has to offer in a way that increases the range of what is possible in the relationship.

A mediator can make good use of this phenomenon. The search for unique outcomes can include responses to what the other person has already said or done, even in the mediation itself. We find it useful in mediation to ask regularly for each person's reflections on what the other person has said, and to stay on the lookout for opportunities to elaborate on these and incorporate them into nascent stories.

For example, a mediator might notice one of the parties looking surprised or thoughtful in response to what the other party has said. A useful skill to foster for noticing such things is to scan carefully and regularly both parties' nonverbal behavior. It is easy to focus attention only on what the person speaking is saying, but it is equally important to keep looking at what the person listening is doing in response at any given moment.

When such responses are noticed, or even when they are not but may be guessed at, a mediator can ask for the kind of verbalization that helps the speaker know they have been heard:

- You are looking a bit surprised. Was there something Melissa said that was news to you?
- You look a bit thoughtful at the moment. Was there something Mike said that gives you pause for thought?

Moments of careful listening and understanding of the other person are often in themselves unique outcomes, given that conflict stories do not encourage protagonists to include perspectives alternative to their own. It is more likely in many disputes for people to become convinced of the rightness of their own perspective and less tolerant of, or willing to listen to, another's perspective. Therefore, against such a trend, respectful listening can be a newsworthy event. The mediator can dwell on such moments briefly rather than allow them to pass unnoticed. The mediator can also refer them back to the other person so that person can make meaning out of them:

- Did you feel like he heard what you were saying?
- What difference does it make to be heard?
- Does this kind of interaction make some kind of agreement more likely or not? Why?

Even in situations where such listening does not appear to have happened, the mediator can request it. One party can be asked to step outside of his or her own perspective for a while and make room for the other person's perspective. He or she can be asked to put himself or herself into the other person's shoes and make meaning from there:

- Can you imagine what all this must seem like from Melissa's position?
- If I were to ask her to comment on what you just said, what do you think she would say?
- What do you imagine Mike would appreciate most about the ideas you just mentioned?
- What do you both imagine all this sounds like to me?
- What do you guess I appreciate most in what you have been saying?

## Internalized Other Questioning

Internalized other questioning is an extension of this idea.[10] In this process, one person is invited to step into the persona of the other. The mediator asks questions and the person responds as if he or she is the other person, who is sitting by and listening for the time being. Later the roles are reversed. After a few minutes of conversation in this vein, the mediator can stop and ask the person whose perspective is being represented to make further meaning of what has been said. Here's an example.

*Mediator:*  Jim, could you be Janet for a little while and answer some questions as if you were her? Are you willing to try this out? Thanks. OK, Janet [*to Jim, role-playing her*], what do you think are the main issues we still have to work out here, and what, for you, is standing in the way of making some progress with them?

[*Jim responds as Janet.*]

*Mediator:*  So, Janet, what was it like listening to Jim speaking as you? To what extent did he understand things as you would understand them? Is it a surprise that he could put himself in your shoes to that extent? What does it mean to you that he could do that? What do you think it means for the chances of you both working out better ways to handle this problem?

The unique outcome here is in relational terms. It is hard to maintain a stance of antagonism or stubbornness about one's own position when one is being asked to speak in the other person's persona. It is also hard for the person listening to someone talking in her persona to maintain a picture of the speaker as an antagonist. The shift in perspective that this exercise encourages is toward feeling the other person's position from the inside and demonstrating understanding of this experience in front of the other person. Conflict stories do not usually feature such relational empathy very highly.

Internalized other questioning is therefore a very powerful tool for opening the space needed for a different story to emerge. It needs to be handled carefully, however. It should not be attempted too soon before the parties are willing to make such a leap. It requires a degree of trust in the process and can be sabotaged if someone decides to speak in the other's persona without adopting that person's viewpoints. If the opportunity is used simply to score points or make sarcastic remarks, huge damage can be done to trust. However, this element of risk in the use of this process can also provide it with the edge that makes it highly memorable when it does work. Everyone senses that it requires trust and respect; therefore, if that trust is honored, the relationship is advanced toward mutual respect and understanding, which are good bases for the resolution of issues.

The opening of space in a seemingly closed story of conflict, or more commonly, in two separate stories of a dispute, is a first step toward the creation of a different future. This task is achieved in a narrative framework by seeking out gaps in the watertight stories of the conflict. Because no story can ever contain the complexity of human relations, such holes are easy to find if a mediator is alert to them. Even if different perspectives are not readily visible to the parties in a mediation, they can be constructed in the conversation that takes place in the mediation. Once holes in the story are opened up, the mediator faces the task of working to increase the flow through such holes rather than stemming this flow in favor of a monological account.

At the same time, it should be clear that the mediator who seeks out unique outcomes that offer a different perspective on events is being selective in the process. There is an ethical dimension to such choices. We believe that a clear bias toward respect, agreement, and equity should guide the ethics of what gets selected by the mediator. Otherwise, unique outcomes could be selected that would give rise to a story of subjugation of one party by the other, or of intensification of the conflict. The conflict could even be spread to new areas of the relationship between the parties that didn't exist before the mediation began.

Opening some space in the dominant story of the conflict is not enough, however. Small holes in an entrenched story can easily clog up again. In the next chapter we address the task of developing an alternative to the conflict-saturated story. This involves elaborating on what has been opened up and inviting the parties to step further into it.

## Notes

1. Henriques, J., Holloway, W., Urwin, C., Venn, C., and Walkerdine, V., *Changing the Subject: Psychology, Social Regulation and Subjectivity* (London: Methuen, 1984).

2. White, M., and Epston, D., *Narrative Means to Therapeutic Ends* (New York: Norton, 1991); Monk, G., Winslade, J., Crocket, K., and Epston, D., *Narrative Therapy in Practice: The Archaeology of Hope* (San Francisco: Jossey-Bass, 1997); Freedman, J., and Combs, G., *Narrative Therapy: The Social Construction of Preferred Realities* (New York: Norton, 1996); Dickerson, V., & Zimmerman, J., *If Problems Talked: Narrative Therapy in Action* (New York: Guilford Press, 1996); De Shazer, S., *Putting Difference to Work* (New York: Norton, 1991).

3. Davies, B., *Shards of Glass: Children Reading and Writing Beyond Gendered Identities* (St. Leonards, Australia: Allen & Unwin, 1993).

4. White, M., *Narratives of Therapists Lives* (Adelaide, Australia: Dulwich Centre Publications, 1997).

5. Bruner, J., *Actual Minds, Possible Worlds* (Cambridge, Mass.: Harvard University Press, 1986).

6. White, M., "Deconstruction and Therapy," in D. Epston and M. White (eds.), *Experience, Contradiction, Narrative and Imagination* (Adelaide, Australia: Dulwich Centre Publications, 1992).

7. Bateson, G., *Steps to an Ecology of Mind* (New York: Ballentine Books, 1972); Bateson, G., *Mind and Nature: A Necessary Unity* (New York: Bantam Books, 1980).

8. Roth, S., and Epston, D., "Consulting the Problem About the Problematic Relationship: An Exercise for Experiencing a Relationship

with an Externalized Problem," in M. Hoyt (ed.), *Constructive Therapies II* (New York: Guilford, 1996).

9. White, "Deconstruction and Therapy."

10. Tomm, K., *Internalized Other Questioning: Workshop Presentation* (Hamilton, New Zealand: University of Waikato, 1996); Epston, D., "Internalized Other Questioning with Couples: The New Zealand Version," in S. Gilligan and R. Price (eds.), *Therapeutic Conversations* (New York: Norton, 1996).

# Chapter Eight

# Building Momentum

*Little drops of water, little grains of sand*
*Make the mighty ocean and the pleasant land.*
*So the little minutes, humble though they be*
*Make the mighty ages of eternity.*
(JULIA CARNEY, "LITTLE THINGS")

*I dwell in Possibility—*
*A fairer House than Prose—*
*More numerous of Windows—*
*Superior—for Doors.*
(EMILY DICKINSON, NO. 657)

The previous chapter was about the opening of space in a tightly knit story of conflict that had prevailed in the recent history of a dispute. We now address what to do with such space once it has been opened. Unique outcomes can be discovered in the landscape of any dispute, but they do not constitute the end of the differences that have led to the logjam. More work than that has to be done to shift the logs.

Our focus here is on what is required to build a story out of such unique outcomes. If stories form the basis of the ongoing performance of meaning,[1] then what people who want to find a way out of a dispute need is a story that can serve as an exit pathway. Such a story must be well-enough formed to be able to carry the necessary weight of both disputing parties' hopes for something different. It needs to develop the qualities of a good story. So what are these qualities?

First, a good story must have a story line. This implies a coherent series of plot events that hang together rather than a random collocation of chance happenings. The story needs to be plausible as a story, not just to the mediator but to the disputing parties as well. This suggests a careful crafting process that sustains a certain level of suspense so that the participants in the story are drawn forward toward some sense of denouement.

For such narrative momentum to be sustained, the protagonists in the story need to be challenged to develop characterizations that fit the story and yet still honor their histories. These characterizations may well be foreshadowed by previous events in the parties' lives. Indeed, the discovery of unique outcomes and the making of meaning about those outcomes are key steps in the crafting of an alternative story, but such snippets of story do not constitute works of art in themselves. What they foreshadow needs to be developed. The past is a resource on which to draw for this development. But the developments must come forward into the present and project a future in order for the plot momentum to be plausible.

A story also requires thematic consistency. A mediator who is aware of this need should attend to the development of key themes in the building of momentum for the counterplot to the conflict story. These themes should express the preferences of the parties for the path forward. They should also serve as counterpoints to the themes of conflict and disharmony (or the like) that have been featured in the previously dominant story. For example, themes such as equity, agreement, cooperation, or respect may be featured and woven into the plot developments that are taking place. In a recent mediation about a conflict among members of a school board, the idea of working together as a team emerged as a theme that the participants preferred as a future focus for their work. The challenge then was to seek out expressions of this theme in the plot developments that followed.

Focusing on the qualities that constitute a good story distinguishes a narrative mediation process from a problem-solving one. Rather than having an instrumental focus on solving problems or a goal-fixated desire to settle a dispute, narrative mediation aims to create a relational context in which different story lines emerge and develop. Often, rather than being settled, the dispute starts to dissolve as the discursive conditions that have supported it are weakened. Change resembles dissolution rather than solution. On other occasions, the story of cooperation or respect starts simply to supplant the conflict-saturated story in the minds of the protagonists. Its salience in the mediation conversation invites the protagonists to begin to live more intentionally into its possibilities.[2]

We would not want to suggest, however, that the mediation of disputes does not, or should not, include attempts to reach agreements or settlements. Disputing parties often enter mediation wanting solutions that will ease the pain of the conflict in which they are caught. We are not of the school that would secretly substitute a "higher" goal of social transformation for the solving of the problems that preoccupy the disputing parties. Rather, we think that social transformation takes place through the negotiation of more satisfying stories. It also takes place through the explicit privileging of cultural discourses and the discussion of their influences on the parties in the mediation conversation.

We also believe that agreements, where they are made, are simply plot developments in a story. They must later be incorporated into the warp and weft of life. As this happens, a story of agreement evolves that is more than what ever gets written into the documents drawn up within a mediation process. Such an agreement is a lived experience rather than a one-dimensional paper description. Narrative mediators are concerned more with the production of this lived experience and the storying of it than with the production of a piece of paper containing a set of promises.

Ironically, we find that this shift from focusing on the production of agreements to focusing on the production of alternative stories leads to a process of forming agreements that actually happens much more quickly and easily. Attention to the relational and narrative context leads to a much quicker phase of designing solutions than has been our experience of the same phase in a problem-solving process.

## An Example of Building a Good Story

To demonstrate this process of developing an alternative story and building momentum for it, we offer a particular story as an example. This is a transcript from a role-played mediation based on a real scenario. It is the story of a dispute between two roommates. Here is an outline of the events that led to the mediation.

*The Scenario*

Mark and Chris live together in a house that belongs to Mark's parents. It is Mark's family home but his parents are currently living overseas and he is acting as landlord for them. Mark and Chris have been friends since their school days.

Chris has fallen behind in rent payments and has amassed a sizeable debt with Mark's parents. Chris has spent large sums of money on repairs to his car, which has required major mechanical work.

Mark has become increasingly concerned about the size of Chris's debt and feels that what started out on his part as flexibility with a friend has turned into a situation in which his friendship is being taken advantage of. He is feeling responsible to his parents and worried about letting them down. He is worried that Chris seems still to be spending money on his car rather than paying his rent.

Mark has tried to express his concerns to Chris, at first by making jokes about eviction and then by confronting him. At this point a yelling match ensued.

Chris has been feeling anxious about the debt and does intend to pay the rent. But he has needed his car to be running so he can get to work. He feels frustrated that Mark does not appear to believe him when he gives assurances that he will pay the debt, and he finds Mark's jokes a source of pressure that he could do without. Therefore, when Mark confronts Chris angrily, Chris reacts angrily.

## The Mediation

Let us follow the creation of an alternative story through a joint mediation session with Mark and Chris. The alternative story in this example begins from the earliest moments of the meeting. After an initial greeting, the mediator asks the two disputants what they are hoping for from the mediation. The following conversation ensues.

*Mediator:* So, it was your initiative to have this conversation, wasn't it?

*Mark:* It sure was, yeah. I'm just getting a bit hacked off that he hasn't paid his rent.

*Mediator:* So what do you hope will come from this?

*Mark:* That he'll pay his rent.

*Mediator:* That's the main thing?

*Mark:* Yeah. And he knows that because I keep telling him about it all the time.

*Mediator:* Are there other things you're hoping to get out of this as well?

*Mark:* Oh, well, we used to be really good friends, but we might be a bit too far down the track to do that now.

*Mediator:* But if you weren't too far down the track, would being good friends be something you would still want to happen?

*Mark:* Yeah, I suppose, yeah.

*Mediator:* [*To Chris*] And out of the listening you said you were prepared to do [*Chris had announced at the start that he had agreed to come to the mediation only to listen*], do you have any hopes for what might happen here?

*Chris:* The thing that was important, the thing that I'm pissed off about is that we used to be friends, and that doesn't work any more; the money's only part of it.

*Mark:* Yeah, but it's a big part of it.

*Mediator:* Let's get that clear. You used to be friends and, like, the money isn't the most important thing here. Are you saying that—I mean, imagine that we could make some difference here, that being friends would be something you could hope for again?

*Chris:* I think that probably what's happened is that the friendship will never be repaired. It's gone. It's gone, what we used to do together.

*Mediator:* That's how it seems right now.

*Chris:* Yeah, I just think that's where it's at. What's made me sour is that it's gone this far, but I don't think that it had to go this far. In fact I—

*Mediator:* So you said you were here to listen?

*Chris:* Yeah.

*Mediator:* You're pissed off that it's gone this far. You feel sour about that. But you're here, and you're here to listen. Do you have some hope about what you might hear as you listen?

*Chris:* I expect we've all got hopes.

*Mediator:* OK.

*Mark:* Yeah, his hope is that he doesn't have to pay the money.

*Mediator:* Hang on, hang on. He can speak for that.

*Chris:* Well, I will agree to pay the rent, but I can't get blood out of a stone. I haven't got it at the moment. The car broke down.

*Mediator:* So what might be your hope?

*Chris:* Some sort of solution that I can pay, and I've agreed to pay the money off, but some sort of solution that stops this asshole of a situation we've got.

*Mediator:* OK. So some sort of solution is something you, Chris, would want. And you, Mark, want the money paid, that's what you said before? [*Mark nods.*] And you'd also want to, you're not quite sure about this, whether it's possible, but something about the friendship. Is that right?

*Mark:* Maybe.

*Mediator:* Maybe, yeah, OK. You are both here with certain hopes for what we might do, and obviously there are some things that you both are alerted to that really stand very much in the way of those kinds of hopes at the moment.

## Articulating Hope

It is evident in this segment of conversation that the dominance of the conflict story exerts a pull on both parties so that even statements of hope that things might be different are hard to make. In these statements of hope, as they are eventually elicited by the mediator, lie the glimmers of an alternative story about the relationship between these two friends. The narrative perspective encourages us as mediators to have faith in the possibility of things being different if events can be constructed differently or organized into an alternative account. This faith leads the mediator to be persistent at times in the pursuit of the alternative story, even when it seems in danger of being overwhelmed by the dominating force of the conflict story. In this segment of conversation, the question about hopes has to be repeated several times, and tangential answers that refer back to the conflict story have to be negotiated around before even the faint hope for things to be different can be articulated.

Once these hopes had been established, the mediator sought to keep alive the story of hope in the next phase of the conversation, in which the problem story needed to be explored.

*Mediator:* You are both here with certain hopes for what we might do, and yet obviously there are some things that really stand very much in the way of those kinds of hopes at the moment. So I'm wondering if I—I don't know much about the problem as it exists at the moment. You've mentioned just a few things about it. So could you help me to understand a little bit about how things got to this point?

Here the mediator has invited the two parties to define themselves and their relationship differently. Rather than viewing the relationship as defined by the problem, this statement opens the possibility that the relationship might be defined by their hopes, and in the process frames the problem as an obstacle. It prefigures the process of objectifying the problem in an externalizing construction. In this way the momentum of the previous exchange about what the parties hope for from the mediation is not lost and the momentum of the fledgling alternative story, which is still far from being airborne, is maintained.

## Locating the Problem Story in a Historical Context

The next phase of the conversation is about the telling of the problem story and the conflict that emerged. Even here though, the mediator is alert to news of difference. One source of this, as discussed in the previous chapter, is in the history of the relationship.

*Mark:* So, we came to an agreement about how much rent was going to be paid and we thought it was fair, and we worked out how much we might get from some other roommates coming in.

*Mediator:* This was two and a half years ago?

*Mark:* About two and a half years ago we did that, yeah.

*Mediator:* OK, yeah.

*Mark:* And then we started going to the university, and things were pretty good, and then it all turned to shit.

*Mediator:* So when did it start to turn to shit?

*Mark:* When he stopped paying the rent.

*Mediator:* Which was when? How far back?

*Mark:* Well, I don't know. When did your car break down?

*Chris:* About five months ago.

*Mediator:* So for just over two years things went okay, and then the last five months it's gone downhill.

*Mark:* Yeah.

*Mediator:* I'd like to come back in a minute to how things were before it all fell apart. But first, his car broke down, and what happened then?

*Mark:* Well, I mean, friends always have disagreements. Sure, we've had a few, but we seemed to work them out in the end, somehow.

*Mediator:* OK. You seemed to work out those other disagreements, right?

*Mark:* Well, I suppose they just went away. Get on, and go back to the university, and get caught up with assignments and things—you just tend to forget about it.

*Mediator:* So you had these few disagreements, you seemed to work those out. Do you mind if I make a note of that?

Here the mediator is working to create some distinctions, between the time since the conflict started and the time before that, and between the experience of handling disagreements and "working them out" and the current experience of a conflict that seems to defy being worked out. The momentum of the alternative story will be built here by harnessing the experiences of handling conflict successfully and by contextualizing the conflict story inside a wider story of relationship in which most disagreements are worked out.

It is worth noting that the dominance of the problem story is still evident in the comment that the previous disagreements "just went away." The implication is that neither party played any active role in such resolutions—an account that supports the current experience of the impossibility of restoring the friendship. The mediator's response is to ascribe these successes to the two protagonists ("You seemed to work those out") rather than to chance, and then to lend the point extra significance by asking permission to write it down. He could build further on the momentum at this point by asking both parties to explain how they made the disagreements disappear, and by detailing the skills and thought processes that go into "You just tend to forget about it."

## Mapping the Effects of the Problem

The mediator then moves on to asking about the effects of the problem in order to map its influence in the lives of the two parties. Watch here for the use of externalizing language to subtly separate the persons involved from responsibility for the ongoing influence of the problem. This contributes to the momentum of the alternative story as well. The separation of the people from the problem undermines bit by bit the dominance of the conflict story and the parties' entanglement with it. It also sets up a context out of which different accounts of the relationship can be chosen and elaborated.

*Mediator:* So, if, as you say, it's a simple issue of getting the payments in order—like, if he was to do that, would that be enough?

*Mark:* No. I don't know if it would be really.

*Mediator:* What do you mean then?

*Mark:* It's sort of like dragging on and dragging on. It's a bit like he said at the beginning—I don't know if we can ever get it back to what it was like before.

*Mediator:* So it's sort of like there's the problem with the money, but there's also the problem of the whole thing dragging on, and the damage that it's done to your friendship along the way?

*Mark:* Yeah.

*Mediator:* What else?

*Mark:* It would be pretty hard for me to trust him again, wouldn't it? What's to say he starts paying it again and then something else goes wrong with the car and the next thing I'm forking out the rent for the next six months.

*Mediator:* So trust is one of the things that's been damaged by this whole problem, right?

*Mark:* Yep.

*Mediator:* Any other effects of this whole thing for you?

*Mark:* Well, it's all the pressure I get from the family and—

*Mediator:* Yeah. What effect does that have on you?

*Mark:* Well, huge, because they're at me, they're bleating at me about him paying his rent. And yeah, there was a bit of a flexible agreement in there, but not six months' flexibility. You've got to be realistic about these things.

*Mediator:* OK.

*Mark:* There's all that, so they're at me. And then the other roommates are going, "Oh well, if he can get away with it for six months, I might give it a go."

*Mediator:* So there's a spreading effect to the other people?

*Mark:* Yeah.

Clearly a simple settlement-oriented approach will not be enough to address in a satisfying way an issue that is being defined in these terms. A narrative perspective helps us include both the money issue and the trust issue. It rejects the separation of money and values into two separate worlds (for example, a division into facts and emotions) and instead treats both as expressions of meaning. It is in this context of meaning generation that the momentum for the alternative story is being built.

## Responding to Unique Outcomes

As the mediator turns to Chris to pursue the same kind of questioning, an interesting piece of information pops into the conversation.

*Chris:* We had a good couple of years, nothing seemed to go wrong. Yeah, we all have arguments, but healthy ones. And then, really the trouble started the first time my car broke down. I had to put a new motor in it. We worked out how to do it and it would be about two months before—

*Mediator:* Sorry, when you say "we worked out," do you mean you and Mark discussed all that?

*Chris:* Well, we talked about it. Yeah, we talked about. There'd be a couple of months there that I could have some room on the rent, then I could pay this motor off. That was the only way I could see doing it. But at that stage I thought we'd agreed on something that was workable.

*Mark:* Yeah, but there's a big difference between two months and six months.

*Chris:* Yeah, OK. But all the other expenses were kept up to date.

*Mediator:* That would be like power and phone?

*Chris:* Yeah. No shortage of that. And in fact, some months there I'm sure I paid all the phone.

*Mark:* How could you have paid all the phone when there's four of us in the house?

*Chris:* The bill came to me, I paid it.

*Mark:* Yeah, your portion of it.

*Chris:* No, I paid the whole bloody thing. I'll show you.

*Mark:* Yeah, I'd like to see it.

*Mediator:* So, is there something you're saying about the significance of that, that you did pay the phone bill then? What does that demonstrate? What would you like it to demonstrate?

*Chris:* What I was trying to get through there was that it was only the rent that's outstanding, nothing else; all the other bills were paid.

*Mediator:* OK. And that means something about your faithfulness and your honoring of commitments, or something, in that area?

*Chris:* Well, I hope so.

From a problem-solving perspective this might be an irrelevant piece of information. But from a narrative perspective, it is significant precisely because it does not have significance in the ongoing problem story. Hence, still hearing Chris through the meanings constructed within that story, Mark is not keen to grant it much significance. The mediator, however, is alert to the relational meaning of this information for a different story, that which includes the hopes for rebuilding trust between the two parties. He therefore asks the landscape-of-meaning question about what Chris hopes his comments demonstrate.[3] Again, the fledgling alternative story is kept moving, this time by inclusion of an historical reference that achieves thematic significance in the present.

## Creating a Grammatical Alignment Between the Two Parties

*Chris:* The new motor we put in the car blew up.

*Mediator:* Where did that place you?

*Chris:* That put me in a situation where I couldn't start paying rent two months down the track. And we ended up not seeing each other in the apartment for a month. We came and went and we never talked to each other. So I thought, oh well, I'll go with what we've been doing and then, as I say, I was getting all these sarcastic comments and I thought, if I'm going to get such comments, I'll ignore them for a while; and I thought, oh well, eventually something will happen.

*Mark:* I kept leaving him notes, though, too.

*Mediator:* So this is how it developed, right? This whole thing between you. There was the agreement, and then the further problem with your car, and then the month where you didn't see each other much, and the whole thing was just lingering there. And then you, Chris, started to get some comments, some written comments, and sarcastic comments, and then what?

*Chris:* Oh, got my back up. I thought, damn it. I won't pay for a while, make him sweat.

*Mark:* Yeah, and now he owes two grand. I'd like to know how he's going to pay that off.

*Mediator:* It's like this whole thing has just been snowballing, hasn't it? Is that right? And along the way it got your back up, Mark, and got you, Chris, into a place of thinking, "Well, I won't bother," or what?

*Chris:* Well, I don't know. We always used to be able to resolve things, and I thought we'd eventually do that, but it didn't happen this time.

*Mediator:* Like, somehow you kept having some hope, based on your previous experience, that you would be able to resolve it?

*Chris:* Well, I mean, we've known each other, what, six years now? Since high school.

*Mediator:* So did you have the same kind of thought there? Did you hope that because you've been able to sort things out in the past, that would happen this time?

*Mark:* Yeah, but that was never money. Money was never involved.

*Mediator:* So somehow this particular difference between you sort of tricked you in some ways because in the past you'd been able to deal with all these other things? Is that right?

*Mark:* Oh, I suppose, but I don't know if I want to be his friend anymore.

*Mediator:* Yeah. I'm just trying to get at how this kept going, getting bigger, and kept escalating and snowballing.

*Mark:* Yeah. Oh well. I suppose he was never there, I was never there, and we were trying to sort it out. I don't know. I got pissed off with him, really.

*Mediator:* Right. Was it like, it got to the point for both of you that it started to get too big for you?

The story of what happened between Mark and Chris is further elaborated here. But it is told in a particular way. The externalizing of "this whole thing" and the inclusion of both parties' actions in a recursive scenario that is bigger than either of them individually is juxtaposed to the preferred theme of hope. This theme is an echo of the opening discussion about hope and serves to maintain the momentum of the alternative story. The impression created by the development of this frame around the events is that Mark and Chris have both been trying to sort this problem out, even though their efforts have been somewhat feeble at times. The conflict is talked about not as an expression of their relationship but as an enemy of it. And they are both aligned, grammatically, as recipients of its malevolent designs.

*Mediator:* So, coming back to you, Chris, how would you summarize the effects of this whole thing on you?

*Chris:* Made me a bit bitter.

*Mediator:* Do you want to tell me a bit more about that? What do you mean by bitter?

*Chris:* It seems to have reached an impasse. I've got a block we just can't seem to get past. Every time we, one or other, wants to do something about it, the other one gets in a snoot.

*Mediator:* So, from your point of view, you've wanted to do something about it and it got to an impasse when you tried and you couldn't get past that, is that right?

*Chris:* I tried organizing an automatic payment. It was like I wasn't being listened to.

*Mediator:* So you tried to organize an automatic payment? Was that one thing that led to an impasse? You were trying to do something to solve it and it didn't work?

*Chris:* Well, I wanted to get at least a current rent going so that it wouldn't get any worse.

*Mediator:* So, OK, that's an example of something you tried, that you were trying to move things in the direction of dealing with this thing and because you couldn't get the number, that left you frustrated, and—

*Chris:* Yeah.

*Mediator:* And that's where the bitterness started to come in? Is that right?

*Chris:* Well, I don't know whether *bitter* is the right word. It could be, like he doesn't seem to care, so I don't seem to care. I'm bitter about the friendship, but I don't give a damn about the money.

*Mediator:*  Hang on, I just want to be clear about this. You feel
bitter about the friendship, but what's the other bit?
*Chris:*  Oh, feeling like I'm numb about the money.

We said earlier that an externalizing construction served the
purpose of grammatically aligning the two parties against the objectified problem. Here the momentum of the alternative story is
maintained with a grammatical move as well. Chris is spoken to as
the subject of a series of actions, all aimed in the direction of his
hopes for things to be different. As the subject of the sentences in
which these actions are described, he is invited to think of them as
subjective acts and to step into a subjective view of himself as someone who wants to resolve the conflict. By contrast, the conflict story
is grammatically depersonalized and objectified. It becomes a series of static nouns and pronouns (bitterness, impasse, it, this
whole thing) while the alternative story features more grammatically in the verbs of these sentences. Verbs carry ongoing processes
forward.

In this grammatical context, which the mediator is quite actively building, a unique outcome appears (the automatic payment) and assumes some significance. It is noteworthy that this
information about the attempted automatic payment enters the
conversation at this time. We suggest that it is not coincidental. At
some level, Chris is conscious that mentioning this action helps
construct him as active rather than passive in the ongoing plot.

*Mediator:*  And that numbness, what's that lead you to do?
*Mark:*  Not pay his rent here.
*Mediator:*  So it's like, the dispute kind of grew. Does that fit with
how you're understanding it, too?
*Chris:*  Umm-hmm.
*Mediator:*  The dispute grew, and then it kind of got you to feel
more and more numb to that whole issue. And the
more you did that, the more you didn't pay, couldn't
be bothered to deal with it and pay the rent. I imagine
that when you had this idea of the automatic payment
then couldn't get the number, you felt, well, stuff it,
I'll give up, almost.

*Mark:* Yeah, but about that automatic payment. I tried to tell him that it's got to go through my bank account, and he just didn't want to listen, he wanted my parents' bank account.

*Mediator:* OK. So did you try and talk to him about that?

*Mark:* Yeah, but he just wouldn't listen.

*Mediator:* So when Mark was saying this about the bank account, and that he wanted the money to go into his bank account, what did you do? Did you just not listen to that, or argue with it, or—

*Chris:* I switched off.

*Mediator:* So, is that like the numbness, the switching off? Is it the same kind of thing?

*Chris:* Yeah.

*Mediator:* And when the switching off takes place over here, where does that leave you, Mark?

*Mark:* I get bloody angry. He just takes advantage. I've been trying to sort it out, but it just goes on and on.

*Mediator:* So, for both of you, you tried to do something to get it sorted out. He switches off, and then you're just left frustrated, right?

*Mark:* Umm-hmm.

*Mediator:* That's sort of how this has snowballed backwards and forwards and left you both in a real impasse. I'm just summarizing things here; is that fair enough? Does that feel right for you?

*Chris:* Yeah.

*Mediator:* It's like this whole thing just kept growing bigger and bigger. And despite you both having thoughts that you'd like to solve it, it just kind of kept growing?

*Mark:* Umm-hmm.

Again we go back to mapping the effects of the problem story, but this time in finer detail and in a way that traces the plot events as they are woven backward and forward between the two protagonists. Each person's actions in the conflict story are constructed as part of a larger relational whole that has caught them up and driven the conflict forward. This construction aids the developing story of two former friends who have basically honorable intentions that have been subverted by the more sinister designs of the problem story, which is consistently externalized by the mediator as a distinct entity. What gets disrupted here is the interpretation of each other's actions as intentionally provocative. Instead, they can come to be understood as products of the discursive world out of which the relationship has been produced, products that neither individual is primarily responsible for.

## Establishing the Platform for Change

*Mediator:*  So, what's it like just to think about that right now?

*Mark:*  I just want my money.

*Mediator:*  You want to get out of it, right?

*Mark:*  Yeah.

*Mediator:*  You want to get out of this whole bind?

*Mark:*  Yeah, and whether that means we go our separate ways, or whatever, I mean I've got this two grand debt that I owe to my parents. I can't afford it.

*Mediator:*  Yep. [*Turns to Chris*] So, what's it like for you to sit and think about this whole thing, and how it's grown and just taken over like that, and gotten bigger and bigger? Do you kind of want to get out of it?

*Chris:*  No, I don't really want out of it, but I would like it over.

*Mediator:*  You'd like it over?

*Chris:*  Umm-hmm.

*Mediator:*  Are you saying, then, that it's not really acceptable to you that this thing just keeps on snowballing?

*Chris:*  No.

*Mediator:*  Is that right? And I think you're saying something similar. In a way, its not acceptable to you that this just keeps getting worse.

*Mark:*  No.

*Mediator:*  Because you want, as you say, you want your money, you want it solved.

*Mark:*  Yeah, just the rent. He's still living there. All his gear's there. Each week that goes by there's more rent. So, if he's not going to pay his rent, then he'll have to go.

*Mediator:*  So would it be fair to say, then, you're actually, in a sense—I mean we haven't solved this in any way but

> there is some agreement between you that this thing just keeps on getting worse is not acceptable to both of you?
>
> *Mark:* Yeah.
>
> *Mediator:* Is that right? You'd agree on that? OK. Does that mean that you have, both of you, at this moment as we sit and think about it, some sort of motivation, at least, if not ideas about how—some motivation to actually get this thing shifted?
>
> *Chris:* Yeah, I'm keen to get it sorted out.

At this point the platform created by the process of an externalizing conversation is ready to be stood on. The effects of the problem for both parties have been mapped and the recursive patterns of conflictual interaction have been traced. Here the mediator asks a series of small questions that lead the parties into making a statement of an intention to resolve the dispute. In a way, this statement revisits the declaration of hope that each party made at the beginning of the conversation, but it also builds the momentum for resolution because this time the declarations are made in the context of having visited all the negative effects of the conflict. The pain caused by the dispute itself is now harnessed to the wagon of change rather than to blaming each other. At this point, another piece of news pops into the conversation.

> *Chris:* I've got a couple of month's rent in the bank, just sitting there waiting. Until I saw a different attitude I wasn't going to part with it.
>
> *Mediator:* Right. [*To Mark*] Does it make any difference to know that he's got the money?
>
> *Mark:* Yeah, he can pay it now, get his checkbook out.
>
> *Mediator:* Are you willing to do something?
>
> *Chris:* Yeah, well, I said I wanted to solve it.
>
> *Mediator:* So you have two months' money there?
>
> *Chris:* Yeah.
>
> *Mediator:* Are you saying that you are willing to start solving this by paying some of that, that two months' money that you've got? Is that what you are saying? I don't want to jump to conclusions.

*Chris:* Well, yeah, but I want to see a change in attitude, I want the comments to stop; I mean they just got worse.

*Mediator:* Have you heard anything that Mark has said today that fits into the sarcastic comments?

*Chris:* The attitude's the same, it hasn't stopped.

*Mediator:* So what do you mean by sarcastic comments? I'm not quite sure.

*Chris:* Oh, little digs, little windups. Just annoying little things, little references that just target things.

*Mediator:* Have you heard him say some other things that don't fit with the sarcastic comments, or the windups, or the things that get to you? Have you heard him say anything else that's more like the kind of attitude you'd like to hear?

*Chris:* Well, there's what he said about a couple of years of living together. To hear him go on, I thought it was like a bloody marriage, jeez.

*Mediator:* So you heard that as, what, as him talking about your friendship in glowing terms over those years?

*Chris:* Yeah. And our friendship was good, and we did spend a lot of time together.

*Mediator:* So, when you heard him talking about your friendship, as he did, OK, it may have been a bit much for you, almost, hearing that; but was that more in the direction of the kind of attitude you're wanting to hear?

*Chris:* Yeah, yeah.

*Mediator:* Anything else Mark has said today that is more inclined toward an attitude that you're going to hear as being helpful in this situation?

*Chris:* Oh, he seems to be under a lot more pressure from the family than I understood.

*Mediator:* So was that news to you to hear some of that?

*Chris:* I didn't know that he was under that much pressure.

*Mediator:* Knowing about that, does that make a difference in some way? Like, does it alter your understanding?

*Chris:* Well, it might have made a difference about that initial two months of rent.

*Mediator:* Right. Okay.

*Chris:*  We might have had to look at, well, I would have a
        look at another way. If there's going to be that much
        shit go down over it, I'd have had another look at
        another way about paying off the motor.
*Mediator:*  So, that knowledge back then would have made
        quite a difference to how you would have dealt with
        it? Is there room for that to happen now, like could
        knowing that help give you some inkling of a way
        forward?

A problem-solving attitude might direct us to focus here mainly
on the money in the bank and what might be negotiated to get it
paid. A narrative emphasis, however, equally foregrounds the relational issues.[4] There are a series of unique outcomes in Chris's
responses. One is the news that he has a significant amount of
money in the bank. Another is that he has seen some evidence of
a different attitude from Mark that eases the way for him to make
moves in the direction of settlement. Then there is the gesture of
understanding he makes toward Mark about the family pressure
the problem has caused. These are relational moves that the mediator asks about further in order to hear them echo through the
relational chamber.

## Building Shared Meanings

Questions about what difference a unique outcome makes are subtle moves into the landscape of meaning. These questions do not
take for granted the significance of anything; they build the momentum of the story of resolution slowly, piece by piece. Nevertheless, the mediator assumes that there will be some significance
to each unique outcome, and such questions at times invite creation of that significance rather than simply ask for it to be reported. The curiosity is therefore purposeful in developing
momentum for the story of hope. The next step in the building of
this momentum is to ask about the significance of what Chris has
been saying to Mark.

*Mediator:*  What does that mean to you to hear that?
*Mark:*  Well, hopefully that means he's going to pay the out-
        standing amount.

    *Chris:*  Well I never said I wouldn't.

    *Mark:*  Well you haven't done it to date have you? I'd just like to see it resolved. I'd just like him to work out some way of paying the money back.

*Mediator:*  What I'm hearing here from both of you is that there are two issues. One is sorting out the money thing, and the other is the attitudes and exchanges and comments and stuff that go on between you, or the meaning that you make about the problem with the money, that seems to have got in the way all the time of you actually addressing the money problem. Mark, I'm wondering if there's anything you're hearing Chris say that gives you some inkling of a way forward in terms of sorting out the attitudes that will get the money paid?

    *Mark:*  Yeah, well, I must say I did say a few sarcastic things, but I'd just had a gutful of it.

*Mediator:*  So, the whole problem led you into saying some things that normally you wouldn't say, is that what you mean?

    *Mark:*  Well, yeah, yeah, I suppose so.

*Mediator:*  Do you even regret saying some of those things?

    *Mark:*  Not really.

*Mediator:*  You wouldn't go that far? Would you prefer not to have had to get to the point where you had to say them?

    *Mark:*  Yeah, exactly, yeah.

*Mediator:*  Are you hearing Chris say anything that's giving you any kind of encouragement at this point?

    *Mark:*  Yeah, he's got two months' rent in his bank account.

*Mediator:*  That helps, right? Anything else?

    *Mark:*  Oh, well, at least he now seems to understand that I was under pressure from my parents.

*Mediator:*  Does that make a difference, do you think?

    *Mark:*  Yeah.

*Mediator:*  What difference does it make?

    *Mark:*  Well, now he believes me. He didn't seem to believe me before when I was telling him that my parents were on my back about it, but he seems to believe it now.

*Mediator:*  So is that, like, a start?

    *Mark:*  Yeah, I suppose it is, yeah.

*Mediator:* What do you think it might be the start of?

*Mark:* Oh, well, I don't know if we're going to be able to repair our friendship back to where it was, because it's been six months of this going on. Sure, he could stay there and we could get the rent going regularly, and we could see how it works out, but I don't know if it's going to.

*Mediator:* Do you have any ideas about what it would take to get the friendship, maybe not back to where it was but started a little bit again?

*Mark:* It's been ongoing. I don't know how we could start it off again.

*Mediator:* What if it wasn't ongoing?

*Mark:* Well, if it hadn't been ongoing we most probably wouldn't have gotten to this situation.

*Mediator:* I guess I'm thinking about what things would be important for you to hear from Chris.

*Mark:* Well, that he's sorry might be a start. He seems to think that I was in a position to be able to carry him for six months, so an apology would be decent.

*Mediator:* OK, that would be some recognition of the pressure?

*Mark:* Yeah. I was trying to be a good friend, trying to do the best for him by letting him get his car fixed, because I know he needs his car for work. But he took advantage of me, and that's what's landed us here today.

*Mediator:* Did you understand at the time that Mark was doing that as a friend rather than as a landlord?

*Chris:* No, I didn't see the distinction.

*Mediator:* So Mark's just made a distinction. Does that mean anything to you, that distinction, as he makes it now, or does it add to your understanding of what happened?

*Chris:* Well, I suppose if you ask me to decide where he was coming from I'd say it would be as a friend.

*Mediator:* OK, so you did recognize that?

*Chris:* No, I'd say if you asked me now.

In these exchanges the mediator weaves deliberately back and forth between the two disputants. One person's statements become opportunities for the other to make new meanings. The mediator asks questions to elicit the meaning making. That this is done in front of the other person is important. Each person speaks into the context of the other's hearing. Even when they speak to the mediator, they are constructing each other as an overhearing audience to the utterance. Knowing that the other is hearing adds another layer of significance to what is being said. The mediator then seeks to make this layer explicit by asking something like, "What does it mean to you to hear him say that?" Each statement invites a reflective response from the other. The mediator facilitates this response, which then becomes a statement for the other to respond to.

The mediator is acting like a conductor orchestrating the playing of a piece of music. In the process, the momentum of the story of hope for the friendship enters a new phase. For the first time the two former friends are considering openly in front of each other the possibility of a future friendship.

| | |
|---|---|
| *Chris:* | Well, even just talking about it here, some of how we used to feel about each other, I can feel that again. The coldness that was there when we walked in has gone. |
| *Mediator:* | Wow! And instead you feel some—what? |
| *Chris:* | Some kind of response. |
| *Mediator:* | So you feel some kind of response now? Could you name that response? |
| *Chris:* | I don't know how to label it. The numbness has gone. |
| *Mediator:* | [*To Mark*] What's happened for you while we were talking? |
| *Mark:* | Well, we might be able to be friends again, I don't know. I hadn't figured friends did this to each other, so— |
| *Mediator:* | There has to be some pretty major repair work before that could be possible from your perspective? |
| *Mark:* | Well, we just have to get this sorted out, and then, whether we remain friends—but as long the issue remains, if that can be resolved, then maybe we can go on. I don't like to hold grudges or anything, and we have been friends for a long time. |
| *Mediator:* | OK. So are you at a point where you've got ideas about what you can do about this? Whether we can start to talk about some of those things? |

*Chris:*   Well, I think we need to get the money thing sorted out first.

*Mediator:*   You've got some ideas there.

*Chris:*   Yeah. I probably think I want to sleep on it.

*Mediator:*   When you say "sleep on it," if we were to come back tomorrow, for example, is that what you mean? And actually discuss how to deal with the money, is that what you mean?

*Mark:*   So is he saying that he's going to sleep on it, but does that mean, yes, he is going to pay it tomorrow, or is he going to sleep on whether he pays for it or not?

*Mediator:*   What's your concern?

*Mark:*   Well, we might be sleeping on it for another five months. He hasn't committed to anything yet.

*Mediator:*   So you want something a bit more in terms of good faith, or something like that?

*Mark:*   Yeah, I want something a bit more set in concrete at this stage, yeah.

*Mediator:*   Given that you've been waiting for five months, is what, waiting until tomorrow going to make a lot of difference?

*Mark:*   No. No. It's not so much that it's going to make, that it's another day—okay, because we have been waiting for that long; but it's just like, oh here we go, it's another day again.

*Mediator:*   You're looking for something today that's going to ease that sense of pressure for you?

*Mark:*   Yeah, yeah. Exactly.

*Mediator:*   [*To Chris*] Is there anything you can say in response to Mark's concern about the pressure he's still feeling that would give him some sense of reassurance?

*Chris:*   I'll say, you'll get an absolute definite answer tomorrow, and if that two months is there, that can be the first payment.

*Mark:*   OK.

*Mediator:*   We're at a point where we do need to stop for the day. Would it be okay if we left it at this point for the day and came back tomorrow and worked out what you're actually going to do to sort this out?

At this point in the mediation, the relational context was built and had gathered enough momentum for the working out of the details of the money dispute to take place relatively quickly and easily. The two former friends met with the mediator the next day and within minutes had worked out the payment of most of the rent arrears as well as a payment schedule for the rest. Chris also undertook to write to Mark's parents and take responsibility for the problem. He did in fact move out of the house, but he and Mark also agreed to do some social things together that they had not done for a long time.

The point that needs to be underlined about a narrative approach to mediation such as the one illustrated in this chapter is that the settlement negotiation happens relatively effortlessly and usually quite quickly. It is not so much through the negotiation of outcomes that the relationship is restored (in disputes in which there is a possibility of ongoing relationship between the parties). Rather, the relational context itself is addressed as a site for narrative development and the settlement negotiation is treated as a natural outgrowth of that context.[5]

## Notes

1. Bruner, J., *Actual Minds, Possible Worlds* (Cambridge, Mass.: Harvard University Press, 1986).
2. White, M., and Epston, D., *Narrative Means to Therapeutic Ends* (New York: Norton, 1991); Monk, G., Winslade, J., Crocket, K., and Epston, D., *Narrative Therapy in Practice: The Archaeology of Hope* (San Francisco: Jossey-Bass, 1997); Freedman, J., and Combs, G., *Narrative Therapy: The Social Construction of Preferred Realities* (New York: Norton, 1996); Dickerson, V., and Zimmerman, J., *If Problems Talked: Narrative Therapy in Action* (New York: Guilford Press, 1996).
3. Bruner, J., *Actual Minds, Possible Worlds.*
4. Winslade, J., and Cotter, A., "Moving from Problem-Solving to Narrative Approaches in Mediation," in G. Monk, J. Winslade, K. Crocket, and D. Epston (eds.), *Narrative Therapy in Practice: The Archaeology of Hope* (San Francisco: Jossey-Bass, 1997); Winslade, J., Monk, G., and Cotter, A., "A Narrative Approach to the Practice of Mediation," *Negotiation Journal*, 1998, *14*(1), 21–42.
5. Winslade and Cotter, "Moving from Problem-Solving to Narrative Approaches in Mediation"; Winslade, Monk, and Cotter, "A Narrative Approach to the Practice of Mediation."

Chapter Nine

# Getting Unstuck

*All is vanity and vexation of spirit!*
(ECCLESIASTES 1:14)

*Now here, you see, it takes all the running you can do, to stay in the same place. If you want to get somewhere else, you must run at least twice as fast as that!*
(LEWIS CARROLL, "THROUGH THE LOOKING GLASS")

*. . . I have never made friends but by spiritual gifts,*
*By severe contentions of friendship and the burning fire*
*of thought.*
(WILLIAM BLAKE, "JERUSALEM")

In this chapter we address some of the more difficult aspects of mediation. We want to look at some places where the process can get stuck and where there can be threats to undermine it altogether. The kinds of difficulties we speak about here include the barren desert where there is little goodwill, the threat or fear of violence, the mire of traded insults and putdowns, the obstacle of defensiveness, and the absence of compassion and empathy. We concentrate our attention on the field of mediation between separating couples because it is in this field that we have seen intense examples of these kinds of relational impasses. A number of narrative ideas can be useful at such points. We offer a smorgasbord of suggestions for mediators to consider as tools to help them and their clients get through such difficulties.

---

This chapter was written with the help of Wally McKenzie.

# Absence of Goodwill

When couples are separating, goodwill can get to the point where it is largely used up or seems to be in very short supply. Both parties are in places of intensive defense of their positions. This becomes manifest in the throwing of garbage over each other in the form of resentments from the past. As one person drags up an incident that proves what is wrong with the other person and why they can't be trusted, the other person is prompted to do the same. The logic of such exchanges is very much an internalizing one. Each move in the cycle of blame and resentment focuses attention on the internal characteristics of the other person and seeks to pin an interpretation of the problems of the marriage, or of the separation, on these characteristics. Such exchanges can lead to rapid escalation of conflict, and whatever goodwill still exists can seem to fly out the window at this point. Mediators need to be ready to respond to these situations rapidly.

Michael White describes an innovative way of interrupting this kind of exchange and of using an externalizing conversation to make room for goodwill to come back into the room. He tells of a couple who started arguing in front of him with little invitation to do so. He listened for a little while and then interrupted, thanking them both for being so open about the problems they were having with each other and "for providing such a clear demonstration of how things go for them."[1] The couple heard this, paused briefly, but took little notice and soon commenced to argue again. White repeated his message. He thanked them again, saying he believed he had a reasonable understanding of their experience of the relationship, and informed them that "further demonstrations of this will be unnecessary." Patterns of conflict have a momentum of their own, it seems, because the couple continued to argue. White reports that he repeated his interruption twice more before the couple was prepared to stop arguing and listen for a minute while he asked some questions.

White spoke about their "pattern of interacting" in an externalizing conversation. He asked the couple to what extent this adversarial pattern of interacting was dominating their relationship, how it was influencing their perceptions of each other, and whether it was having them do things to each other that were against their better judgment. This led to both parties making statements that this adversarial pattern of relating was not their preference. After further deconstruction of the supports for this pattern of relating, they began to enter into a conversation about their preferred way of dealing with the outstanding issues of their relationship. They anchored this preferred path in their own history and then employed it to address the issues of access, custody, and property.

Another approach to this issue is to negotiate a way of structuring the conversation to avoid these exchanges. This idea comes from Wally McKenzie.[2] As the mediator, McKenzie might say to the woman, for example, "Do you mind if I have a conversation with your husband for a while? You don't have to join in this conversation. It won't be that I am being rude to you. In fact, can you just really concentrate on listening for a while and see if you can hear anything that strikes a chord with you or that might be a basis for a small piece of hope in what he has to say?"

Then, turning to the man, McKenzie might ask, "Is it OK with you if I talk to you for a while and ask her to listen?" He would then interview the man about the history of goodwill between him and his wife, inquiring about what he has noticed about their goodwill, such as when it is more available and when it is less available. When has he felt more goodwill and what has helped that to emerge? At the end of this conversation, which might take some time, McKenzie would thank the man and ask him if he wouldn't mind listening for a while as McKenzie asks the woman some questions. He would then turn to the woman and interview her about goodwill while the man listened and reflected on what he heard her say. This inquiry would include asking the woman what she found of interest in what the man said. At the end of this conversation, McKenzie would ask the man also to reflect out loud on what he heard his wife say.

Along the way McKenzie would add some further checks. He might ask the person who is listening if it is okay to talk for a while longer to the other person. He might ask the person who has been talking about goodwill whether there is anything else he or she could say that might be helpful to notice, perhaps something that the mediator missed asking about.

Several things are achieved by this approach. One is that the pattern of defensive reacting is interrupted and the need to defend a position is removed. Instead, a more reflective conversation is initiated in which interruptions do not dominate and the participants have more room to speak their minds. They are also invited to listen more attentively, without the distraction of feeling compelled to respond immediately. When they do eventually respond, they have had the chance to reflect on their responses and to process them in the light of the additional information they have received from the other person. Moreover, the mediator's questions would hopefully have invited each participant to say some things that have never been said before in the relationship, especially not in the context of conflict. Another difference in this approach is that the focus is shifted from a cycle of blame to a cycle of hope because the subject of the inquiry is not problem-focused. The very nature of a conversation about a person's relationship with goodwill generates an externalizing conversation that does not take goodwill for granted as an internal characteristic of an individual. Instead, goodwill is conceived of as related to context and history and as happening in the social spaces occupied by discourse between people.

## Motivation to Attend a Mediation

Sometimes one party is more motivated than the other party to attend the mediation. If the invitation to mediation comes from one party to the other, the conflict itself can set people in opposition about the mediation process. From the perspective of someone in a conflict who is firmly set against another person, the proposal to mediate might be seen as a foolish idea simply because it is being proposed by the other person. For this reason, it is important for mediators to consider carefully the assumptions they make about people's motivations for participating in mediation. For example, many times we have seen the situation where one party predicts with absolute certainty that the other party will not be at all interested in participating and yet when we talk to the other person, he or she is much more willing to play ball than the other person predicted.

Another assumption to be avoided is that motivation is a stable, internal characteristic of an individual. Descriptions of people as "motivated" or "not motivated" are, from a narrative perspective, problematic notions that rest on a psychology that is very different from the assumptions on which the narrative approach is built. These are classic internalizing descriptions that reify a conclusion drawn from a relational context and account for it by referring to it as an internal attitude. From this perspective, what is being expressed in the relationship is regarded as a simple representation of the internal attitude of low or high motivation. A social constructionist interpretation might lead us to a quite different account. This reading might account for the presence or absence of motivation as a product of the relational exchanges that are taking place. If motivation is in short supply, we might wonder what is happening in the relations between people that is diminishing it.

This perspective is quite similar to the view of motivation proposed by William Miller and Stephen Rollnick in their exposition of the principles of *motivational interviewing* in the field of alcohol and drug counseling.[3] They argue against the usefulness of what is in effect an individualistic, internalizing conception of motivation and in favor of a definition of motivation as a "state of readiness" produced in a relationship between a counselor and a client. In mediation, then, we might consider a person's motivation to attend the mediation as a product of the conversations in which the mediation process is being discussed. This is consistent with the constructionist idea that discourses get mapped onto the psychology of individuals rather than the psychological dynamics of the individual getting expressed in discourse or in relations between people.

From this perspective, it follows that the mediator is not let off the hook by ascribing the responsibility for a motivation problem to an individual. The challenge remains to craft the kind of relationship that invites into existence the motivation to participate. There may be many situations where other relations (such as those in which the conflict is embedded) or sets of relations (such as established influential patterns of relations between men and women) operate to construct people's expectations of mediation in ways that make the generation of motivation difficult. At times they may make it impossible. However, the mediator should not assume that this will be the case. Such assumptions carry with them what amounts to a subtly disrespectful attitude that can easily be read as calling a person into a position in which they will be treated as difficult from the start. When read this way by the person concerned, motivation is more likely to decrease. Conversely, the ethic of respect requires a mediator to approach the parties with an expectation of motivation that is set slightly higher than either of the parties might feel free to express, while still paying attention to the forces that can operate against motivation.

Here, then, are some conversational moves that might embody this kind of respect. Many of these are borrowed from *Motivational Interviewing: Preparing People to Change Addictive Behavior* by Miller and Rollnick.

- Affirm the person's right to choose whether or not to participate and indicate that you will respect their decision not to do so if that is their choice.
- Avoid getting into persuasive talk, which can simply invite stubbornness forward.
- Express interest and respectful curiosity about low levels of motivation rather than expressing disappointment.
- Acknowledge ambivalence and empathize with it.
- Acknowledge and pay respect to the forces that would decrease motivation to participate.
- Invite the person to present to you the reasons for and against participation and then invite them to weigh these against each other.
- If the person is feeling more strongly persuaded by the reasons against participation, ask if there are any possible assurances that could be given that would lead to a change of mind.
- Roll with resistance and treat it as a stance that makes a lot of sense to this person at this time, rather than treating it as an obstacle to be overcome or engaging in an argument with it.
- Ask someone who is leaning away from participating to think forward in time and consider whether in two months (or six months or a year or whatever period seems relevant) they might possibly look back at this point and regret not having taken part.
- Accept a decision not to participate and repeat an affirmation of the person's right to choose that option.

Later in this chapter we show how using motivational interviewing by avoiding persuasive talk and rolling with resistance leads to a desirable outcome in a mediation.

# Treading on Eggshells Around an Issue

Sometimes people come into a mediation so nervous about the conflict and its effects that they stand back from expressing their feelings. Rather than directly addressing their central concerns, they skirt around the most sensitive issues over which they differ. This caution can assist the mediator to establish rapport with the parties and engender an atmosphere of respect and cooperation early on. However, after a while the mediator can start to sense that there is a large gap in the conversation. It is as if an elephant is sitting in the room taking up a lot of space but everyone is pretending to ignore it.

In this context, the mediator might sense that something is not quite right but may not be able to establish exactly what is amiss. Conversely, if the mediator has met separately with each of the parties before the joint meeting, she might very well know what is not being spoken about. We now explore some strategies a mediator might use at this point.

The first strategy is to preempt this eventuality by preparing the parties carefully for the joint meeting. This preparation can be achieved by using the separate meetings before the joint meeting to address the sensitive issues and discuss each person's relationship with the issues. Nervousness can be spoken out loud and externalized as an issue that might enter the room like a third party to the mediation. The mediator can ask the person what would be necessary to keep nervousness from taking charge of the meeting and silencing the person.

A second strategy, applicable in the joint meeting, is for the mediator to use *immediacy*.[4] This involves interrupting the discussion of substantive issues to talk about the process and how people are experiencing it. The mediator may wonder out loud about whether nervousness or anxiety is affecting everyone and preventing some things from being spoken.

Sometimes, of course, there are some very sensible reasons for someone keeping quiet about something. There may be a threat hanging over the mediation that the mediator does not know about. Threats of violence, for instance, might very well inhibit the possibility of substantive progress being made on the sensitive issues. Mediators need to be alert to these possibilities and should avoid trying to force people into opening up when it might not be safe for them to do so. If the mediator senses that violence might be lurking in the background, it is better to call a halt to the mediation, at least until safety issues are clarified. Our preference would be to meet separately with each party at this point.

Another strategy is based on the narrative idea of *negative explanation*. From this perspective, the mediator does not inquire about positive causes of the silence. However, negative restraints from speaking openly are made the subject of inquiry. The mediator might ask what is holding the people back from speaking about important issues. This inquiry may take place in the joint meeting or it may require a separate meeting with each of the parties. In either case, the restraints that are identified can be externalized rather than internalized as essential feelings or characteristics of the persons concerned.

Finally, *internalized other questions* can be useful at this point.[5] Both parties can be invited to say what they think the other person might be concerned about that has not yet been spoken. The most powerful approach is to ask them to speak as if they were the other person and to comment on what has been said so far and what might need to be addressed. This strategy achieves several purposes at once. First, it is likely to bring out into the open what is being politely stepped around. Second, it lets each person know that the other person understands his or her concerns. In this way, it assists the development of empathy and cooperation between the parties. Third, it ensures that the expression of the issue does not in itself become an inflammatory concern.

## Not Taking the Other Person's Concerns Seriously

Suppose that in the context of a separation a woman has been endeavoring for some time to get her husband to pay attention to some issues in the relationship that she wants to change. Given the dominance of patriarchal ideas and the attendant assumptions of male privilege that easily produce an exaggerated sense of entitlement for men in a relationship, it is not uncommon for this to be the way things are. The woman is unhappy with the organization of her marriage around such patriarchal assumptions and wants to challenge this situation. She makes a series of attempts to have her voice heard. She becomes frustrated, however, at the way her attempts are shrugged off and not taken seriously or treated as her problem and not her husband's. In the end she resorts to separation as an expression of this frustration.

How can a mediator respond to such a situation? Armed with a social constructionist analysis of power relations, we cannot take a neutral stance on the issue of subjugated voices deserving to be heard. We would support the woman in her challenge against patriarchal privilege, but we would not express this support in ways that objectify or pathologize the husband if we are not simply to recreate another form of colonizing. Nor would we express support for one party's views in a way that would set up a barrier between us and the other party or that is disrespectful of or disrupts our relationship with the other party. Simple advocacy, therefore, is often not enough. An approach is needed that is evenhanded and responsive to both parties, even while supporting the process of having one of the party's concerns taken seriously and addressed.

Wally McKenzie has developed ways of telling stories in these situations. Rather than speaking about his own opinion and risking the start of a debate, he tells a story of a similar situation from another client and then asks the man what he thinks of this story. Here's an example of a story that McKenzie might tell.

I wonder if you might be interested in the story of another man in something like your situation. He sat in that chair and his wife sat in that chair. His wife said to him, "I'm leaving because I've been talking to you about these things for months and months and not getting anywhere. So I'm leaving for now but I am not yet leaving the marriage. I've got an apartment and I'm going to go and live in it, but if we can sort some things out I will come back. I want to come back, but right now I am leaving because I want you to take this seriously."

Her husband then asked what was wrong. He wrote down on a piece of paper the things she had said and appeared to be taking them very seriously. But next time they met he had made no changes whatsoever and she was very disappointed and upset. At the end of the session he made a derogatory remark to her. I said, "When I hear you make that comment I wonder if you feel that you're tempting fate a bit here, pushing the limits fairly hard, given the seriousness of the situation? I'm also wondering what you think your wife might make of that comment."

"Oh, no, no," he said. "It's just a joke, it's all right."

At the next meeting he came on his own and there were tears running down his face when he came in. He reported that she had phoned him three nights previously and told him that it was over. "I never believed she would do that."

So I asked him why he didn't take it seriously enough. He replied, "Oh you know, us men, we think, 'She'll get over it.' It's one of those woman things. Time of the month or something like that. I can't believe how stupid I was. I didn't take it seriously, and now it's too late. I've lost her."

At the end of telling this story, McKenzie would ask the man, perhaps in front of his wife, "That's what he told me. What do you think of that story?" Other questions can follow that get at the man's understanding of what this story means. McKenzie reports one client in particular who responded to this story by saying, "I don't think I took her seriously enough either."

On other occasions the story might be about children's perspectives. These stories can be useful in discussions of custody and access issues between parents, especially when the father is focusing on his own preoccupations and not taking the effects of the issues on the children seriously. In this case, the story might be about an interview with a child in which the child's knowledge of what he or she wants from his or her father is expressed in a direct and powerful way.

For example, one story McKenzie uses is of a six-year-old girl, Fran, who told him that she was unhappy with how her father yelled at her and smacked her if she did something wrong. McKenzie asked Fran what her father would need to do to make him a great dad. With McKenzie's help, Fran made a list of things she would like from her father. The list had such an impact on her dad that Wally has developed the list with the help of other children who are troubled by ongoing conflict between their parents. It has become an excellent resource that has had the effect of inviting parents to look quite differently at the cost of conflict for their children. Parents can take a copy and place it on their refrigerator door or bulletin board to remind them what most children want from their parents when they separate. We present this list here with McKenzie's permission.

*My Dream Mom and Dad*

1. They would let each other see their children as much and as often as they can.
2. It would be great if Mom and Dad just got along—not even as friends would be OK.
3. They would encourage the children to have a good time with the other parent.
4. They would not swear at their children.
5. They might punish their children a bit if they are naughty and that's OK. But they wouldn't hit us.
6. They will appreciate and love their children by telling them so when they come and stay or call up and talk.
7. They would try to create a home where the children would look forward to coming back and want to call them up.
8. They would talk about parent things with each other and not talk to the children about parent things.
9. They would swap or share birthdays and Christmases in a helpful way without getting angry at each other.
10. They would keep their promises to us.
11. They would not bad-mouth each other.
12. When they get angry with each other it messes up their love for us. Hating each other makes it harder for children.
13. They would both talk to all our teachers—maybe not together though.
14. They would be really busy loving their children, not fighting over them. They would know that there was enough of their children to love and go around for everyone.
15. They would each sit down with their children from time to time and ask them "How's it going?" and "How could it be better?"
16. Parents should have to go for a tune up from time to time for being separated parents. How else do they know how they are doing?

Mothers, fathers, and caregivers can be asked about their reactions to the "My Dream Mom and Dad" list and to think about the implications these views have for their children. After presenting these ideas, it is possible to ask the parents what their children would include on their own list of what would make their parents great. The implications of the children's views for the custody and access issues can then be explored. In addition, in a separate meeting the children can be given the list so they can think about which items apply to their situation and what they would like to add.

Another strategy that can be used to give people an opportunity to take each other's positions seriously is the use of internalized other questions. We mentioned these earlier in another context. These questions invite a person to speak from the other person's point of view. The mediator can ask the man to answer some questions as if he was the woman and vice versa. For example, a mediator might ask, "If you were Margaret, what might you be concerned about that hasn't been discussed yet?" If the man is asked to step into the woman's experience and answer questions from her point of view, the likelihood is increased that he will take her concerns seriously. It becomes more difficult to stick rigidly to an exaggerated sense of entitlement after experiencing through role-play the feelings that accompany the other person's point of view. The door is opened to a compassionate understanding growing between people, and such compassion greatly assists the mediation process.

## The Specter of Violence

The presence or threat of violence or abuse in a relationship can exert a huge influence on the course of a mediation. There are many who would say that such a threat makes it impossible for mediation to take place. Certainly there are many contexts in which we would agree. We are inclined to use caution in this area especially because of the reports in some New Zealand studies of violence happening before and after mediation meetings.

There are many stories, however, of violence being addressed in conversations constructed in the right ways that suggest the impossibility of making a rigid rule on this subject. For example, restorative justice mediations in which victims and offenders, including violent offenders, are brought face to face have proved to be powerfully successful events that make a difference for both parties. Similarly, Alan Jenkins's work on the renegotiation of relationships after violence or abuse suggests the possibility of creating a safe context in which violence can be addressed.[6]

Safety is the key. If safety does not exist, then all the best efforts at mediation are likely to be undermined. A sense of safety might sometimes be created by the parties themselves before they come to mediation. This is possible in some situations where the violence is at a low level and stands in contradiction to other qualities of the relationship. We would urge mediators to be cautious in making this assessment and to do so in careful consultation with the person who has been the recipient of the violence or abuse. It is wise to remember, too, that safety is not a fixed state of being. By its very nature it is relative to current events. Complete safety can never honestly be guaranteed, and legal options cannot guarantee it any more than mediation can. Mediators are wise to be alert to the fluctuations in the sense of safety that people experience and to be ready to interrupt the mediation process at any stage to protect the safety of the participants. It is crucial that safety issues be given higher priority than the desire for settlement.

Safety might also be created by moves the mediator makes. Here are some examples:

• *Negotiation of a contract to address safety issues.* If the mediator has any inkling at all that intimidation, violence, or the threat of violence has been a feature of a couple's dispute, separate sessions are always the safest option in the early phase of the mediation process. Usually it is the female in a disputing heterosexual couple who is feeling in danger, although this is not always the case. If some indication of violence is provided by the referral source, we would tend to meet with the woman first. During this first meeting, we would ask the person who is at risk to speak explicitly about his or her fears of being hurt by the other party and what shape this could take. We would want to know which topics in the dispute have the potential to escalate the possibility of violence. In many instances, it may be unwise for the mediator to risk a joint meeting. The person experiencing the greatest sense of risk will usually know what they need to make them feel safe in a joint session. This discussion makes it clear to the person who has been violent that he or she must take full responsibility for his or her behavior and be aware of how he or she can intimidate others. The mediator can negotiate a contract with the person who is at risk of contributing to any future violence, with the expectation that no violence, threat, or intimidation of any kind would be shown in the mediation process. These descriptions can be defined with examples. Included in the contract should be an agreement that the person who is at risk of being hurt would not have to ask or answer any questions in the mediation session that he or she thought would leave them unsafe. It can be negotiated ahead of time that if the contract is broken, the mediation process will end immediately.

• *Arranging the seating to maximize safety.* If someone is concerned about his or her safety in a joint meeting, there are some physical arrangements that can be made to minimize, if not remove, the threats to safety. Often a person who feels afraid of the other person will prefer to sit near the door in order to make a quick exit if it is required. This can feel quite different to being caught on the opposite side of the room with one's exit route potentially blocked by the other party. Sometimes it is also worth negotiating that one person arrive five minutes late and leave early in order to prevent confrontations in the waiting room or outside.

• *Use of immediacy.* The skill of bringing up for discussion the immediate process issues is a useful one for mediators to develop in order to be able to address issues of safety. This might need to be done repeatedly at regular intervals. It involves checking with the participants about how the process is going and asking them to express their experience of it. If one person is looking decidedly uncomfortable and appears reluctant to participate, there might be some very good reasons for this. It may not be possible to address these issues in the presence of the other party, but they could be brought out in a separate meeting. The mediator can lead the discussion into this issue by expressing her own experience of the process. For example, she might say, "I'm a little unsure about what is stopping us from getting very far right now. This is frustrating me a little and I'd like to ask if you can help me sort this out." If one of the parties is behaving in an intimidating manner, the mediator can overtly name this by saying, "I am starting to feel intimidated by you," or "I find your behavior threatening. Is this your intention?" If the person states that it is not their intention, they can then be asked if they are willing to listen to how the mediator has come to that conclusion. This gentle form of confrontation often challenges the person to be more respectful in the mediation process. It is also often a good idea to mention to parties that it is okay to have a time out if the interactions become too intense. Thus, if a party is overly upset and leaves the room, the mediator has already made it acceptable to do so without disturbing the process.

• *Facilitating externalizing conversations about violence.* In the process of speaking about violence, an externalizing conversation can be developed in which it is clear that violence and its effects are the problem and that the person (both the perpetrator and the victim of the violence) is not the problem. The effects of the violence on each of the parties can be fully mapped and the preference for everyone to live without violence can be made clear. The hangover that violence can have in people's minds and the possibility that this hangover can be exploited to support an exaggerated entitlement needs to be respected in this process. People who are not on the receiving end often underestimate the effects of violence on others. But the effects of violence need not be measured only in terms of their internal psychological effects either. They can also be spoken about in terms of their effects on relationships, even their effects on the mediation itself. People can also separate themselves from the effects of violence. The experience of protesting the violence that has been done to them and having that heard and acknowledged by the person who perpetrated it can help prevent the effects of the violence from being ongoing. We have seen this technique used successfully on numerous occasions in mediation conferences designed to be alternatives to school suspension.

• *Having the violent party acknowledge their preference for nonviolence.* It is preferable not to assume when speaking with people who have perpetrated acts of violence that violence speaks the whole truth about who they are or about their preferences for relationships. In our experience, it seldom does. Even those for whom violence and abuse have become commonplace or a habit in their lives usually have a preference for more respectful ways of relating. It can therefore be useful, as Alan Jenkins acknowledges, to bring forward this preference from the start and then talk about the violence and abuse as *restraints* on the expression of this preference, rather than risk the implication that the violence and abuse is inherent in a person's character.

• *Using separate rooms.* Sometimes safety, or more specifically, one person's sense of safety in the presence of the other person, can be increased by meeting with the two parties separately and having the mediator convey messages between them. This can be achieved by using two separate rooms and having the mediator go back and forth. Although this is not ideal in terms of the possibilities for conversation, there are circumstances in which it is a pragmatic option that is better than nothing. An advantage of this approach is that the mediator can suggest a different arrival time for each party to avoid them having to confront each other in the waiting room. The person who is concerned about his or her safety can also be given the opportunity to leave the building at the end of the meeting while the mediator is talking to the other party. This avoids the problem of confrontations taking place outside the mediation room that can themselves turn into violence.

• *Acknowledging the role of support persons.* Support persons can be invited to the mediation meeting to bolster the position of the person who is feeling intimidated by the hangover of violence. In the session with the person who has exhibited violent behavior in the past, the mediator can explicitly discuss with this support person the safety of the participants in the mediation if joint meetings go ahead. This move can help strengthen a sense of entitlement in the person who has been the recipient of the violence that might otherwise be undermined (thereby making room for an exaggerated sense of entitlement in the person who perpetrated the violence to hold sway in the relationship). Support persons can be asked to perform the task of monitoring the interests of the person they are supporting in the joint meeting.

## Working with Fundamentalism

One of the assumptions that a postmodern approach to mediation assumes is that the world of meanings we inhabit is a fluid one. Sure, there are meanings that come to dominate within a particular cultural milieu, but these are often contested and the balance of influence of dominant and subjugated meanings is always subject to shifts and changes. New meanings are always evolving and developing.

However, even this view of the world is not uncontested. Many people view things in black and white terms and prefer to adhere to fundamentalist perspectives of various kinds. From these perspectives, meanings are fixed and nonnegotiable. They are constituted by authority (such as the authority of God) that cannot be questioned without threatening the whole system of meaning for that person. When such people come into a mediation, they present particular challenges for mediators, because they sometimes appear resistant to participating in a process of meaning negotiation. The challenge is to continue to demonstrate respect for someone's view of the world while at the same time seeking to open up some space for meaning negotiation.

In divorce mediation, for example, this can lead to some impasses in which a person rigidly states a point of view (perhaps about gender roles in the care of children) and justifies it on the basis of spiritual authority. We advocate for an approach that avoids directly confronting a person's fundamentalist beliefs and also openly and actively works to create space for new meanings to emerge. Wally McKenzie's work in this area has been very helpful to us.[7]

McKenzie's emphasis is on making explicit statements about the process of mediation not being about theology. He invites a discussion about how a person engages with an authority figure and repositions the person as an active participant in relation to that authority (God, for example) rather than as a simple parrot of this authority or as a passive recipient of the authority's help. This can be done within the story as it is framed in the person's own worldview.

Consider an example. Laurie has separated from her husband, Angus, who has been opposed to the whole idea of separation and regards her move as a sin against God's creation of the institution of marriage. When shortly after the separation she enters a new relationship with another man, Angus is filled with righteous anger and seeks custody of their eight-year-old daughter. His reasons for seeking custody rely mainly on the idea that Laurie has sinned and deserves to be punished.

How can a mediator open a conversation with Angus in a way that also allows Laurie's voice to be heard but stops short of challenging or undermining Angus's Christian beliefs? In individual sessions, Angus could be asked if he would be willing to explore the role of God in this mediation to help address the issues of custody and access. If Angus agrees, the mediator might ask him the following questions:

- Knowing that God means different things to different people, what is the meaning of God in your life?
- What led you to have these ideas of God (and not others)?

- How does God view you and your life as it has been?
- What is God's view of this dispute and what is God's assessment of the part you are playing in resolving this conflict?
- What do you think God would make of this conversation and my genuine interest in your views about how to address outstanding issues?
- Would God favor your role in helping settle this dispute and be outraged by your ex-partner's and children's views?
- How is God communicating to you this degree of certainty? Has there been any circumstance in which you have experienced, even for a slight moment, a spark of uncertainty about what God wants of you in any particular circumstance?

These questions are designed to name overtly the private certainties that a person with a fundamentalist viewpoint might hold. We are not interested in the theological implications in this particular instance but are seeking to open even small spaces for a person to consider alternative descriptions of the conflict as it has unfolded. We are working with Angus to assist him to recognize that other views, including Laurie's, might have some validity in the conflict.

Many fundamentalist views on separation and divorce are shaped by patriarchal discourses. These may range from the man insisting that he should have custody of the children because he is the head of the household and the provider, to the man or woman believing that women are the rightful caregivers, based on the assumption of God-given gender duties. In many mediations, both parents presuppose that the mother will be the sole caregiver for the children.

In these instances, fathers often disengage from a parenting role, for a variety of reasons. They may disengage from their children as a punitive act against their ex-partners or feel so discouraged by their peripheral role in their children's lives that they withdraw altogether. In many mediations, resolution is reached between separating parents simply because one of the parties (in a heterosexual partnership, usually the man) opts out. Thus the dispute is "resolved," but at considerable cost to the children, who are intimately affected by the parent's resolution. We have found that in many instances the mediator plays a critical role in advocating for the children's right to have both parents continue as caregivers in their lives amid an acrimonious separation and divorce.

Wally McKenzie and David Epston have recently been exploring ways to engage fathers in a greater role in parenting their children following separation and divorce.[8] McKenzie was concerned about the way fathers became bewildered by the fading away or even disappearance of their children from their lives. He devised the following set of questions to help engage fathers in maintaining and strengthening their relationships with their children during and following the family mediation process.

- As you look back on your history with your own father, how would you describe your relationship with him?
- What differences do you think there really are between good mothering and good fathering?
- What has led you to think that?
- What difference would it have made to you, to your mother, and to your father if the fathering you had received had been more like the mothering you received?
- What would it have been like for you if the mothering you received had been modeled on the fathering you received?
- Where did your father learn about fathering?
- Do you think he found fathering difficult or easy? Why?
- Did he ever ask you as a child how he was doing?
- What advice would you have given him if he had?
- How often did your father tell you that he loved you?

These questions are designed to invite fathers to reflect closely on the quality of their own experience of being fathered and then to make some connection between that and what is taking place with their own children. This approach indirectly challenges fathers to play a bigger role in their children's lives by building empathy with their children's circumstances and their own childhood experiences of being fathered. Additional questions can be asked to connect fathers with a parenting role postseparation. For example:

- Are you compelled to repeat your own early history of having your father absent from your life or do you want to begin to take a stand against history repeating itself? (This question is obviously relevant only to those fathers who were brought up without much fathering.)

- Are you open to receiving your own children's suggestions about what kind of father they are pining for?
- What excuses do you think you are most susceptible to that will encourage you to be on the periphery of your children's lives?
- What ideas do you have to help you manage the anguish of your family breaking up that will lead to you not opting out?
- Who do you know that could assist you with "father ideas" to step forward rather than backward into your children's lives?

Although these questions sound like they are more fit for a counseling relationship than a mediation, we think they still have their use in mediation. In New Zealand, this boundary is blurred anyway because mediation work for the family court is usually given to counselors and called counseling rather than mediation. The use of narrative questions such as these introduces important additional perspectives into the conversation without the mediator telling the parties what they should do. However, when mediators ask these questions, they are clearly operating from a partial child advocacy position. We think this can be an appropriate role for a mediator involved in a parental caregiving dispute.

In this chapter we have discussed some of the more challenging domains in which mediators must work when addressing conflict. Getting parties unstuck often occurs when the mediator finds a way of motivating the participants to get fully involved in the mediation process. However, mediation is not about going in search of the participant's motivational potential. Motivation is not an intrinsic commodity possessed by some individuals and not others, as we noted earlier. Nor is motivation attained merely by the mediator pumping enthusiasm into the process through the force of their personal presence or charismatic charm. Although these qualities may help the process along, the main skill of the mediator in building motivation and commitment to the process is his or her ability to create openings for the participants in the conflict to experience greater levels of understanding of themselves and the other party. These openings are created in a variety of moves during the mediation process to address issues such as distrust, defensiveness, ambivalence, violence, and fundamentalism. However, despite the broad range of challenges that confront the mediator, we suggest that there is an underlying orientation that is effective across all conflicts. We hope that we have demonstrated in a variety of ways how the mediator must address the discursive context in which all of the problems described here have been fashioned.

## Notes

1. White, M., "Deconstruction and Therapy," in D. Epston and M. White (eds.), *Experience, Contradiction, Narrative and Imagination* (Adelaide, Australia: Dulwich Centre Publications, 1992).
2. Wally McKenzie, personal communication with authors, March 1999.
3. Miller, W., and Rollnick, S., *Motivational Interviewing: Preparing People to Change Addictive Behavior* (New York: Guilford, 1992).
4. Egan, G., *The Skilled Helper: A Systematic Approach to Effective Helping* (4th ed.) (Pacific Grove, Calif.: Brooks/Cole, 1990).
5. Tomm, K., *Internalized Other Questioning: Workshop Presentation* (Hamilton, New Zealand: University of Waikato, 1996); Epston, D., "Internalized Other Questioning with Couples: The New Zealand Version," in S. Gilligan and R. Price (eds.), *Therapeutic Conversations* (New York: Norton, 1993).
6. Jenkins, A., *Invitations to Responsibility* (Adelaide, Australia: Dulwich Centre Publications, 1990).
7. Drewery, W., and McKenzie, W., "Therapy and Faith," in I. Parker (ed.), *Deconstructing Psychotherapy* (London: Sage, 1999).
8. McKenzie, W., and Epston, D., *Psychological Open Heart Surgery for Severed Father-Children Relationships Following Marital Separation/Divorce* (Hamilton, New Zealand: New Zealand Association of Counsellors Conference, 1999).

# Chapter Ten

# Documenting Progress

*But in this page a record will I seek.*
*Not in the air these my words disperse . . .*
(LORD BYRON, "DON JUAN")

*Writing, when properly managed, . . . is but a different*
*name for conversation.*
(LAWRENCE STERNE, "TRISTRAM SHANDY")

In their book *Narrative Means to Therapeutic Ends,* Michael White and David Epston established a landmark reputation for narrative therapy in the construction of therapeutic documents.[1] By therapeutic we mean that which increases the possibility for people living in satisfying ways. In mediation, this might mean escaping from the tight grip of a conflict and achieving the amount of resolution necessary for the relationship to move on. It is worth noting that the original title of White and Epston's book was *Literate Means to Therapeutic Ends,* which stressed even more the role of the written document in facilitating change.[2]

Problem-solving approaches to mediation have of course made use of written agreements produced as an outcome of the mediation process. When signed by the parties to a dispute, they serve as reference points for future adherence to the understandings reached in a mediation meeting. Because people can refer back to and hold each other accountable to their written

This chapter was written with the assistance of Alison Cotter and Tim Clarke.

agreements, the chances of the conflict becoming inflamed again are reduced.

A narrative perspective on written documents expands on their use and places written agreements into a different context.[3] Rather than being end products of the mediation process, written agreements are more like milestones or signposts in a narrative journey. They serve to advance the plot and develop particular character traits in the protagonists. Viewed from this perspective, written agreements are tools for ongoing narrative development rather than goals of the process. Moreover, for this purpose, documents other than final agreements can be contemplated as well. We have found that letters written by mediators to participants at various stages in a mediation process can serve a crucial function in securing small progress and preventing slippage back into the conflict story between mediation meetings.

In this chapter we demonstrate some of the things that can be achieved in such letters and other documents and comment on the different purposes they can serve. We begin with a sample letter sent to two people involved in a mediation about a workplace conflict.

> Dear Danny and Lance,
>
> We have met with each of you once and also with both of you together. Before we meet again, we wanted to write to you and review what we have covered in our sessions, what you have accomplished, and what remains outstanding.
>
> An overall reading of the situation is that the dispute has you both feeling that you are at the end of the road with regard to working together. The change in your relationship seemed to be tied to the restructuring that took place in the institute in recent months. It was almost like the changes and stresses were too much for your working relationship to bear.
>
> Yet you both conveyed the strong impression that until recently you had respect and regard for one another and had placed value on your association, over a ten-year period. Danny, you said that you were "still wanting to find a way out of this mess." Lance, you had

serious doubts about whether this was possible, but you did wish "things had never gotten so bad."

Danny, you told us how the dispute led you, against your better judgment, into a state of bloody-mindedness and how this has affected productivity in the unit. Little things have been subject to unnecessary delays as a result. You expressed concern about standards of work slipping and saw it as your responsibility to maintain those standards. This has made you more critical of others' performance than you used to be.

Lance, you expressed a feeling of not being appreciated over the years for the contribution you have made to the team. You want not just a restoration of things as they used to be but a much better opportunity to make decisions on your own and have them respected by Danny and others. You wanted the experience you have built up acknowledged and valued. The dispute between you two was preventing this from happening.

Both of you reported other effects of the whole dispute as well: your general enjoyment of life being reduced, a depressing sense of hopelessness starting to take you over, and a procrastination habit growing bigger.

Frankly, we are wondering whether at this point hopelessness has not completely taken charge. For example, is hopelessness overshadowing everything so much that even when positive developments do appear you find them hard to recognize? Yet we also noticed you both being willing to continue to explore these problems in the hope that something will change.

What we did notice that you came up with, and we are interested in discussing it further with you next week, were the following ideas, perhaps flying in the face of hopelessness.

1. The idea of a scheduled weekly meeting to discuss upcoming work issues.
2. Danny, you identified that Lance needed a junior assistant to take some routine pressures off him.

3. Lance, you appreciated this as a helpful suggestion from Danny that would make a difference to your feelings of being appreciated and your ability to make decisions on your own.
4. You both agreed to discuss with the manager some changes to the appraisal and review process so that this dispute does not infect that.

We are still wondering about the significance of these steps. Do they put a small or a large dent in the side of hopelessness? We also have several ongoing questions for you to consider and for us to discuss next week.

1. Do these developments and agreements mean that you are starting to reformulate your working relationship in ways that you would prefer?
2. What kind of experiences and attitudes would be more present in your workplace if hopelessness was to take more of a back seat?
3. Have there been any hints of such experiences happening that would be worth talking about next week?

These are just some thoughts to mull over. We shall look forward to talking them over with you next Tuesday.

Sincerely,
John and Gerald

## Commentary

The externalizing language of this letter will not come as a surprise to readers at this stage. The conflict is separated from any kind of blaming language and spoken about as having a life of its own and as affecting the lives of the disputants and their relationship. Thus the letter serves to elaborate the perspective with which the mediators have enjoined the participants in the conversation. Having this approach documented and available to be read and reflected on after the meeting creates the opportunity for it to be extended in everyone's minds.

What is also extended is the relational alignment of the parties against the designs and devices of the problem or conflict and the contextual circumstances (the restructuring in the institute) that have contributed to the conflict. All these language shifts create a conversational context that allows a different set of meanings about what has happened to emerge. The letter stipulates the new meanings and creates a record of them for future reference.

The effects of the conflict on each person are acknowledged in summary form, too. This personal acknowledgment, expressed in ways that do not ascribe blame to the other, is foundational to the development of news of difference.

Another purpose served by this letter is that of personal acknowledgment of the best intentions of each of the parties to the dispute. Conflict situations seldom provide opportunity for people to acknowledge such things. People in dispute are more inclined to downplay each other's best intentions and to assign malevolent intentions to each other. The acknowledgment of people's best intentions can be built on any small act, even the act of participating in the mediation itself, and storied in conversation before being extended and documented in such a letter. The letter also implicitly invites each person to join the mediator in acknowledging the best intentions of the other, at the very least by not disputing such ascribed intentions. In our experience, such acknowledgments serve to cool the heat that can be generated in conflicts.

The letter also attempts to open space for further developments in the relational story. These attempts are made in the form of wondering about possibilities for extending small moments of difference mentioned in the mediation session by each party. These ideas are framed under the general heading of "flying in the face of hopelessness." Each idea is subjected to some questions about the meaning or significance of the idea. The assumption behind these questions is that the greater the significance attached to an idea, the more likely it is that the parties will embody that idea in future meaningful action.

Life will have continued on since the mediation meeting. During this time, further unique outcomes can arise. It can reasonably be expected that the meetings with the mediator will have had some effect. Indeed, if an alternative story to the conflict story has been developed in the mediation meeting, it might be expected to have undergone some narrative development after the meeting. Plot features might have been added or characterizations expressed at the mediation meeting may have been elaborated. The letter concludes by inviting the two parties to notice what has happened and to make meaning of it, especially meaning that lines up against hopelessness.

## Advantages of Putting Things in Writing

There are some features of the place of the written word in the modern world that lend themselves to the writing of such letters and render them of more than passing usefulness. White and Epston argue for the writing of such letters because they make use of the authority of the written word in contemporary cultural traditions.[4] Although such authority is not inevitable (and may sometimes be culture specific), White and Epston suggest that people in the modern world frequently place greater store in things that are written down than in things that are just spoken. Greater truth status is granted to written documents than to oral pronouncements. The written word tends to get counted as trustworthy knowledge. Hence, White and Epston suggest that professional practices that make use of this aspect of modernist culture are likely to enhance the effectiveness of those practices.

They also propose that people who are seeking to make changes in their lives and relationships need "mechanisms that assist them to plot the events of their life within the context of coherent sequences of time."[5] In other words, in order for meaningful change to occur, people need to notice it happening and give it credence. One of the mechanisms Epston and White propose is the use of written documents designed to enable this kind of noticing.

Another argument for the use of written documents as part of the change process is based on the limits of memory. We are limited in how much we can retain of the many subtle but important shifts in meaning that can take place in a mediation meeting. White and Epston argue that the use of literate means allows for the more "deliberate organization of linguistic resources" than can be achieved orally so that changes or shifts in meaning can be retained and revisited.[6] Such revisiting, as the records created out of a mediation meeting are read by the participants, serves a purpose like that of photographic fixing chemicals, strengthening the impact of the oral conversation and allowing the images created there to be held and remembered. People often report that before another meeting they thoroughly and frequently read the documents produced from the mediation. In their own time they are able to digest the meaning of what has been written down more completely than they could in the heat of the moment in a mediation meeting.

There can also be a downside for mediators in the use of letters and other documents after a mediation meeting. We are thinking of the time it can take for the mediator to compose a letter. Institutional demands or client funding agreements often do not allow mediators the luxury of spending time writing to their clients. However, we have had enough experience of people finding such letters valuable to consider the time spent writing them worthwhile in the long run.

Such letters can also serve as official documentation and note taking. The discipline of writing to the client creates a record of the professional relationship that can serve many administrative purposes. Further note taking becomes redundant as a result. The ethics of using letters to clients as notes also promotes respectful behavior among mediators. It ensures that what gets written in the notes is in the clients' interests (because the notes have been written directly to them). Secret files of information are not kept behind clients' backs and the tone of what gets filed is prevented from deteriorating into disrespectful language that could not be spoken in front of the clients.[7]

## Specific Purposes of Letter Writing

Letters and other documents produced out of mediations can serve a variety of specific purposes. We describe some of these here and give examples of letters and extracts from such letters that illustrate these purposes.

## Acknowledgment

One purpose that can be embodied in written words is that of providing each party with a sense of personal acknowledgment. Acknowledgment demonstrates personal respect (and therefore fosters trust in the mediators), validates things that might otherwise be subject to self-doubt (especially in the midst of conflict), and encourages the further development of what is acknowledged. It is best if such acknowledgment is as specific as possible.

The effect of this acknowledgment is enhanced when it is formalized in writing. What is more, the acknowledgment is given in the knowledge that the other person or people involved in the dispute will also be reading it (on principle, we would not write separate and different letters to either party). There is therefore a sense that the acknowledgment is being "published" or announced publicly, even if the audience amounts to only a small group of three or four people. If what is acknowledged for each person is done so evenhandedly, its public nature enhances its meaning.

So what might we want to acknowledge people for? One simple but obvious acknowledgment is for their willingness to participate in the process. Goodwill and courage can be noticed, as can honesty and integrity and willingness to adhere to process agreements. Here are some examples drawn from actual letters written after mediation meetings:

> We want to communicate our respect for the commitment, time, and energy you put into addressing the issues that were concerning you, and what you put into identifying more productive ways of working together. You told us that tensions in your work environment were interfering with your work relationships, productivity, time, and energy. Yet it was obvious to us that you had not lost a sense of pride in your work, or a sense of regard for the contributions of others.

> We especially admired your willingness to hear each other's points of view and, in spite of the tensions that were obviously there, to listen respectfully to what was upsetting each other.

> We respect the courage it took for you to raise these difficult issues and were left wondering what it meant about the importance to you both of the work you do.

> Even though it was tough for you both to hear what was said at the meeting, we want to acknowledge your willingness to speak honestly and address these significant issues.

Sometimes the acknowledgments do not need to come from the mediators. They can be drawn from the participants themselves by asking questions such as the following:

- What have you appreciated about how the other person has gone about things in this meeting?
- What are you pleased about in the way you have handled yourself in this meeting?
- What about the spirit of this meeting would you like to carry over into the next meeting?

The answers to these questions can be written down by the mediators and included in a letter after the meeting. For example, in response to the last question, one group of participants wanted these things to carry over:

- The reasonable level of goodwill
- The level of commitment to getting things sorted out
- The effort to hear what others have to say
- The focus on the well-being of the organization
- The participation level

It is worth noting that in the process of saying that they wanted these qualities to be present in the next meeting, they were implicitly acknowledging each other for the presence of these qualities in the previous meeting.

Another opportunity exists in the writing of narrative letters to reinforce a fine distinction that can be made orally but assisted to register more strongly by being acknowledged in writing. We are referring to the distinction between people's intentions and their behaviors. Even if someone's actions can be referenced to the problematic conflict story, sometimes their intentions can be separated from their behavior and spoken about as openings to an alternative story, one that has been subjugated by the conflict from seeing the light of day. These good intentions can be rescued, spoken about, and referenced differently in terms of the possible alternative actions to which they could conceivably give rise. A letter that records and supports this interpretation can go a long way toward making such good intentions more likely to be embodied in future actions.

- It was clear in your comments that you had every intention of communicating your appreciation to Ann, but the argument, as it developed, interfered with that intention.
- It sounds like this conflict got you doing things that were against your better judgment.
- It was clear from what each of you said that there was no shortage of desire to contribute to the functioning of the team, even if recent events might not give that impression.

Expressions of the desire for change or motivation toward it are also worthy of acknowledgment. Writing down such acknowledgments seals such statements in and weakens the pull of inertia. The publicizing of such statements (to the participants in written form) makes it harder to go back on them.

Here are some examples from narrative letters of such acknowledgments:

- Each of you was clear that you wanted things to change and that you were prepared to "do your bit."
- You each said that you were dissatisfied with the recent history of your relationship as colleagues and that you had a desire to make changes.

## Mapping the Influence of the Problem

We spoke earlier in this book about the questions that can be asked to support an externalizing conversation by tracing the effects of a problem rather than hunting for its cause. Again, the less-blaming perspective introduced by the externalizing language can be reinforced by its repetition in writing. The effects noted may be emotional responses, relational exchanges (or their absence), personal experiences of stress, implications for people other than the disputants, impending decisions, or meanings of which people have become convinced.

The recording of these effects in writing creates a record that can serve as a point of reference for noticing change. It can also serve to bring together into one document a variety of effects spoken about at different times in the mediation meetings. The juxtaposition of all these effects can serve to highlight the extent of the problem's effects in a way that has not previously been notice-able. Here are some examples from letters sent to people noting these effects:

> You each told us of the effects of the difficulties you have experi-enced. These included hurt feelings on both sides and general ten-sion between you at work. The difficulties had also gotten you to be really wary of each other and this was affecting the work you needed to do together. For you, Eva, this problem was affecting your sleep. It had you fretting at night and worrying about it. And Grace, you suspected that your recent illness had been brought on by these difficulties. You were both starting to notice that the chil-dren for whom you are both responsible were starting to be a bit more difficult as the problem spread its effects, even though you have both tried to stop it from affecting them.

> You both spoke to us about the effects of this dispute over your father's will. It caused a considerable amount of hurt when in the wake of the loss you could have done without this extra element of pain. You have both felt this hurt and have expressed it in your own ways. Another effect has been on the relationships among the wider family, which traditionally have been quite close. It seems that the bad feeling has spread beyond you two and has caught other family members in its web. You have not seen as much of each other's families as you would have previously and the children are missing out on seeing their cousins as much as they used to. The dispute is also costing you in terms of legal fees as well.

> All of you mentioned some similar things that have come from this conflict on the board. You have all felt constrained by the tension in the air at board meetings in recent months and have held back from volunteering contributions in the meetings when potentially controversial issues have arisen. The result has been that decisions that have been made have not had everyone's input and no one is really happy with the outcomes. You also spoke of some of the more personal effects, such as long-standing friendships that have been disrupted, personal questioning of why you are doing this work, and some accumulated stress effects becoming manifest in minor illnesses.

## Historicizing the Problem

Letters can also be used to locate the conflict in its context, especially its temporal context. As the participants come to an understanding of the sequence of events in which they are caught, they are in a better position to consider possible departures from that chain of events. Sequences of events are often complex and the task of reaching an understanding of them as linked together in a single sequence is not easy. A letter can bring together the disparate details of a conversation and organize them into a meaningful sequence. It can therefore help the participants achieve an overview that can become the foundation for a change in trajectory toward a preferable future. Here are two examples from letters that serve this purpose:

> It seems that this problem had small beginnings in the difference of opinion between you over the meanings of the staff survey. Then the differences erupted in a staff meeting and you, Maryanne, said some things in anger that you later regretted. But the fallout from that meeting meant that you, Jocelyn, were approached by several other staff members who wanted to complain about Maryanne. Wind of this got back to you, Maryanne, and you thought that Jocelyn was fomenting discontent behind your back. You challenged Jocelyn about this and you, Jocelyn, were offended by this implication and took particular exception to the remark about "not being professional." Your concern about this was such that you consulted a lawyer, who wrote a letter threatening legal action against Maryanne. This shocked you, Maryanne, and you began to feel that it was unsafe to actually work with Jocelyn at all. As a result, the current standoff has ensued.

> This was how you described the conflict sequence developing. An incident happened that resulted in one person feeling angry. This anger made others withdraw. They didn't understand or approach the person directly. Barriers and blocks went up. The first person felt disregarded and unimportant. She withdrew and wondered if she was being punished for getting angry. Others saw her as difficult. And so the cycle continues, feeding itself as it goes.

## Holding up Unique Outcomes to the Light

Another purpose that can be served by communicating with the participants in a mediation in writing is that of holding to the light the new shoots of growth that represent the counterstory to the conflict. Writing about such unique outcomes can be considered an act of nourishment, granting sustenance and life to these new shoots. Although these outcomes at first might fall short of agreements that constitute a lasting exit from the conflict, they may need to be given the kind of status that is accorded to the written word in order to take firm root in the context of people's lives. Writing them down for repeated reading enables the ripples they create to circle wider and accumulate greater significance. The greater the significance that accumulates around such unique outcomes, the more likely it becomes that agreements can be reached. Here are some examples of such purposes drawn from narrative mediation letters in the middle of a mediation process:

> We want to acknowledge in writing the importance of the things you both said that might be the seeds out of which the cooperative relationship you both prefer could grow. Sam, you mentioned your willingness to stop the clowning around and jesting that has confused Tania, especially in stressful situations. You recalled the differences on the occasions when you had taken notice of her requests for you to take her seriously. Tania, you offered to stop the "kicking out" in semiserious jest that you had been doing, which had upset Sam. You could see that this was not helping the working relationship between you. We asked you how you had arrived at these decisions. You both said that you had been thinking seriously about your relationship between our first and second meetings. We wondered what this serious thinking indicated about the value you both place on your working partnership. Does this valuing indicate a way forward? Are there other ideas for changes in your patterns of relating that might grow from such thinking?

> Natalie, you spoke of the difference it made when Martin phoned and spoke to the children. It felt like he was taking an interest in them and that they weren't completely abandoned by him. You indicated that you do not want to stand in the way of that at all.

Martin, it was news to you that Natalie did not want to interfere when you phoned and you appreciated that she was not hovering around the phone supervising the phone call. We were interested in the significance of this occasion as a model for the possible ways out of your parenting standoff it offers you.

Sometimes the new shoots of growth in the counterstory are not reported events but ideas or suggestions that the participants make about ways to resolve differences. They might be statements about their vision of the kind of ongoing relationship they would prefer. They might be memories of how things used to be. Or they might be principles on which they would like to build in the creation of a different future. Again, the committing of these ideas to paper gives them added status over the spoken word. Here are some examples:

> In answer to our question about the features of the cooperative re-
> lationship you would prefer, you each came up with a series of ideas
> that overlapped considerably. Greg, your list featured discussing is-
> sues together early before others got involved, discussing initiatives
> before taking action, sending apologies if you can't make a meet-
> ing, and aiming for a collegial spirit. Rowena, your list featured
> dealing with issues when they arise, respecting each other's feelings
> and ideas, and negotiating more things in your meetings rather
> than taking them for granted. We are interested in talking further
> with you about these ideas, particularly about where you see it pos-
> sible to implement them, or indeed where you have already been
> implementing them.

> We asked you about the big picture of how you would prefer a
> good working environment among all of you at the rest home to
> look. Here is a summary of your answers: everyone is kept informed
> of what is happening, people are receptive to new ideas, staff are
> willing to help one another, expectations from management are
> clear, everyone takes satisfaction in taking care of the residents,
> companionship is valued among colleagues, and people feel that
> they are trusted. We went on from there to discuss the instances
> when these qualities were evident, despite the designs of some
> forces that worked against their progress.

## Reinforcing Process Agreements

Process agreements or arrangements can also be usefully attended to in the course of a letter during a mediation process. In saying this, we do not want to make a sharp distinction between process and content. We do not believe that processes are simply neutral containers in which the content of a mediation sits. Process shapes content. Significant shifts in the process, in how interactions get played out in the mediation, can alter the meaning of what gets said. As a result, it is often useful to ask people to make meaning out of the mediation process itself. This can be done by asking them to reflect on what has been happening, particularly the aspects of it that they are appreciating. These relational processes can then be projected into the relationships outside the mediation context. Here are some examples:

> After considering some concerns about how we would talk together in the mediation, you decided to adopt the following process agreements: address issues, not the person; respect each other's point of view; take time to explore and understand; give each other the opportunity to complete statements without interruption; and take time out if necessary when conflict feels too intense.

> During our meetings, we heard you both wondering in different ways whether or not it would be easier just to give up and walk away. Yet you have continued to be committed to staying and seeing the process through, addressing problems through respectful communication and perhaps in the process repairing some of the damage that the conflict has wreaked on your relationship. Maureen, you actually spoke about this when you said you did not think you needed to reach some sort of agreement so much as you needed practice at regenerating your relationship in these ways.

## Recording Agreements

Most of the written documents we have canvassed so far have been letters and have been referenced to midpoints in the mediation process. The drawing up of written agreements is another form of producing written documentation out of the interactions that take place in mediation. Written agreements are usually created later in the process. Their use needs little introduction to those who have knowledge of mediation from the problem-solving perspective. What is different about such documents from the narrative perspective is the context from which they are understood. Rather than being considered endpoints in the process, as an instrumental approach to mediation would suggest, written agreements are simply records of plot development up to a particular point in time.

They are like snapshots taken at a particular time and, like photographs, can serve as reference points for things we want to hold onto and remember from that time. The story of a relationship continues after the recording of agreements, just as life continues after the taking of a snapshot. The record of an agreement can serve as a departure point for future development, as well as the culmination point for a mediation narrative. The goal of mediation from a narrative perspective is not to produce an agreement but to advance the ongoing developmental narrative for both parties. The agreement should serve this narrative purpose rather than the narrative development serving the purpose of producing an agreement or settlement. With this emphasis in mind, we can look at some agreements that have emerged from some narrative mediations.

The following are the agreements you reached in answer to the question, Where to from here?

1. We will all monitor and check our progress with these agreements.
2. Harley will be available to consult with the other members of the team.
3. Important memos will be circulated to all staff rather than just posted on the wall.
4. New work will be distributed to those present at joint meetings.
5. Harley will arrange a meeting with Michael and Alison to summarize for them the outcomes of this meeting.
6. During Harley's absence next week Tristan will assume supervisory responsibility.
7. A review meeting will be held on June 15 to check out the progress you have made with these agreements and to discuss further developments you would like to make in your working relationships.

There were several matters that we did not manage to resolve in the time we had available yesterday. These were:

1. Staff training needs
2. Use of the boardroom
3. The requests for updated job descriptions from several staff
4. The concern about lack of clarity in relation to lines of authority in the organization.

We will be interested in whether you manage to make any progress with these issues before our meeting on June 15, and we will focus on these issues then.

## Deconstructing the Techniques of Power

Sometimes a letter or other written document can be a vehicle for helping people consider how their conflict has developed in the context of power relations that are often sanctioned in wider social discourses, such as sexism or racism. The purpose of such deconstruction might be to invite people to take steps out of such pervasive social discourses, and out of the techniques of power that support them.

An example arose in a school mediation that involved a local community group and the school principal and board of trustees. One of the members of the community group (she was Maori) accused the school administration of racism in its decision not to reemploy her as a teacher's aide for a child with special needs. From the school administration's point of view there was a simple explanation for this decision: the child concerned had left the school. However, the matter could not be dismissed as just a simple misunderstanding, and the concerns of the community group were wider than this single incident. In the mediation, we took the overt stance that racism exists and is likely to be in the background of issues such as this. However, we also invited the school administration to express its opposition to racism and its desire to work against racism with the community group. The focus of the mediation then became the negotiation of what this might mean in relation to this issue and some others. Here is part of a letter that summarized this process:

Let us reiterate the statement we made in the meeting, which you all accepted, that racism exists. Therefore, when events like these happen, it is not surprising that questions are asked about its influence. We want to support the legitimate asking of such questions rather than assume that conflicts arise only out of personal interactions. However, we also did not hear any indication of racism being a personal commitment on the part of anyone involved. To the contrary, we heard you all express in various ways your desire to combat racism and its effects in your school, even if you do not always agree on exactly how. When we meet again, we would like to ask you to consider further how to work together against racism and how to prevent it from entering into relations in your school community.

## Putting It All Together

Finally, let us draw all these purposes together again in a single letter. You will no doubt have noticed that these purposes differ according to which process stage a mediation has reached. Some letters serve the purpose of drawing people further into the process of the mediation. Some emphasize process arrangements for the mediation so far and propose a map for going forward. Others highlight little rays of hope that have appeared so that they do not get lost. Still others seek to underline achievements in the mediation or eventually to cement agreements that point out a path toward the future. The letter that commenced this chapter was drawn from the middle stages of the mediation process. The following letter comes from the later stages, after the formulation of some agreements:

Dear Dawn and Graham,

We have come a long way in the six meetings we have had and I want to acknowledge the commitment you have made to stay with the process during this time. It felt like there were many distractions that kept inviting your attention away from the main issue you both wanted to sort out, which was about the care of your children now that you are living apart.

The separation itself had left you both with strong feelings and depleted energy and had affected your trust of each other. It even had you questioning each other's parenting in different ways. Dawn, it had you doubting Graham's commitment to the children at times, and Graham, it had you wondering whether Dawn was poisoning the children's minds against you.

These doubts have not always been so strong, however. In the first three months after you separated, they were not as powerful in your minds as they have been recently. We all agreed in the end that since you had commenced a new relationship, Dawn, tensions had increased between you and Graham. Neither of you liked the direction in which things were going and you both wanted to shrink these tensions down in size.

In spite of these tensions, you were able in our meetings to continue to talk to each other with respect and with the children's needs in mind. We speculated about how this could be explained and you both spoke about the qualities of your relationship that had not been destroyed by the tensions that had arisen toward the end of your marriage.

Graham, you made it clear that you did not want to be bound by the common patterns of noninvolvement by fathers with their children after a marriage separation. You wanted to demonstrate that you still loved your children, even in the face of some suggestions from two workmates that you should just walk away and leave them to your ex-wife. Dawn, you said that you appreciated this stand and that you wanted to see it built into the understandings reached in the mediation for care of the children.

During our meetings we reached the following understandings that you have agreed to put in place:

1. The children will continue to live with Dawn but will spend one month over the summer school holidays staying with Graham, as well as two weeks during the winter school holidays.

2. The children will also stay with Graham on alternate weekends and will visit him after school every Wednesday until 9 P.M., when they will be driven home to Dawn's place.

3. Dawn agrees not to make negative remarks to the children about Graham.

4. Graham agrees to give Dawn two weeks' notice of any family events at which he would like the children to be present.

5. Graham agrees to take the children to their music and drama lessons and to pay the fees for these lessons.

6. Dawn agrees to send Graham a photocopy of all school reports and letters and to inform Graham by phone about any medical problems that require the children to be seen by a doctor.

7. Graham agrees not to visit Dawn unexpectedly when he wants to discuss some aspect of the children's welfare. Instead he will phone first to check that it is convenient for Dawn. If it is convenient, they will meet to discuss the issue at a neutral venue that they both agree on.

Here are a few questions I would like to ask you to mull over. We are interested in how these understandings sit with you after you have had time to think about them. Do they work in practice? Are there any other ideas you have had since we met that need to be included? Have there been any events in the last two weeks that have helped you believe that these agreements will continue to work in the children's interests?

I will be interested when we meet next Thursday to check whether any of these questions interest you or lead you to any further thoughts. I'll also be interested in how these understandings have been working in practice.

Yours sincerely,
John

This chapter has demonstrated the use of letters and agreements as documents that promote change in mediation. There are other possible uses of the written word as well. No doubt creative mediators will continue to develop these uses. We hope that these examples serve to widen the value of the written word in mediation. The discipline of writing these letters is sometimes demanding. But we believe that the rewards often make the time required well spent. The task of writing in this way has an impact on the mediator's thinking, too. It requires the mediator to adopt a reflective stance in relation to the mediation conversation, and it disciplines the mediator to select the aspects of the conversation that most deserve to be developed into an alternative account. These selections can then serve as the basis for a future meeting.

Finally, such documents serve a rounding-off purpose for the parties to the dispute. They bring to completion the outcomes of a conversation, even in circumstances in which there will be further meetings. These documents can also serve a rounding off purpose for mediators. They close the description of the narrative mediation process in this book.

### Notes

1. White, M., and Epston, D., *Narrative Means to Therapeutic Ends* (New York: Norton, 1991).
2. White, M., and Epston, D., *Literate Means to Therapeutic Ends* (Adelaide, Australia: Dulwich Centre Publications, 1989).
3. Epston, D., "Consulting Your Consultants: The Documentation of Alternative Knowledges," in D. Epston and M. White (eds.), *Experience, Contradiction, Narrative and Imagination* (Adelaide, Australia: Dulwich Centre Publications, 1992).
4. White and Epston, *Narrative Means to Therapeutic Ends.*
5. White and Epston, *Narrative Means to Therapeutic Ends*, p. 37.
6. White and Epston, *Narrative Means to Therapeutic Ends*, p. 37.
7. Bird, J., "Talking Amongst Ourselves," *Dulwich Centre Newsletter*, 1994, *1*, 44–46.

# Epilogue

So, dear reader, we now reach the end of this particular journey together. As we do so, we step out of the positions of author and reader that the discourse of publication offers us and we take with us into other areas of our lives some meanings forged in the process of writing and reading. Meanings are forged, as we have often stressed, in conversation, in discourse. This is no less the case in the process of writing a book than it is in a mediation. This book has been produced in the context of a series of conversations, between each other and between ourselves and our colleagues who are interested in mediation. But we have also held an imaginary conversation with you, the reader, as we have written. We believe that to reach this point in the book, you must have done something similar. The process of reading is surely one of engaging in conversation with a text. It is at best an active process in which you no doubt have had much to say.

We are curious about what you have said while you have been reading. We presume that you have found some things here that speak to your interest in the practice of mediation. Perhaps some features of the kind of practice we have outlined have intrigued you. Perhaps some of the ideas presented here will enter into other conversations in which you become involved in your professional capacity.

We want you to know that writing about these ideas has intrigued us further as well. We would not have bothered writing about this subject if we did not feel excited about what narrative thinking has to offer the process of mediation. But you have already influenced us into further development of these ideas simply by being there in our imaginations as we have written. We have imagined you asking along the way for a clear explanation of how this approach differs from previously published models. In this way you have called us to sharpen our thinking. So we have ended up with some clearer distinctions than those we had in mind when we started writing.

Let us emphasize these distinctions one final time. From our perspective, a narrative approach to mediation stresses the following:

- The privileging of stories and meanings over facts
- The hearing of people's stories of conflict as they are produced in discourse
- The clear separation of conflict-saturated stories from stories of respect, cooperation, understanding, and peace
- The use of externalizing conversations to help disputants extract themselves from problem stories that have held them in thrall
- The creation of a relational context of change as a primary task of mediation in preference to the pursuit of an agreed-upon solution
- The selection of alternative stories for development as pathways out of disputes

In our experience of mediation, these ideas have demonstrable utility. They are not always easy to learn, however, because they require a philosophical commitment, not just an application of techniques. For this reason we have dwelled carefully on the philosophical and theoretical issues. We claim that the theory we are proposing is robust. Although not everyone will warm to these ideas, we would like them to be respected as a coherent account of a credible practice. We also imagine that this practice can contribute to the production of a different kind of conversation, and in the end, to a different kind of community. The kind of community we speak of is founded on a commitment to dialogue, to the shared creation of meaning, rather than on the privileging of individuals in competition with each other to have their needs met. It is a community in which power relations are always open to contest and where respect flourishes. It is a place where people are curious about one another and where new meanings are always being created in response to the challenges provided by constantly changing contexts. It is a world in which people are encouraged to have a voice in the production of the discourse that shapes them.

Have we contributed to the creation of such conversations and communities? This judgment lies in your hands, dear reader, not in ours. It is in your reading rather than in our writing that this book needs to make sense, and it is in your practice that this sense will become evident. We imagine people who work as mediators taking up these ideas and developing them further so that we too can learn more about them. It is in this sense that we look forward to your response.

# About the Authors

John Winslade is director of counselor education at the University of Waikato in Hamilton, New Zealand. Gerald Monk, previously on the faculty of the University of Waikato, was recently appointed director of school counseling at San Diego State University.

Winslade and Monk have been key developers of narrative mediation. They are principal authors and editors of a general text on narrative therapy, *Narrative Therapy in Practice: The Archaeology of Hope* (Jossey-Bass, 1997), and have recently published *Narrative Counseling in Schools: Powerful and Brief* (Corwin Press, 1999). Both Monk and Winslade have written articles and conference papers, and have taught workshops on narrative therapy and mediation in New Zealand, Australia, Great Britain, Canada, and the United States.

# Index